COMMUNITY AND DIFFERENCE

Studies in the
Postmodern Theory of Education

Joe L. Kincheloe and Shirley R. Steinberg
General Editors

Vol. 261

PETER LANG
New York • Washington, D.C./Baltimore • Bern
Frankfurt am Main • Berlin • Brussels • Vienna • Oxford

COMMUNITY AND DIFFERENCE

TEACHING, PLURALISM, AND SOCIAL JUSTICE

EDITED BY
ROBERTO A. PEÑA,
KRISTIN GUEST,
LAWRENCE Y. MATSUDA

PETER LANG
New York • Washington, D.C./Baltimore • Bern
Frankfurt am Main • Berlin • Brussels • Vienna • Oxford

Library of Congress Cataloging-in-Publication Data

Community and difference: teaching, pluralism, and social justice /
edited by Roberto A. Peña, Kristin Guest, Lawrence Y. Matsuda.
p. cm. — (Counterpoints; v. 261)
Includes bibliographical references.
1. Critical pedagogy—United States—Case studies.
2. Discrimination in education—United States—Case studies.
3. Multicultural education—United States—Case studies.
4. Social justice—Study and teaching—United States—Case studies.
I. Peña, Roberto A. II. Guest, Kristin. III. Matsuda, Lawrence Y.
IV. Counterpoints (New York, N. Y.); v. 261.
LC196.5.U6C66   370.11'5'0973—dc22   2003054621
ISBN 0-8204-6844-4
ISSN 1058-1634

Bibliographic information published by **Die Deutsche Bibliothek**.
Die Deutsche Bibliothek lists this publication in the "Deutsche
Nationalbibliografie"; detailed bibliographic data is available
on the Internet at http://dnb.ddb.de/.

Cover photo by Ramon Peña
Cover design by Dutton & Sherman Design

The paper in this book meets the guidelines for permanence and durability
of the Committee on Production Guidelines for Book Longevity
of the Council of Library Resources.

© 2005 Peter Lang Publishing, Inc., New York
275 Seventh Avenue, 28th Floor, New York, NY 10001
www.peterlangusa.com

Printed in the United States of America

TABLE OF CONTENTS

FOREWORD

The world will be saved not by one big story but by the telling of hundreds, thousands, and millions of small, individual personal stories and then some-day what Buddha, Jesus, Mohammed and others have been telling us for all those years will come true. We must respect ourselves and others as our-selves or the world as we know it will no longer continue to exist.

Pete Seeger

For those of us who are involved in rethinking established educational prac-tice through research or reflective inquiry, this book offers further evidence of the power and promise of narrative storytelling as a means of enlighten-ment and transformation. We are introduced to the storied lives of the au-thors and invited to share private wounds inflicted by those whose charge it is to nurture, shepherd, and encourage but rather have contributed to dark so-cietal phenomena such as indifference, alienation, prejudice, and apathy. Readers will find themselves embraced in the warmth of honesty as tales of personal struggle and awakening emerge. They may even connect vicarious-ly to the experiences of social injustice wrapped tightly with the clever rib-bons of oppression. The voices of the storytellers are strong, compelling us to listen in the spirit of coming to know others and ourselves in our collective journey toward understanding.

Noteworthy here is to place the premise of *Community and Difference: Stories about Teaching, Pluralism, and Social Justice* with others who share common beliefs about the importance of a way of being that embraces story-telling. Those like Thomas Barone, Nelson L. Haggerson, Maxine Greene, Nell Noddings, Mary Beth Spore, G. Lynn Nelson, and Mary Rose O' Reilley have found other voices who believe stories possess the capacity to heal our lives by care-full listening and reflective conversation.

For many years as a middle school literature teacher, I taught a book called *The Bracelet*, written by Yoshiko Uchida. It is a story about a young Japanese American girl in 1942 whose family was first sent to an internment camp located at the Tanforan Race Track on the West Coast. Later, the au-thor and her family were sent to the Utah desert for the duration of the war.

It is a painful story about discrimination, rejection, and alienation. But it is also a story about bravery and determination and unwavering dignity.

For the most part, my students had no understanding of this chapter in American history and appeared to be genuinely shocked that this could happen in their country. Uchida writes, "I was tremendously hurt by these incidents, they color a child's outlook on life enormously. One never forgets." The story traces a girl named Ruri through her experiences in the relocation camps and her family's ability to survive the abusive treatment delivered in the name of national security. In a section called "Notes and Comments" at the end of the story, the reader learns that Uchida (Ruri), although traumatized by her treatment, goes on to graduate with honors from the University of California but was not allowed to attend the ceremonies. Instead, her diploma was sent to the camp in a cardboard tube. "That your own country would put you behind barbed wire without any trial, simply because of race, is a real tragedy." Probably most telling for my students were the photos accompanying the story, compliments of the National Archives. What is it, they say? A picture is worth a thousand words? These pictures speak volumes. They are tragic accounts of man's inhumanity toward man.

So we think about this and we talk and we listen in an effort to put our heads around this injustice. My students shared a collective outrage and I hope they have learned a small lesson, a lesson on what it means to be a part of a whole and what it means when someone in that whole can't appreciate differences great and small. It could be that the experience of meeting Ruri and hearing her story had the effect of raising a red flag when they witnessed some injustice through their years. It is all I can hope for.

The nature of this book is couched in heuristic inquiry, meaning that it is an effort to discover or find some truth. Heuristic methodology is grounded in phenomenology and seeks to discover meaning through the lived experiences of those involved in the inquiry. The authors represented here are heuristic scholars in that they are passionate about the world in which they live, they are curious individuals who constantly seek to understand and make sense of human nature, and they have chosen paths of personal discovery. They find their research inquiries as a juxtaposition between self-discovery and an understanding of the world in which they live.

You will read that Roberto Peña learned great, albeit tragic, lessons about self from Ms. Cohen and that he learned gentle lessons about pride and self-worth from Ms. Boyle. He learned that even the most valued of all possessions, one's name, can be easily dismissed as irrelevant by a teacher's casual mis-pronunciation. Kristin Guest discovered the best way for her "to respond to injustices in the world" is for her to be a model in her classroom and with her colleagues. Lawrence Matsuda remembers being invisible and that "with liberty and justice for all" doesn't necessarily apply to children who may have slanted eyes or dark skin. Althe Allen describes her struggle to discover her self through her work with students who face enormous challenges in life. She reflects on her life as an adopted child who never felt as though she belonged. Jacque Ensign describes her lifelong struggle with identity and place, Katherine McNeil writes about what it means to growup ADHD, and Cleo Molina and Hutch Haney describe teaching social justice in partnership.

These are passionate, involved, and inspired people who have chosen a path of self-discovery through the genre of personal storytelling. While very different in terms of life experiences, they seem to walk in the same direction in their search for self, hope, understanding, and peace. Moreover, the contributors to *Community and Difference* seek to reveal injustice and to support those who have been singled out for differentiated and inferior treatment.

The use of narrative storytelling in qualitative inquiry is being given more attention in academe in terms of a paradigmatic approach to research. It is said that the stories we write about our lives provide a sense of meaning and authenticity often not found in traditional approaches. We are able to find a sense of connection to the world; we belong, we matter. We become totally immersed. Using the metaphor of the stream, we are the stream, not merely an observer watching neither from the shore nor even as a boat in the water. We become known by our stories. Said differently, we begin to know because of our stories. Nel Noddings writes, "The story fabric offers us images, myths, and metaphors that are morally resonant and contribute both to our knowing and our being known."

The writer who crafts a story from the experiences of a life acts in much the same way as a skilled stonecutter who brings forth a dazzling gem from the shards of an ancient rock. Each seeks to hold the completed piece up to the light, to allow the warmth of its clarity to stir our passions and to learn from the final reward. Storytelling can at once suffocate us with crushing pain and breathe healing life into our faded spirits. Some literature tends to suggest that the writing of our storied lives helps us to define and more clearly understand who we have been, who we are, and even who we might become.

I believe the writers of this book have traveled long roads on their personal journeys of coming to know and understand themselves. Their purpose is to weave the pedagogical structures of narrative writing and its accompanying transforming effects with educators' rich life experiences, which here focus on the notions of prejudice, alienation, discrimination, and social justice. The fabric that flows from this literary loom offers timely and significant enlightenment for behaviors displayed inside and outside of the educa-tional setting. As with good qualitative research, it begs us to ask more ques-tions than we can answer. It causes us to hold our actions to the light. It compels us to consider the implications of allowing the wounds to reign freely in social engagements. The message for us here is that incidents such as those at Columbine High School and even the events of September 11th are not serendipitous; they don't happen without a root cause, and without action or change, they will happen again.

The authors of *Community and Difference: Stories about Teaching, Pluralism, and Social Justice* have taken great personal risk to tell their stories. They have with boldness and resolve connected the dots between theory and praxis. With honest voice they have shown us there can be a huge chasm between what we think we are doing and how it is ultimately interpreted. They offer good evidence that in the very notion of difference, one finds unity and strength rather than weakness.

But telling our stories is not sufficient to change harmful attitudes and long-standing social ignorances. We must also be willing to listen. We must attend to these and other stories like them with a notion Mary Rose O'Reilley calls *deep listening*. Without one to listen, to complete the circle and be changed, the process is stifled and we silently perpetuate our flawed and hurtful customs; writ-large social injustices will continue to grow unchecked like weeds on an empty piece of ground. I especially like how Terry Tempest Williams puts it in her book *An Unspoken Hunger: Stories from the Field* (1994) when she says, "Writing becomes an act of compassion toward life, the life we so often refuse to see because if we look too closely or feel too deeply, there may be no end to our suffering. But words empower us, move us beyond our suffering, and set us free. This is the sorcery of literature. We are healed by our stories."

In these times of social unrest, a book such as this offers us a rare gift— that of hope. We are beckoned to consider what power our stories possess to help us secure a stronger sense of self, to ensure a sustainable future for our children, and to help provide a peaceful coexistence among the people of this planet. As for me, I think at the very center, this book is about healing ourselves, helping others, being kind, and finding peace.

Marsha D. Harrison, Curriculum and Instruction, Arizona State University

ACKNOWLEDGMENTS

Our stories grew from life experiences that shaped our hunger for justice. We appreciate each other for the opportunity to become acquainted in ways that would not have been possible if not for the dialogue promoted by writing this book. We thank our colleagues and friends who joined in the writing, and we thank the editors at Peter Lang Publishers for their faith in the pursuit of this project.

Roberto wishes to thank his parents, brothers, and sisters, his wife, Lisa and their three children, Julia, Alex, and Rose. I love and cherish you deeply. I miss you, Dad.

Kristin wishes to thank colleagues and students who, over 25 years, joined me in the teaching/learning experience where I could learn as well as teach; my parents who were my first models for justice work; my children, Andrew and Mary, who have taken on justice work so challenging that I am in awe of their commitments; and my husband, Pete, whose love and support continually sustain me.

Larry wishes to acknowledge his wife, Karen Matsuda, Roberto Peña, Kris Guest, and Dean Sue Schmitt for their help, support, and advice in the process of writing his chapter and coediting the book.

Thanks to Wileen Maniago and Sommar Kramer for their support in the completion of this book and to Julie and Santos Rivera for making this book possible.

Thanks for permission provided by:

CHAPTER ONE

Water Is Clear like Me: A Story about Race, Identity, Teaching, and Social Justice

Roberto A. Peña

I have been a university professor since 1993. Not a very long time. Since then I have conducted research and helped others to complete their research studies. This effort has involved using various methodologies and has involved me in assisting and supervising many other approaches. More than that, conducting, directing and chairing dissertation and my own research introduced me to heuristic inquiry, the approach to be used here.

To avoid being redundant, I will not describe what heuristic inquiry means in this writing. Others, including Clark Moustakas, Nelson Haggerson and Marsha Harrison, have done a very good job of that. Rather, the call for following a question through to its end is what compels me here. Further, the promise of increased self-awareness that heuristic inquiry gives may be enough to keep me alive. For me, other approaches to conducting research seem less meaningful, honest and important. Debates about procedures, subjectivity and objective truth, while enormously significant and intellectually rich, nonetheless seem guilty of draining attention away from the truths that some social scientists seek to understand. What's left for me is staying my course and my heart's beat, writing this story, and following what it is that I most need to know through to its end. I confess I do not know enough at the time of this writing to write that question which I hope to address. I do know, however, that while writing this journey, I will find some meanings that possibly address who I am and why children, truth, freedom, justice and teaching are so vital to me.

A Boy

Strawberry Summers
Growing up in a poor family,
I learned at an early age
how tough life could be.

Every summer from the time I was ten,
strawberry picking was my way of life,
from morning til night.
Sixty scrawny pounds, working harder than three grown men.

Cut and swollen fingers,
filling the strawberry rack,
the straw boss cursing and yelling
and a sun blistered back
dominated my young life.

Exhausted, hot, thirsty,
on my hands and knees,
I would stop for a moment and look,
but there was no end
to the infinite rows of strawberries,
as I continued to dream
of playing with my friends.

Forty-two years later,
I hold back the tears
as I recall those five long years,
when poverty enslaved me
and strawberries robbed me of my childhood.
I haven't eaten a single strawberry to this very day.

Francisco Rey Davila, Buffalo, New York

Issues that motivate me touch on belonging and kinship. Belonging and kinship are the essence of family, and given that I'm the youngest of nine, belonging and kinship describe two feelings that my siblings and parents and I knew best. Belonging and kinship and the warmth that was generated, my earliest and fondest memories are of these.

In the Baker Homes on 7 Wilmuth Street in Lackawanna, New York, I knew belonging and kinship first. I remember Eddie, for instance, the tall, skinny kid who lived on the other side of the alley. Eddie was running and running around *Joe Ball's* dumpster one day. I recall my brother, Raymond chased him until the dumpster quit, falling and pinning Eddie to the ground by his frail, slender right shoulder. I remember Eddie cried. His buckteeth and cheeks wet with fear. I remember too Raymond bending deep at the knees, pushing and pulling with his own fear to get the dumpster off. Then, I remember Eddie's mother and his two sisters running. I remember my mother and father and my brothers and sisters running, too, pushing and pivoting the dumpster up on its green steel wheels. Eddie was free and there was no talk about doctors or hospitals or lawyers or even police. Instead, Eddie was laughing and crying and his face shined with wet. I remember our families laughed and cried and embraced Eddie and each other too and like Eddie, we were happy and warm and free. That and other times in the Baker Homes were times when all stood right with the world. That and other times were when your muscles felt strong and when the air was thick with the warmth that comes from belonging and kinship. Powdered milk and roaches,

Father Fri and hand puppets at Christmas time, those were experiences and times to remember.

Mom and Dad did not move from the Baker Homes because they were asked to leave or because they wanted to. I look back and think on it now, and I know that we moved because Mom and Dad saved enough money and we could afford to. The Baker Homes was where we lived and where things seemed peaceful and equal and right. Moving in the station wagon with the wood on both sides meant being with my family again, and looking forward to more sunshine, warmth and better times.

On the other hand, moving to Alturuia Street on the south side of the city meant learning we were different, though, that we didn't and couldn't fit in. We learned that we were mostly not as good as the other families who were whiter who knew more about things and who knew more—like brethren—about each other. Moving to Alturuia also meant learning to be ashamed: ashamed of my parents, ashamed of my family and ashamed of myself in a place where there were no dumpsters, where there was no alley, where Eddie was gone, and where the houses were not joined at the sides with each other. Moving to Alturuia Street meant leaving a warm embrace and breathing and living with belonging and kinship and happiness no longer.

Learning More about Learning Less

Living on Alturuia also meant learning I was slower and mostly lesser than the rest. It didn't take long to learn these things well and it didn't take long to learn how cold they crept. When I was six I learned to hate being Puerto Rican in a world where there were no Puerto Ricans and on a street where being Puerto Rican meant that *you stink*. I learned to hate the smells of Spanish seasonings and the sounds of Spanish words and music. I learned to hate being outside in the sun and the rain and I learned to hate my family, my home and myself.

I never hated until we moved to Alturuia. I knew somehow that hating was an evil and forbidden thing to do, like lying or swearing, being untrue or talking back or disrespecting your elders. I remember learning hating, and I remember loving too. On Alturuia loving meant adoring white skin, straight hair, eyes that were not brown, and all of those things that separated me and that kept me from being human. Filth and dirt and evilness and life without worth were not what I had known but what I had become.

This was the new me and the beginning of my new future and life. This was the beginning that would not let me go and that forced me to want to go back. No more Eddie and no more Baker Homes. I hated everyone for taking these away. More, I hated Eddie and I hated the Baker Homes for not being white and for lying about being right with the world. Mine had become one shade of darker, dirtier skin where innocence and heaven did not belong; instead, it belonged to those without woolly hair and dark-black eyes like mine. On Alturuia I learned I was the son of the devil: a nigger and a bitch, suspicious, dirty, evil and not worthy of belonging. I could not know kinship and I deserved to never ever be trusted again. I was suddenly not worthy of being or ever being believed.

Indeed, this was the beginning of my very new future and the start of my very new life and I hated everything and everyone for putting me on this not-white, nihilistic track. Knowing and having learned to trust no one, not wanting to breathe, being white. These meant everything. But more than that, not being white meant everything too. Dirtying myself, learning when, where, how and whether to smile, hating and enjoying kinship and belonging with white, denying myself love, these were those things that became my idol. Worse, this was not only the track that I lay before me, this was the track that I wanted and prayed to follow.

Marking the Beginning of my Very New Life in School: First Grade

I remember my first day of school at P.S. 29. Mrs. Boyle, my kindergarten teacher from the year before at Roosevelt Elementary in Lackawanna, wrote on crisp, white paper that it might be this way when we moved and when I started first grade on the Irish Catholic south side of the city. I didn't understand.

Mrs. Boyle wrote:

Dear Roberto,

You have greatness in you.

Remember this and never forget. The school you attend in first grade will have more money than Roosevelt…more things…but this does not really matter and it should never hurt you. You must not worry about where you came from, what you have and don't have, who you are and if everyone tells you you're different and not good enough. You're a good and kind young man, respectful and very very smart and you should be proud. Not many children read…and so well before they start the first grade. Be strong. Don't get discouraged and everything will turn out fine.

Yo lo bendigan…Senora Boyle

With this, Mrs. Boyle handed me the thin, blue book and I read *The Old Man and the Sea* that night and I thought about Jesus Christ. Looking back on that first day in my new school, I recall Hemingway was more tattered then when I first received the book before. My mom said to show my book to my *new* teacher in my *new school* to show what I read and that I knew how to read.

At first, I feared bringing my special book with me to P.S. 29, but then I knew that before in the Baker Homes Mom and Dad were always right.

I think back then when I stood in front of the green door at P.S. 29 and it appears glossy and bumpy, covered in thick paint before me. Reaching up on my very most tiptoes, I recall I could see through the crack underneath the blurry Plexiglas window. My shirt was pressed stiff and hard from starch; my thin black tie was tucked into the front of my cuffed, wooly slacks. I remember Mom made me wear a light jacket that morning but that I ditched it and would have nothing to do with it before my new school. The sleeves were frayed and the zipper didn't zip, but on one side, and no matter how often she said, "Just being clean is good enough," I knew that if I'd told her, Mom would bring warmth and Mom would bring understanding to me. Just being clean wasn't good enough, I realized. Not anymore. I remember stuffing the coat up beneath the front seat of Dad's Chevy and running away quickly to my new school. Two hours early so I could be first in line, I felt clean and new and crisp like the morning dew, and I remember feeling proud or maybe good inside for not having to be embarrassed about wearing the light and tattered and imperfect coat.

Stars Are Children

Stars. Other children and some adults crowded behind me but I would not stop being first in line. I knew. The other side of the green door, heavy and locked tight, was where stars were grown inside. I imagined fits of sparkle dust and teachers and other adults filling the students' bodies and heads with wonder, taking them in warm and close. I imagined the teachers making the students into molten-hot, ivy-like stars, stars of white, and stars of diamond and belief. Mrs. Boyle told stories the year before of how first grade would be warm like this. In tight circles, shoulder to shoulder, we would sit legs crossed and we'd listen to Mrs. Boyle say how we were stars already and how next year in first grade we would shine even more brightly. I pressed Hemingway and Santiago close to my heart, wiping my shoes on the black of my trousers as the green door opened heavy and wide. Magic. When you looked in, you felt it and could smell and taste and see there was plenty of warm honey bread to go around.

"Slow down, don't run," the thin lady said as she stood taller and smiled. I remember I stood taller too, with hands together, waiting to be invited inside. "What's wrong, little boy?" the new lady asked. "Don't you *want* to come to school today? And where's your jacket? Didn't your mother think to dress you right this morning?"

I glared at the dull metal stairs leading up and inside the school, watching as beneath my stare the stairs fogged up and began to melt away. Watching, I remembered Mom said how to never cause a scene, how to never intrude or go inside even if invited. I was dazed. I knew to go to room 104 as Mom and I visited P.S. 29 some weeks before. Walking slowly, the smash of metal locker doors loud around me, I wondered how the students did not know to respect, to be quiet; how the students could interrupt the learning place and be so thoughtless and rude. I remember filling rich with excitement and I remember like yesterday Principal Cohen blocking my path. "Come with me," she pressed my warmth sternly. Observing that she was dressed in a gray wool jacket and starched white skirt, I watched her black shoes and felt her dry breath, knowing not to look a grown-up in the eye. I'd never seen a lady with a tie before.

"What's this?" she asked, tearing Santiago from my hands. "What grade are you in? Did you take this from someone, from the school library? Students your age don't read. You don't read this."

I swelled with fear, afraid to breathe, to ask why, to ask about the bathroom.

The office smelled like Comet. Mom and my sisters and I caked the green, powdery stuff on the sink and tub and let it stand before scrubbing away the grime, so I knew what Comet smelled like. "It's *The Old Man and the Sea* by Ernest Hemingway," I became certain that I'd done something deeply and very, very wrong. "I *do* know how to read," I continued. "Mrs. Boyle said I could have it and my mom said..."

"Never mind about that," I remember the school principal said. "I can read. Now look at me when I talk to you." Ms. Cohen squinted; her eyes, razor sharp and without color, cut hotly through the thick fish glasses and sliced me. "Do you see my name over there on that door? Do you know who I am? Do you know how to read? I'm the principal of this school and this is my office and we don't like stragglers and smart-mouth, know-it-all kids in the school to make noise and crack wise. Do you understand me?"

"Do you know who the principal is?"

I knew I did wrong but did not know what to say or do. Should I answer? Look at her eyes? What should I say? Should I say I was sorry? Maybe beg for Santiago back? And the note, should I say something about the note? Would she read it? Would she take it away, maybe understand? What I did wrong, like water, began to fill me. I was so ashamed and so wrong and so out of place. I reached for the frayed sleeve of my coat but it was not there. Except for delivering the attendance card, I had never been to the office before, but I knew, like everyone else knew, that the principal's office was for kids who were bad. Only bad kids were in the office and the office was where bad kids got dealt with and hurt, and the principal's office was now and big and hot and prison with fear inside me.

"What's your name and what room do you go to?" the principal said. "My name is Roberto and my teacher is room 102." I said it wrong.

"Not you," Ms. Cohen pushed, pointing to the wooden bench beneath the large gray clock. "I'll check your room number, then *I'll* be walking you to your room where you're supposed to be. You're not to be seen or heard or trusted to go by yourself."

Some time passed before Ms. Cohen took me by my shoulder to the room next door. The office beat without air and sweat trickled down my neck thick and hot like summer days. My feet hung above the floor while I sat and I remember my new shoes looked dull and felt tight. I held my body still and small, knowing that if I did not move, no one would see me and know who I was and maybe guess what I did or possibly even see me in the school principal's office. I wished not to be seen or heard or alive. Invisible. Being alive meant being oily like an overused rag or some dirty, evil, grungy kind of thing. I couldn't stand up.

"This is what happens when you don't do the right thing and go directly to your homeroom," Ms. Cohen said. She pushed me forward inside the door. I recall her wiping her hand on my neck, and I remember bending smaller when the students laughed and the teacher turned and saw me and shook her head. "Mr. Penna, this is your teacher Mrs. Feerlicks. We apologize for interrupting you on the first day of school, Mrs. Feerlicks. Some students don't know how to behave, *where they belong*. Mr. Penna will take a seat in the back and know not to dawdle or interrupt schooling anymore. He'll sit in the back where no one will see him. Isn't that right, Mr. Penna?"

Yes.

Fourteen squares separated my desk from the front door. I slid carefully and quietly into the wooden seat and folded my hands on top, wanting to crawl into the round hole in the desk's right-hand corner. Writing and deep pen cuts marked the desktop and I knew I would see Santiago and Mrs. Boyle's pretty writing no more. P.S. 29 was where stars were made. Mrs. Boyle said so, so I knew that it must be.

I looked at the bright faces, students sitting upright and forward, all very clean and new and attending to what the teacher said. I saw their faces shining white. Not like my brothers and sisters. Not like my mom and dad and not like me. I was late and missed what happened before and I was not white like the others. I was sully, dirty and dim, like under the refrigerator in a well-lighted kitchen. I missed the early stuff and knew I would have to work much harder to be slightly less bright and slightly less shiny than the dimmest star. I recall knowing then and what seems like forever that I was learning that I could not be.

This was schooling at P.S. 29 and in Mrs. Feerlicks' first grade classroom before schooling had begun. I would be ready before much time passed. I knew I had to be. I would be ready and the first to grasp, hold and know belonging and kinship like I had in schooling and at home before. I would be first, I insisted, to hold and become the diamond star, knowing full well that for some reason I didn't measure up and that school, the principal, my teachers, my parents, family and peers would not let me be. More, I knew then that it was I who had to say no. I was at fault and I was broken, and no matter how carefully placed and how hard the glue, my face and my hands and my hair and eyes were a different color and they would not wash away and they betrayed me. I was not white nor could I ever be enough to even measure up or belong or be even a dimly shining star. Mrs. Boyle and my mom and dad lied to me.

Playing with Peers and Back to School Again: Seventh Grade

"Ouch, that hurts," I thought to myself. I wanted to cry but worked instead to not let the hurt mark my face. Mom said no fighting. Like Jackie Robinson, she said, "Never, never fight mio. Always walk away." Timothy O'Shea held my arm wrenched deep up my back, his white face and red eyes and hair mashed against my brown face and my wooly brown hair. My elbow and shoulder screamed. Smiling and praising Tim O'Shea were the best things to do. I thought to myself, "These were the sure ways to show him and the others that I thought he was great. That they were great. That I knew they were better than I, and that maybe, if I laughed with them and at myself, and if I laughed hard and loud enough, then maybe I could fit in and be somewhat like them and maybe be a friend and belong. If only he would let go." "This was a good pain," I thought to myself, "better than no pain at all." I remember it hurt so much to give yourself away.

It was 11 o'clock on Wednesday morning. Some kind of furniture noise came from the room next door. It wasn't noise like a chair or desk being pushed or pulled across a wooden floor all at once. The sound was heavy and somewhat grinding. It had rhythm, a sort of heat. It didn't last long but I remember it sounded hard then slow then reached a peak again. Curious, I thought about knocking, maybe asking Mrs. Turley or Mr. Tocken if I could help. I remembered to stay seated instead, however. Mr. Tocken, the vice-principal at T. S. White Middle School, gave orders. Loud and clear. He said to sit in the wooden chair next to his desk and "absolutely do not move!" He always seemed angry, so I thought I'd better sit quiet so he and Mrs. Turley could finish moving furniture, finish their work inside.

"Well, Mr. Penna, we've got a problem here and I want to know how you cheated!" My hands were wet as I squeezed the seat and felt my pulse beneath my thighs. I thought I was in trouble for Tim O'Shea beating me. Mr. Tocken tugged his blue vest straight and then his face was in mine. I froze tight; I had to pee and thought how Mr. Tocken's breath smelled like burnt rubber.

"I'm sorry," I whispered to my knees, "I won't do it ever again. I promise." Not knowing what I did, I hoped Mom didn't know or wouldn't find out.

"Nobody finishes the test," Mr. Tocken ordered. "Not even the good kids. It's not made to be finished." He sat all wound up, ready to spring from his seat, and I feared him. "If you think your score is going to count, keep you in honors, well forget about it. You're done. It was a mistake your being put there and I shouldn't have let Mrs. Stargell say otherwise. I knew what to do with you and *now* look what you've done. I want to know how you cheated. I want to know where you got the answers. Did Mrs. Stargell tell you about the ITBS? Tell me. Tell me and I promise it won't leave this room. I won't tell your mother."

"You and Mrs. Stargell think you pulled something off, but it isn't gonna work. You're not gonna squirm away. You're not smart enough to pass and get away with cheating without me knowing how you did it. And you and Mrs. Stargell, working together during lunch and after school, not again. It's not normal. Not in this school. Not in any school. Never! And I promise— it's not kind. You're out of debate, you're out of the speaking contest, and you're out of math olympics, spelling bee and basketball for good. You'd better learn to be like you're supposed to be, and don't think this cheating won't go on your permanent record, because it will. You're gonna see more of me, so you'd better learn to act right and get used to it."

It was November and the gray hung on the wet windowpane. I had the one green spring jacket, but that was alright. It kept the cold out OK. Mrs. Schultz, my newly assigned seventh grade homeroom and English teacher, said to sit in the first seat. I remember I smiled and looked at the floor when Darryl said he was only the second dumbest student now.

"Those advanced honors books won't work for you here or in your other classes," Mrs. Schultz said. "I'll take them and assign regular ones and I don't know when I'll find the time." I covered my suddenly old new honors books with my jacket, folding my hands, feeling ashamed about them; I did not want to give them away. "The other boys and girls are reading from the blue Corwin. It's easier. You look on with Darryl until I can figure out what to do with you and how to catch you up and get you on schedule." I took the test from Iowa seven times that year before I figured out what an acceptable score was supposed to be. The more blanks I left, the more Mr. Tocken nodded and the happier he seemed to get. The more he let me be. My mom told me, "Don't afford no trouble, do what the teachers say without question or making a mess." My mom and dad labored in the steel mills, often with different shifts, so we didn't get to see them together for most of the time, and that meant we had to know better and make no fuss and mostly fend for our-selves. For me, this meant keeping it simple and following the straight and narrow. Causing no stir and staying out of trouble before trouble began were rules to be obeyed. Knowing that adults and especially teachers and schools were right—well, that rule was understood and to be followed exactly to the letter, too.

Looking back, Mom and Dad suffered with me and my brothers and sis-ters, I think. We weren't bad, and never did we dishonor our parents and family name. Nonetheless, I think on it now and I realize it must have hurt them more than it hurt my brothers and sisters and me. Seeing what we were and were not allowed to do; not being fluent and able to defend their chil-dren—these things made Mom and Dad age faster and before their years, I believe.

I learned. High or low test scores became the same back then until one day school and prejudice and being different and worse than the rest sud-denly no longer mattered to me. If grades, high or low, brought attention in any form that was loud and maybe unsettling—well, then, these were to be toned down, made average and inaudible. Staying on the straight and narrow meant not being and certainly being no different. No more than second best at everything was a safe and comfortable place to be.

As I write, I wonder now how Mrs. Stargell might be. I miss her and want her to know I'm making it by not being different; by missing answers on tests; by doing somewhat well; by doing right without letting others see. I want her to know I'm sorry for not finishing seventh grade English with her that year. I'm sorry Mr. Tocken expelled her from school. I'm sorry that it was my fault that he made her leave.

Enrolled in High School and More of the Same

A Mind Gone Awry

Naked memories,
Robbed of recognition!
Blind perception,
Void of understanding!

Confounded confusion,
Lost in tangled webs!

Wounded heart,
Stripped of yesterday!

Empty conversation,

Slowly Feeling
Silenced!

Mary Davila, Buffalo, New York

Vice-president of the ninth grade class. Being elected wasn't really important and didn't really matter. It was only a popularity contest. At least that's what Mrs. Johnson, my ninth grade algebra teacher, said.

High school was easy because the teachers never cared. Not like Mrs. Boyle and certainly not the way they did when I was younger. At South Park High everybody was from other parts of the city, so it mattered less what your teachers or anybody else for that matter said or thought or believed about anything, including me. In the morning Mr. Brown took homeroom attendance; then I was gone. Algebra for period one, social studies for period two, and then English, science; one class after the next and it didn't matter who you were, where you came from, what you believed. In high school all students were equal; dead; mysterious and wanting to be accepted; friends with each other, maybe. Many wandered wanting to be left alone. Nowhere to go, unimportant and nobody to be, high school worked because I could fail, forget my off color, and get lost around everyone and deep inside of me. Free.

In ninth grade I left my parents' home. School didn't matter and anytime I needed to, I could pass the test, make the grade, and achieve. Besides, moving out and sharing a place with a different family meant I could reinvent myself, change and color myself the same or white or somehow different and somewhat alive if so moved. Corned beef and cabbage, potato salad and soup, shopping to buy towels to make a home, a life. These were not Spanish rice and beans but foods of my new life and home, and somehow it followed that I should and could and still had to be so very different from what I was born and had grown to be. The man of the house sleeping alone, sleeping with others I was a grown-up and free at fifteen. I remember I checked in on Saturdays and Sundays, moved back home with Mom and Dad, and ate the rice with the beans.

I remember too that ninth grade during the summer of 1973 was hot with blacktop and rubber. I laid driveway enough to pay Mom some rent money and to buy my first house: a single converted to a double, a chance to be me. Mr. Salamander, the attorney who helped me close on the house, said I was an entrepreneur when he took the $700 check for closing, and I decided I liked what he said. He said I was a credit because I was young and because I had bigger plans than most others of my race. "You're a credit to your people and to your country," he said. I remember I believed him. He was an attorney garbed in the law—justice and what's right and he should have experience and knowledge and he should know what to say and do and especially what was ethical and right. His comment about Puerto Rico being my country wasn't lost and it made me chuckle and feel warm inside. Mr. Salamander told a joke and I felt good because I was in his circle and understood.

Eleventh grade. Made it this far, and then Mr. WeMet ruins everything. I read what he wrote in my yearbook and I knew what he meant. "To Bob. When will you learn the mind is mightier than the mouth?"

Mr. WeMet was my study hall teacher and the only teacher in high school who said things that mattered. He took me aside and asked when did I drop out of school? Why I helped others with school work but didn't do my own? "And what about college?" Mr. WeMet asked. "I've spoken with your teachers and they tell me you know what you're doing. They say you write well, when you write, that you've read the books, that math and science are no problem for you, that you just don't apply. Will you take the test? The SAT? Will you pass?"

I recall Mr. Piñto, my guidance counselor, said not to think about college and the SAT way back in ninth grade. In ninth grade he said to work in the steel mill "like your Porter Reecan mother and father" and "don't worry about books and tuition and school." "Your future is working with your hands," Mr. Piñto said. "Nobody trusts you and nobody will ever believe you and give you a chance, so you better do what's expected and right."

"Your skin is dark and you're just not white, so you know you're strong and can stand the heat. It's God's way of saying what's right and you've just gotta believe." I remember Mr. Piñto advised, "Go through high school, stay out of trouble and you're on your way. Teachers like me—we don't make money. Go make steel and have a family and with your skin you'll go places. It's important that you learn your place while you're still young. Stay off welfare and know who you are. The sooner the better. College is not you. The cost will hurt your family. Go to Bethlehem, make a living and things will turn out fine."

"Look at your parents," Mr. Piñto continued. "They're in labor and they made it good, didn't they? Don't you want to be like them? Are you ashamed of your mom and dad? Don't you know they know their place? What they've done for you? When will you wake up and know your place and decide?"

Leaving home from ninth to eleventh grade meant being different by washing myself almost nearly clean. I didn't want to look Puerto Rican. I didn't want to speak or smell or be near Spanish, and I just felt tired of my life and me. "Mrs. Boyle and Mrs. Stargell didn't say it would be this way," I thought, and I could not bring myself to forgive them both. Mom was not always right any more, and Santiago, Ishmael, Ellison, Lear were liars and phonies in a make-believe book world that wasn't real and that wasn't mine and that no longer mattered to me. Thejrs was a world that didn't exist but on paper and their world would never belong to people who looked and thought and smelled like me. My road was set in blacktop and steel in ninth grade, and what mattered most was observing and obeying and living my life without meaning or question or substance or care. I didn't hate high school, I just didn't know it. And as for college, well 1600 meant keeping my long hair, staying hidden, getting a scholarship and staying out of the Marines.

College Life and After

College life was better than the rest. I applied to two colleges and chose Buffalo State. I remember not really knowing what college was. It seems silly, I guess, but UCLA meant blue and gold and Saturday afternoon football, but not studying and college. What was college anyway? I'd never talked with anybody about how college worked. Closer to my parents' home, my chosen college meant taking two, rather than three, buses instead. Besides, Melville, Shakespeare, Dickinson, Orton and James—I could reread these if I wanted and nobody would ever check or care or know I'd read them before.

Going to classes, not going to classes, C grades and Ds—I'd visit the dean's secretary and she'd sign the permission slip and I was in. Whatever course I wanted. Drama, dance, poetry, absurdist lit—these were not challenging, a blur, and in fact, mostly disengaging for me. I took classes, paid with student loan money, and remained lifeless and unattached as I had grown to be.

One hundred and twenty-one credit hours and still nobody wondered who or what I was: what I studied, what I wanted and what I believed and why. Nobody cared. Especially not me. No major, no meaning. Nothing that mattered, nothing that mattered more or most. Mine was a pulse that was not distinct. I was safe and quiet and unobserved and living in a dry and vacant world. That was where I was, what I practiced, and where I aspired to be.

Dr. Whitehall talked about freedom in American lit class, bigotry and life in America, but who was he and what did he know of these? Could he really know? He said I was smart like Mrs. Boyle and Mrs. Stargell and some others had said before him, but I only parroted what he said, what my college professors said, and I gave them what they wanted from me. I'd learned in first grade—from my mother, father and teachers in school—good and very, very solid and true and clear indeed—smart was what Ellison said it to be. For someone brown and unclean, smart was being close to transparent, being nobody and everybody—impossible to figure about and a shadow that others could barely see.

Bruce Lee talked about water assuming the shape of the glass. Being invisible meant setting no sights and having no sight set upon me. No blood, no bleeding, no killing and no body counts were all that mattered, and while I was certain this was how it was and how it must always be, somehow I knew it could not—and that it should not and that it did not have to be. Ellison said people refused to see him; he said that when they approached, people saw only his surroundings, themselves, or figments of their imagination—indeed, everything and anything but him!

Violence was destruction and indifference cold death, and being meek and trivial and self-consumed and self-effacing and illiterate—all of these things no longer tugged at and worked to determine me. I grew tired of playing the game, the role, and of acting the silence that I was supposed to be. Tired of being nothing, tired of short-circuiting my brain and reacting as others would have me react and acting as I perceived they wanted me to behave, I could no longer repress my emotions and humanity to appear white and as a reflection of what others thought I should be. A walking dream, the most perfect personification of what my race was capable of achieving, I grew tired of knowing and knowing nothing at all except for being certain of what it meant to have no home, no soul, no person, and no right to kneel, stand or even be. Suicide, so I'd understood, was for cowards and while I could not know this, if cowardice was the deterrent, then I knew cowardice and for cowardice, suicide could not be.

When I was close to one hundred credits into my undergraduate degree, I found Eddie at the Truck-Stop Inn where we ate breakfast and dinner before I caught my bus to go to school. Eddie had just finished the midnight shift, and I'd only recognized him because of his still slight build and his large buckteeth. I didn't tell him about college that morning, only that I was catching the bus downtown looking for work. With that we sat and talked. I pushed my backpack and books beneath the table, and Eddie made it clear to me. "Look at you—you're so white you squeak." I remember when Eddie said this and I knew at once he was right. I could not go forward and I could not go back.

Katz (1978) writes that racism has been a part of the American way of life since the first whites landed on the continent. Although the United States prides itself on its ideologies about human rights and particularly on its philosophies of freedom and equality, Katz nonetheless asserts that the bleak reality is that, both historically and presently, the United States is based on and operates under a doctrine of white racism.

This racism can be seen historically in white people's interactions with Native Americans, in the development of the doctrine of manifest destiny, in the establishment of Indian reservations, in the capture and enslavement of Africans, in the wartime internment of Japanese Americans, and in the attitude of most white Americans that nonwhite must *fight* for those rights that white Americans have enjoyed since birth. Racism, Katz argues, is manifest not only in the white ghettos of the suburbs, in the South, and in the North.

Racism escapes no one. It is part of us all and has deeply infiltrated the lives and psyches of both the oppressed and the oppressors.

I respect and admire what Katz said about white racism in the United States, and intellectually, philosophically and as a college professor and researcher, I study, generally agree and admit that I know of ideas like these. Personally, though, I also know that I was raised by my parents never ever to fight, and that in Katz's world of black and white nearly every U.S. citizen has a race and home to which to return and belong. Eddie made it clear that day and helped me to understand that while I pined to belong in a world that was white, I failed and could no longer belong in a world with people of a nonwhite color. I did not and could not fight. I could not know what it meant to be white, and I could not know what it meant to be back home again with those whose brown looks were pictured in me.

Contemporary writers, researchers, teachers and theorists who are sometimes described as great suggest that examining the effects of racism on minorities is not enough, and that what is called for is an examination of the effects of racism on the quality of life of all Americans. Du Bois (1903) examined the effects of racism on blacks and whites over one hundred years ago. Myrdal (1944) described racism as an American dilemma. In 1968 the Kerner Commission said that racism was a white problem, asserting that until the real perpetuators of racism are confronted and educated, little would change. This important thinking and writing seems all fine and good, except what does it mean when a member of your home, community and race says and makes clear to you that you no longer belong with him and other nonwhites? Coupled with that, what does it mean when whites who are in a position to know of such things hold doubts about your credibility, agreeing to accept and acknowledge you only when you give in and agree to act close to but slightly less than white?

While in college, I learned that I was not white, and for many, the majority perhaps, I am a different shade of black. Meanwhile, for some Latinos cut, at first, from the same cloth as me, I learned that to them, I speak and I look a darker shade of white. For them, I am a traitor of sorts who has cursed and given up the good life and the *gente*. I am someone or something that did not adequately carry on the critical Latino fight. Struggling for so long to be invisible, to be accepted and to be what whites thought I should be; struggling to go unobserved and to not fight; I find that invisible for the masses is who I am and that the color of water is what I no longer care to be.

White, nonwhite, off-white, red, yellow, brown and black, for you and others I may be a man—but only to a limited degree. For me, I find that I have no place, no home and only faith and love to make and come home to because I do not fight, and because I have a fierceness for justice and faith and youth that boil deep and now deeper inside of me. I know faith and love and I have learned to endure and to make justice. Race is all important and not important to me. Children and what is good and just are what matters to me.

Given this is what I believe, it means I surrender my home and my place and my life and any chance to discover what is possible and what it might mean to be. I aspire to look on the works of others with fairness and caring and freedom as my matrices, and if they (or better yet) we, do not measure up, then I try harder to be gentle, to be kind, to love, to have love denied me, to cave, to not walk away and to understand. To be good and to be just—the play's the thing. My life and being and future are unimportant, for what matters most is to help others and with that, to trap the conscience of the King.

Teaching Myself Last

Buffalo State said no. I'd taken most, but I did not take the basic composition course. Professor Jekle said I'd ruined his summer when he signed the paperwork that allowed me to graduate, and I nodded and smiled and said thank you and walked away. No ceremony. No recognition. All that was left was being a nuisance to the Buffalo Public School District and getting them to meet with me and give me a chance to teach.

"Wow, Dr. Wile is nice and I can't wait to teach," I remember thinking after the interview. Dr. Wile, the director of English for the district, interviewed me and gave me my first assignment. I would teach seventh grade English and science at Riverside Elementary School. I was the fourth teacher the students had had that year. It was November and Dr. Wile and Mrs. Bork said the students were behind. "The students were assigned to a fourth homeroom class," Principal Bork explained, "and the teachers were allowed to decide who —to get rid of and who —they would keep."

Monday morning and I was to meet with Mrs. Kinsella to discuss what the students had learned. The door to room 304 was blocked by a broken chair. I stepped over it and found Mrs. Kinsella seated, her head on her desk. Students sat in small clusters talking and the noise was loud. One child held Mrs. Kinsella's purse outside the third-story window. Others jumped rope, shoved, harassed and slept in the litter, and I knew I was home. Not thinking about what I should do, I left for the door and returned next to Mrs. Kinsella's desk a wooden slat from the broken chair in my hand.

"Bam!" The noise was louder than I expected it would be. "Good morning." I stood in front of the class. The students were silent. "My name is Mr. Peña, and I'm going to be your teacher for the rest of the year."

The students in room 304 taught me many things. Discipline, love and respect—these were understood and would not be compromised, and I believe the children may have held them in abundance and learned something about holding these values from me. Trouble in or out of class, high-and underachievement, these meant dealing with Mr. Peña, and I sense my presence told the students they had a place to come home to for care. Other educators and parents commented that the students were more disciplined and respectful, that those students who were ridiculed and picked on by the rest were no longer ostracized.

I could not and cannot comment about the role I played. This was not and is not the appropriate thing to do because it is not about me. I'd surrendered myself some years before and was therefore not important. I knew and believed in the students, and what was good was what mattered entirely. Teaching was meant for students and not meant for me. I did not know it at the time, but what once was mousiness and invisibility became *myself last* and maybe what my parents and family meant I should be. I have no way of knowing this. Reflecting and talking about practice—this was not what was meant to happen. We were to be judged (and not by ourselves) by the quality of our work and the success of others.

A nurse proficient in seven languages and a classical guitarist who never graduated from third grade—these were my mother and father and I do not know how this happened and came to be.

Never knowing my aunts, uncles and grandparents, never talking with Mom and Dad and my sisters and brothers about who they were, what they thought, what they wanted, what they believed— this course of my life seems at times to be deterministic to me, as though God or some other being were left in charge. I have faith, but I don't know religion. God as faith surrounds and holds warmth inside, but church holds no place for me.

Being a Professor

When I left Arizona State to study law, I had 60 doctoral students. The max was to be fifteen students to chair, but saying no in education didn't make sense to me. I recall sitting in meetings, being told, hearing others say, and having ASU colleagues tell graduate students before me that beginning professors did not chair dissertations. I'd asked the dean of the School of Education how this made sense, and he had no answer for me. Assistant professors established a record of scholarship. High student evaluations meant teaching was too easy. Community service could not count. I'd gone to Arizona State not to obtain tenure there, but to obtain tenure in any university across the United States.

I was promoted to associate professor and arrived at the recognition ceremony in time to help food service staff clean what remained from the celebration. I was advising dissertations at the time, not because I love the work but because it made sense that there were so many students who needed help and advising students was the place I was supposed to be.

Teaching College Now

I am an associate professor at Seattle University and feel fortunate that I can be. Recently I was told that my scholarship intimidated others and that for promotion I would need to work harder to get others to like me. I've also been accused of seeing everything as having to do with justice and race and not paying enough attention to how my ideas about justice make others feel badly and in ways they do not want to feel. I've been told that I cannot be a professor and study law at the same time as this is too much work and my students would suffer.

I've taught and spoken at conferences with students and helped them to publish, and when colleagues look and know this to have happened, they still insist this cannot be. Be, be, be. For years and so often it has been a struggle of what cannot and what has come to be. I am not sure what I know or what I've learned from drinking in this struggle. It is ongoing, it is unyielding, and still while it defines, I neither know nor do I believe that it is all there is to me.

I study law as I believe that while teaching and education can make for right, law is effective to bare some teeth and to ensure that right comes to those who need law and lack opportunity most. Thurgood Marshall described the nature and intent of law and nestled with teaching and social justice: this is brother and sister and warmth to me. Writing these passages is intensive work, but I know of the potential of these words to heal and make meaning not of myself, but of what others see in themselves and what others might be.

Critical theorist, postmodern paradigm, positivist tendencies—these seem to describe what people are and what people are not, as well as what people want and do not want to be. It seems more apparent that people are one, both, more and all of these, and I wonder how it matters and why they care. Our focus on self and on others for too long has dulled our senses to a different economy, I believe. Many theories of being, it seems, approach this subject packed with explicit and implicit assumptions about the nature of the social world and how it is viewed, investigated, and possibly meant to be. These assumptions raise questions about whether race, for example, is external or internal; whether race is objective or subjective; and whether race is real in the social world. These assumptions raise doubts too about whether race is the product of the individual and/or the offspring of the collective mind, and if lacking race, I wonder if I and others can somehow continue to be.

Still, I study works and find that other assumptions deal with how we are to understand race and how it is that we are to communicate about race to others. These assumptions also inform how knowledge about race is obtained. They determine whether knowledge about race is to be viewed as either true or false; valid or invalid. Assumptions of this sort also focus on whether knowledge is hard and capable of being transmitted, it seems, in concrete form to others. Additionally, assumptions like these focus on whether knowledge about race is soft, more subjective and substantive, social and possibly of a spiritual kind. Finally, assumptions made seem to determine whether social scientists view knowledge about race as able to be acquired, or as knowledge about race as having to be experienced.

Associated with ontological and epistemological discussions like these are a third set of assumptions that have implications for how we go about trying to understand race. Different ontological and epistemological assumptions about the nature of knowledge, and in this case, belonging and race, incline social science investigators to use different methodologies to study race and to know about what goes on with regard to race and other things. This means that the possible range of choices about how to conceptualize and investigate and teach race are probably limitless, and that depending upon the nature of one's ontological and epistemological stance, methods for conceptualizing and investigating and teaching about race are likely to take shape as dichotomies: valid or invalid, distinct or interrelated, and for the most part, at odds and irreconcilable with each other—with you and with me. Some social science methodologies, for example, seem to treat the social world like the "natural world," as being hard, real, and external to the individual. Survey results and census numbers are examples of these. Other methodologies treat concepts like race as more personal, subjective, and possibly as relative in nature. This story may be an example of same.

In any event, this resolve of ontology, epistemology and social science methodology is important, I believe, as it describes being and not being and as it renders identity, verifiability, voracity, legitimacy and possibly immortality to one or another competing groups, and to persons like you and me. Additionally, this resolve seems effective for providing and helping peoples find themselves and their places in the world. Maybe, and possibly without intent, this resolve of ontology, epistemology and social science methodology may also be important for achieving priority. This resolve may be important too as it screams of an individual and possibly a socio-and human pathology. This penchant for focusing on all that is human, in other words, seems somehow less humane, as it oftentimes regards things that are human as being at odds; as it sees those things that are not human as somehow being less; and as focusing for the most part on what is human frames those things that are not, or at least not understood to be, as not being or being of lesser substance and significance in the world, and oftentimes, as not being alive and important at all.

Following is a poem and then a discussion about race and how race is conceptualized. Considering the ontological, epistemological, and methodological character of this discussion is probably relevant for getting at the conceptual and theoretical underpinnings and dispositions that color this discussion and me. Concurrently, deliberating on the nature of the discourse may also only be relevant, as the analyses performed contribute to a more real, humane and appropriate positioning of humanity as something that is as well as something that is other than at the center of the universe.

Concepts of Race: A Beginning or Anthropocentric Approach?

Ozymandias

I met a traveler from an antique land
Who said: Two vast and trunkless legs of stone
Stand in the desert....Near them, on the sand,
Half sunk, a shattered visage lies, whose frown,
And wrinkled lip, and sneer of cold command,
Tell that its sculptor well those passions read
Which yet survive, stamped in these lifeless things,
The hand that mocked them, and the heart that fed:
And on the pedestal these words appear:
"My name is Ozymandias, King of Kings:
Look on my words, ye Mighty, and despair!"
Nothing beside remains. Round the decay
Of that colossal wreck, boundless and bare
The lone and level sands stretch far away.

Percy Bysshe Shelley

The importance of race is undeniable. It defines, binds, nourishes and tears women and men apart. For these and reasons that are more humane, maybe, race belongs and must remain a part of the human conscience. More than that, like class, ethnicity, gender, sexuality and all that is human, race must be included and understood to realize plurality and maybe transcendence, and to realize all that it means to be whole, just and truly humane and good.

Ontological, epistemological, and methodological issues characterize race in discussions and scholarly reports. Additionally, race in interaction is often revealed by discussion, or the lack thereof, of relations among humans, different species, environments, spirituality and what I believe to be grace. Whether predicated upon human nature and/or discussions about human interaction as informed by race, the story about race, while not all told and complete, for the most part, has focused on views that are mechanistic and deterministic as pertains to relations with the human and nonhuman world.

Early and current thoughts about race, and especially concepts like racism, are often characterized by sympathy and understanding, hostility and rejection, and by categorizing behaviors that generally do not account for the in-dividual. Instead, thoughts and actions, even those that are well-meaning, oftentimes condemn the individual on the basis of her or his presumed membership in a group about which others, without sufficient warrant, think depressed thoughts and even ill. This categorizing behavior is neither organic nor ecological. It does not herald the specific, mutual and holistic benefit of race, nor does it stress individuality, unity and the interdependence of society, social systems, spirituality and place. Instead, past and contemporary theories of race and racism often seem more concerned with explaining disequilibria and dysfunctionality, defining socially deviant or nonconforming behavior as pertains to race and on the basis of proximity of race to group, majority, and/or racial (often defined as white) norms.

This tendency to associate race with conforming and nonconforming behaviors, with normalcy and deviance, lays the basis for past, current and future studies of unanticipated and anticipated consequences, I believe, and for similar investigations of social and individual function and dysfunction. Narrowing the achievement gap, as so many school districts are wont to do, for example, while appropriately drawing attention to the nature of testing, different test outcomes and possibly achievement and social in-equities, oftentimes is considered in just such a way as to be socially Darwinist. This approach implies, as Thurgood Marshall argued, that members of one group, as demonstrated by high or low student test scores, do or do not measure up. Moreover, and as a result of thought processes like these, members of that one group or the other are presumed to be naturally and possibly inherently inferior or even superior to members of the *other* group. This approach to thinking about and handling race seems hurtful, unhealthy and grievous to me. The tendency to associate race with conforming-non-conforming and acceptable-deviant behaviors, in other words, has the debilitating effect of attaching inaccurate and inflated perceptions to majority (normal?) populations while just as erroneously and certainly more devastatingly attaching inaccurate, deflated, and damning perceptions to individual and minority (subnormal ?) group members.

Many positive and some critical race theories, as well as theories informed by Marxist and to a lesser extent Weberian traditions, while more or less effective for drawing needed and infinitely overdue attention to matters like race, do so in such a way as to be elitist and mainly anthropocentric. These theories and thoughts about race oftentimes pay little to no attention to organisms like the planet Earth, and to concepts like intimacy, spirituality and possibly transcendence, to name a few. Additionally, and possibly like positivist approaches before them, while critical and like-minded frames do aim to improve the human condition by focusing on those power differentials that infuse and for many dominate life experience, these approaches quite possibly altogether also cannot ultimately realize equitability in terms of matters like race.

Founded upon debate and an approach that is dialectic, critical thought, while superseding positive notions by focusing on privilege and power differentials as pertains to race, cannot deliver equity and the promise of freedom, as creating equalizing structures will likely result in the re-creating of disequalizing structures that are potentially harmful and exclusionary for those with less power and for the powerless. Reminiscent of positivist and other exclusive and exclusionary frames, critical and other neo-postmodern frames seem likely to contribute to that state of *poisoness* which critical and other postmodern theories that are purportedly egalitarian in nature so vehemently work to deny.

Anthropocentrism, then, describes that dual-edged and possibly subtle form of racism, sexism and other isms that survive and that describe what I perceive as the logic of genocide. Anthropocentrism as the logic of genocide starts and ends with the tendency to place human beings at the center of the universe. Genocide seems a right choice of word, for as long as society focuses on matters that, for the most part, are exclusively and predominantly human, and that treat how humans interact with humans at the expense of examining things like how humans interact with the environment, justice, spirit and difference, society will then continue to suffer a logic of genocide that spells the deliberate, slow and mechanistic death of individual, individuality, unity, culture and race. With hands and minds that are well-meaning and intentioned, those who analyze race and matters like race in their past and current contexts possibly suffer most from years of learning and skill in the acquisition and application of thoughts and procedures that are born from competition, rivalry, and callousness, and that are hued by the tendency for making invisible matters like ecology, justice, capability, poverty, spiritualness, sexuality and race.

A more comfortable place, as alluded to by Ellison, Friere, Marshall and others, who speak of what I tend to call grace, might also be better described as "plural" or possibly as "plural theory." Such a demarcation does not abandon previous attempts at improving the condition of women and men. To do so would be to discard knowledge and with that human and nonhuman experience and tradition. Instead, a contemporary pluralist approach is likely founded on improving the human condition by lending primary and concurrent interest to concepts like place, transcendence, difference and possibly other physical and spirit-like matters. Probably of a spiritual yet a non-religious kind, a plural approach might also encourage society to survive primitive constructs based upon competition, market rivalries and their seductions, in favor of concepts like integration, inclusiveness, inter-and intra-dependence, environment, equity, ecology, transcendence, love and finally race as place.

Drinking in law's spirit, writing and speaking and dying one hundred times for the needy and weak—this is what it means to defeat genocide and what it appears I have chosen, had chosen, and what has become of me. I decided long ago not to practice law, as I have no designs on gold culled from the depths of others' misery. Writing, speaking, teaching and caring are what I came to value most and with that star called justice, what I most want to do and be. Writing and teaching and living social justice were and to this day are all of what I bleed. Child, youth, college student; university professor, fit and misfit; for Mom and Dad, Lisa and our children, our weakest and most needy—I sense writing, speaking and teaching social justice are important, and as they are for them, a son, father and citizen, so they are for you, perhaps, and for me.

Resolution

I got "proofed" at the lumberyard yesterday, the yard next to the elementary school where we've enrolled our three children. One day after I lost the ñ in my name, the attendant asked, "Who do you work for?" "Where is your bank?" "Is this your credit card?" "Do you have a driver's license?" "When were you born?" "Where?" "Do you speak English?" "How come you speak English so well?" "Have you shopped here before?" and "How can your employer be reached?"

I nodded my head, smiled and pleasantly addressed each of the attendant's questions. I purchased two hinges, some trim for the door, screws and a nail set: $7.93 including tax. Not a bad deal; and all at a fair price, just for giving away me. I thought of the joy in community-in-difference, and then I looked ahead at the elementary school across the street and felt what he said and believed. I thought about my children and their brown skin and dark eyes, and I worried what might be.

References

Du Bois, W. E. B. (1903). *Souls of black folk, in three Negro classics* (Ed. by John H. Franklin). New York: Avon, 1965 (originally published in 1903).

Katz, J. H. (1978). *White awareness: Handbook for anti-racism training.* Norman, Oklahoma: University of Oklahoma Press.

Kerner Commission. (1968). National Advisory Commission on Civil Rights. New York: Bantam.

Myrdal, G. (1944). *An American dilemma: The Negro problem and modern democracy.* New York: Harper and Brothers.

CHAPTER TWO

From the Outside In:
A Journey toward Justice

Kristin Guest

"Knowledge can generate feeling, but it is feeling that generates action. For example, we may know all about injustice to minorities in our society, but until we feel strongly about it we will take little action. Unless knowledge is related to an affective state in the learner, the likelihood that it will influence behavior is limited" (Weinstein & Fantini, 1970, p. 27). It was many years ago, shortly after I began my now 25-year university teaching career, that I came across this quote in *Toward Humanistic Education* by Weinstein and Fantini. Recently, I heard a similar thought expressed, this time by Fr. Hans Kolvenbach, superior general of the Jesuit order worldwide, speaking to members of Jesuit universities from across the United States: "When the heart is touched by direct experience, the mind may be challenged to change. Personal involvement with innocent suffering, with the injustice others suffer, is the catalyst for solidarity which then gives rise to intellectual inquiry and moral reflection." He went on to say:

> Students, in the course of their formation, must let the gritty reality of this world into their lives, so they can learn to feel it, think about it critically, respond to its suffering and engage it constructively. They should learn to perceive, think, judge, choose and act for the rights of others, especially the disadvantaged and the oppressed (Kolvenbach, 2000).

How do we teach so that our students, in fact, "learn to perceive, think, judge, choose and act for the rights of others?" This is my goal as a university educator, and I struggle each quarter with exploring both the meaning of this challenge and the process toward its implementation.

As an educator, the best ways for me to respond to the enormous injustices that exist in our world, I have decided, are through my work in my classrooms, and with my colleagues within my school and across my university. A South American prayer asks, "For those who hunger, give them bread. For those who have bread, give them a hunger for justice." Most of my students and university colleagues have bread. My goal is to contribute to their hunger for justice. The enormity of the problems, the unforgettable images of pain among my students who taught me a little about what it's like to grow up as a person of color in "the land of the free," of malnourished children in Nepal and Malawi, can overwhelm, and anything I can do by way of direct support is a proverbial "drop in the bucket." But I can use my position of white privilege and my power as a university professor, fortunately at a university that has a commitment to education for justice as a central part of its mission. I can hope that raising issues of justice as I teach, of helping students recognize and, more importantly, have contact with "the gritty reality of this world," has some "ripple effect" as my students may bring a justice perspective to their work as teachers and school psychologists. How did my journey begin?

What Grounds Your Work for Justice? My Formative Years

"What grounds your work for justice?" It was a provocative question, worthy of consideration. The question was posed by our university president at a day of "Dialogue Toward Justice," a conversation among the entire faculty in our School of Education. We were meeting to determine whether we could agree on a common vision of "education for justice" as we work with graduate students in a number of programs ranging from teacher education to counseling and school psychology, teaching English to speakers of other languages (TESOL), and adult education.

To discover the roots of my journey to justice, the grounding for my commitment, I have been trying to return to those experiences that touched my heart, that enabled me to experience the "gritty reality of this world" and, as a result, led to critical thinking and response. My journey is different in some fundamental ways, I think, from those of other authors in this volume. Personal experiences with oppression and injustice played an important role for many of them in planting the seeds for their journeys toward justice. Mine? It comes from a lifetime of white privilege.

While some of the experiences I recount were direct experiences, some were experiences that others shared with me, so, in that sense, they came "from the outside in." It is with some trepidation and anxiety that I write this story as a privileged white woman. I am aware that persons of color may well be suspicious: What can she possibly know of injustice and oppression? Why does she care? How can I trust her? And perhaps hardest of all for me, how can she have anything of value to contribute to a dialogue? While I understand that questions like these may occur and are legitimate for some, it also feels at times like my voice may be discounted and my legitimacy questioned from the start because of my whiteness. Ironic, admittedly, that this is my reaction when discussing issues of justice which arise precisely because persons of color and other marginalized groups have historically so often had their voices discredited. I feel anger at times if I think I will be discounted simply by virtue of who I appear to be before my voice is even heard. But I write, and I teach about injustice and justice because I believe that we can only take steps toward confronting injustice in the world if those steps are taken by persons from all racial and ethnic backgrounds.

Sonia Nieto writes, in her foreword to Gary Howard's book *We Can't Teach What We Don't Know* (Howard, 1999), that she "had been waiting for years for a more public discussion about the responsibilities that White teachers have in challenging racism and creating schools that can accept, affirm, and build on the identities of all students. . .Whites, too, need to engage in the multicultural dialogue" (Howard, 1999, p. xiii). So while I cannot write or teach as a person who's had frequent experiences of oppression, I can write and teach as a white woman of privilege from the experiences that have shaped my life. I can also write of what I have learned from those who live with daily experiences of racism and oppression who have been my teachers about justice.

My commitment to justice comes originally from the outside in. I am a privileged white woman, born into a physically and emotionally healthy, very loving middle-class family of Scandinavian stock in St. Paul, Minnesota, the heartland of America. Our house was a comfortable, modest wood two-story building with a small yard, on a street lined with arching elm trees. A two-block walk took us to Phalen Park with rolling hills and a lake with a large swimming beach. In the park we raked piles of leaves to jump into; we sledded, skied and skated in the winter, played hide-and-seek and swam with neighborhood friends in the summer. It felt safe: no warnings here in these times about not talking to strangers. We freely roamed the streets and the park, knew everyone in our block, and took to the street on summer evenings for games of kick-the-can with neighborhood kids of varied ages, continuing until our mothers called saying that it was time to get ready for bed. I walked to school and home at noon for lunch, meeting up along the way with my largely blond, Norwegian and Swedish Lutheran friends, two of whose fathers were the ministers of two large Lutheran churches on the east side of St. Paul. Diversity in high school came in the form of Italian and a few Polish classmates from the Payne Avenue area—not a lot of diversity in today's terms.

My family never considered ourselves wealthy and my parents, products of growing up in the Great Depression, were always careful with money. When it came time for college, the option for my brother and sister and me was the state university, the University of Minnesota, commuting to school with our father who worked on campus.

Loving, secure, encouraged in my efforts at home and at school, this describes my childhood, and I share the good fortune of these family characteristics with other children of many backgrounds who feel loved, secure and encouraged. Even as a woman growing up in an era when many women were severely limited because of gender, my dreams and efforts were always encouraged by my professional, working parents.

But my experiences have also been different in some critical ways, by virtue of my whiteness, from those of some of my friends, colleagues and coauthors. Part of this heuristic inquiry is an effort to understand how I gained privilege from my whiteness in ways of which I was unaware. As McIntosh notes, assumptions of whiteness gain much of their power by passing as "normal," "an invisible package of unearned assets which I can count on cashing in on each day, but about which I was 'meant' to remain oblivious" (McIntosh, 2001, p. 164). I was white as a racial category based on physical features, and also white "as experience," referring to "the daily benefits of being White in our society," and also white "as ideology," referring to "the beliefs, policies, and practices that enable Whites to maintain social power and control" (Thompson, 1997). I was part of the group of dominant voices in our culture.

So my concerns with issues of justice come not from the inside out but from a place of privilege and from the outside in. In my search to answer our president's question, "What grounds your work for justice?" I cast back to think about those experiences that were formative in the development of values related to justice. Two were, for me, fundamental: my family and my church.

Certainly my parents' influence played a major role in my commitment to justice. While avoiding preaching, they communicated from the time we were young the sense of responsibility that privilege involves. Most powerfully, they modeled the values of commitment to just causes and service to others in their lives. My father, trained as an attorney, spent his life in public service work. As the executive secretary of the League of Minnesota Municipalities, he traveled the state of Minnesota learning about the needs of community governments of all sizes, and then lobbied in the legislature on their behalf. Later, he taught part-time in the Political Science department and Institute for Public Affairs at the University of Minnesota. My mother taught high school English in a small town in the Minnesota prairie early in her career, and then spent many years teaching parent and family life education around the state through the University of Minnesota Extension Division. In addition, my parents volunteered in their community, work ranging from Girl Scout and Boy Scout leaders to service on our church board, and on the boards of the Friends of the Public Library (Dad) and the Minnesota Children's Society (Mom). In both cases, their professional work at times involved taking on controversial issues, something they did without question when they believed the cause was just. They provided my values foundation, but their experiences, like mine, were largely those of privilege. They did experience the Great Depression, but at that time most people were in the same position so elements of injustice or oppression were not prominent.

It was, curiously, the group in my childhood that represented the single way in which I experienced being "different" that was at the same time another potent source of the values that worked their way from the outside in to deepen my concerns for justice. That was the Unitarian church in St. Paul in which I grew up. While all of my Lutheran friends regularly worshipped on Sunday mornings at Arlington Hills or Gustavus Adolphus Lutheran churches, where the two friends' fathers preached, my family got in our car to drive across town to the single Unitarian church in St. Paul, Unity Unitarian Church.

The church is a lovely light sandstone building located just off of Summit Avenue, which runs from the St. Paul Cathedral on a hill to Mississippi River Boulevard. A wide, tree-shaded boulevard, Summit is lined with some of the wealthiest homes in St. Paul, old wealth that dates back to the founding of the Weyerhaeuser timber industry and the Great Northern Railroad. As a child, I loved the sprawling white colonial Summit Avenue home that was the Weyerhaeuser residence, and I was fascinated by the carriage house behind the massive stone James J. Hill mansion. But to get to church, we drove through the single, large "black part of town," the Selby-Dale neighborhood of modest to ramshackle African American homes that stood nearby in stark contrast to the Summit Avenue mansions. We passed the large African American church and often saw families coming or going from or to worship. It was a part of St. Paul that most of my eastside friends never saw, living largely in the several-mile radius around Johnson High School, Phalen Park, and Arlington Hills and Gustavus Adolphus churches. It was a part of town we only drove through on our journey to a church nearby but worlds away in the experiences and circumstances of the congregations.

"May the flame upon the altar of this chapel shine in our hearts always, reminding us of the dark places to which we may carry light and fortifying us in moments of doubt and discouragement." These were words I spoke every Sunday morning in the Unity Church chapel for many years as I moved from kindergarten through high school. I loved that chapel: simple, white walls with a dark wood altar and organ, which I played in high school, cane chairs with dark wood frames, and—what I loved most of all—a beautiful small bronze statue on the altar of a Native American on horseback, arms outstretched in prayer. Something about the beauty and grace of that statue spoke to me deeply, as did the words we spoke and the stories we listened to. The stories were about racism, intolerance, global human rights, prison reform, housing discrimination, and other issues that spoke to my broadening view of the world. They reflected the fundamental Unitarian Universalist values that continue to provide such a large part of the grounding for my commitment to justice.

> We covenant to affirm and promote:
> The inherent worth and dignity of every person;
> Justice, equity, and compassion in human relations;
> Acceptance of one another and encouragement to spiritual growth in our congregations;
> A free and responsible search for truth and meaning;
> The right of conscience and the use of the democratic process within our congregations and in society at large;
> The goal of world community with peace, liberty, and justice for all;
> Respect for the interdependent web of all existence of which we are a part.

These are the basic principles to which members of Unitarian Universalist congregations commit themselves. They are principles which I heard spoken and saw lived by many adult models in our church during my formative years: our minister who served on a Minnesota governor's commission for rights of the mentally ill and advocated strongly for these rights partly as an expression of his embodiment of the principles of the inherent worth and dignity of every person, and of justice, equity and compassion in human relations; in members of our congregation who were active in the fair housing movement in the Twin Cities in an era where discrimination in real estate was still blatant and far reaching; in outreach to the needs of the Selby-Dale community through which we drove each Sunday.

Unity Church provided some of the exposure and experiences that sharpened my sense of injustice in our community and in the world, and deepened the value I had also learned from my parents of our responsibility toward others. The experiences touched my heart; they stirred me and punctured my sense of a safe, fair world in ways that are a part of my own journey toward justice. Two specific memories may illustrate.

The first is from a Sunday morning when I was, probably, in junior high school. In a sermon addressing segregation in the American South, the minister read an extended excerpt from *Killers of the Dream*, Lillian Smith's book rooted in her southern childhood. She describes the book as an attempt to answer the question, "Why has the white man dreamed so fabulous a dream of freedom and human dignity and again and again tried to kill his own dream?" (p. 11) The excerpt, which lodged in my heart and mind, was about an experience Ms. Smith had while directing a summer camp for girls. She describes a conversation she had with an older camper who had spent many summers at the mountain camp and was going to college in the fall.

Earlier in the evening the girls had, with Ms. Smith, created and performed a play that she describes as their attempt to "try their strength against…the ghost of custom and conscience…that still divide our children and southern tradition."

"The girls struggled with how to end the play and, after emotional arguments and help from Lillian Smith in finding a way out of an impasse, they ended the play with a dance portraying the conflict among Southern Tradition, Conscience, Religion and Science. Then the children decided that Chinese and Japanese and Germans and Russians and Negroes could come from all ends of the earth and play with the little Prince." Lillian Smith goes on to write, "It was make-believe and we knew it. But we could not let our play die as so much that is young has died on that old wall, segregation. But at supper, the children looked tired and preoccupied and I knew we had failed to answer the question twisting in their minds."

Late that night, long after the lights were out in the cabins, the college-bound camper came into Ms. Smith's office. She stood for a moment, looking pale and tense, and then spoke words that Ms. Smith said became etched so deeply in her mind that she believed she could write them without distorting their truth.

"'I don't know how to begin; I shock myself as I try. I think you have done a terrible thing to children.'

'Tell me why you think so.'

'You see,' she was sorting the words that had piled up during her sleeplessness, 'you have made us want to be good. *Mature*, you've called it. You taught us to be honest, not to cover up things. You made us think it fine to be like that, even when it hurt. All these years, you've said so much about human dignity—it's a nice phrase. But it's all wrong!'

'You told us we were like all children everywhere; that money and color, the church you go to, don't make any difference. And the kids here believed you. You said the only real differences have to do with values and interests and tastes. And you said that the most precious right a human has is his [sic] right to be different. Even his [sic] right to be dull.'

'We liked that. And we believed you. We loved you for giving us ideals that we could be proud of. We wanted to live them. They seemed so fine.' She laughed a bitter little laugh, then added softly, 'But I almost hate you tonight, for letting us fall in love with beliefs that I see now we can't possibly live. Why did you teach us to want to be mature when you knew there was no place down here for such people?'

'When I go back to my town, how can I live these ideals! Tell me, if you can—oh, but you can't! That's what I have just realized. I saw it today as we worked on the play. For the first time in my life!'

'It was as if somebody had swung a bright mirror in front of us. The whole thing opened up in that moment! How it would be—if we tried to live the way we have learned to want to live. Can't you imagine my town—if I were to go home and invite a colored girl to Sunday school? Or even try to get one of the girls in Mill Town in my sorority? They'd think I was crazy. Suppose I said to a colored girl, 'Let's go in the drugstore and have a coke?' Can't you see their faces—Mother's and Daddy's—and everybody's! Well, I can—especially if they arrested me and put me in jail.'

I said, 'You think it's wrong—what we have learned here together?'

'I think it's useless. It just tears us up inside! Makes us so raw. Oh, I hate to say it, but I do think you have harmed us. You've unfitted us for the South. And yet, this is where we shall live. Unless we run away.'

'I haven't told you about last winter. Daddy took me to New York—we were in the dining car—had just finished our soup—when I saw the steward seat the president of that college in Atlanta behind those curtains. I had heard him make a speech at a church meeting. I said, 'Daddy, did you see that? He's the president of a college!' And Daddy said, 'That's where colored folks are supposed to sit. You mustn't get silly notions, honey.' I couldn't finish my dinner. I know it was morbid, but I kept looking at all those faces wondering why they felt they had to have a curtain between them and the president of a college, just to eat their dinner. And it began to seem so crazy!'

'You see,' her voice had quieted, 'I want so much to go home and be decent about things. Not make folks mad—just live what I believe is right. But how? Tell me how! What shall I do when I get on a bus—go to the front with the white folks? Or shall I speak to the motorman and make a little scene each time I get on? Shall I keep on going through White doors? Can I persuade my class to invite a colored girl to Sunday school? Suppose I get that far—will the minister let me? I don't think he would—he would say, 'These things have to come slowly, my dear,' and he would mean that they must not come at all, as long as there is any risk in it. If I do these things that seem so important to us up here, everybody at home will be furious. I can't take it.'" (Smith, 1949, *Killers of the Dream*, pp. 42–48).

In this excerpt, Ms. Smith showed me how segregation played out in the South. Her camper's painful struggle with reconciling her ideals with an institution much bigger than she touched my heart and would not let go of my mind. How could I respond? There were no black children in my personal world. But my family and I could do small personal things over the years: go to welcome the single black family who moved into our neighborhood; have a black student from Mississippi live with our family for a period one summer at a time when this was unheard of in our community; have an exchange student from Indonesia live with us for a year; befriend the only black student in a class when I got to college; work in the civil rights movement; volunteer to live one college summer in Columbia Point Housing Project in Roxbury, outside Boston, working at a day camp program for the resident children who were almost all black; and voluntarily bus our own children to a highly integrated elementary school rather than our predominantly white school in Seattle. I could also hold on to the images Lillian Smith so vividly provided of an unjust society to inform my work later as a professional educator.

The second memory from my religious education is of Joseph Redenbaugh, who touched my heart and troubled my mind while I was a member of the church high school youth group. My recollections of the specifics may not be accurate 45 years later, but the impressions remain vivid. Feeling like a religious outsider as a Unitarian among my high school friends, all Lutheran save one Catholic who had become my closest friend, I realized increasingly during those years that my fundamental values were more aligned with the church youth group than with the largely Lutheran worldview of these school friends. One of these views concerned the death penalty.

Armed with the zealous convictions typical of adolescents, I was firmly opposed to capital punishment. Then I met Joseph Redenbaugh. He came to speak to our high school youth group. Attendance was high, and more than a few of us gathered with sweating palms and hearts beating faster than usual. You see, we were coming to hear from a man of about 70 years, just released for good behavior after serving 40 years of a sentence for murdering his wife with a butcher knife. What would it be like to sit in a room with a convicted murderer? Following our usual supper and social time, we waited in anticipation and Joseph arrived.

I can still see him: perhaps 5 feet, 8 inches, thin, stooped, soft-spoken, and with one of the saddest faces I'd ever seen. That face was anything but violent or angry; it spoke rather of deep pain and resignation. As he spoke, we learned that his crime had been committed in a fit of passion. And although it was the ultimate crime, it was not one that was likely to be repeated from what I have learned since. So Joseph had worked in prison for 40 years, a model prisoner, model worker, supportive of others. He had been free only a few days, and was trying to adjust to a radically changed world. He didn't know about stoplights, he said; there were none when he was first imprisoned. He didn't know where he was going to live or what he was going to do, how he was going to readjust to a world where he felt like a stranger. And then he said what shocked me to my core: "I think it would have been more humane if I had been put to death." He was not speaking about the societal costs of capital punishment versus life in prison, nor about keeping society safe, nor about punishment or retribution; he was speaking as a human being who believed at that moment that his suffering in prison was greater than the value of his few remaining years of freedom: "It would have been more humane if I had been put to death."

I have thought about Joseph and about that evening many times over the years. Was justice served? What is the humane and compassionate response to such crimes? I'm still opposed to capital punishment, and this feels like a contradiction to me with what I've just written; the issue is so complex and really puts our values to the test. But what was perhaps most significant to me about meeting Joseph was that here, at the church of my youth, I was learning to ask questions about issues of justice and compassion and responsibility, to confront issues of our communities and of our world in ways that contributed to my work toward justice. "When the heart is touched by direct experience, the mind may be challenged to change."

Transitions

Our years in college and graduate school followed. We, along with so many in the Sixties generation, vigorously protested the war in Vietnam, stuffed envelopes and marched in Madison, Wisconsin, and in Washington, D.C., as part of the civil rights movement, wept and mourned at the assassinations of John F. Kennedy, Martin Luther King, and Robert Kennedy, and became very involved in Eugene McCarthy's presidential campaign. Those continued to be formative years, years in which our country was torn apart by growing internal divisions and questions about racism, war and violence. We listened to Gandhi and Martin Luther King preach non violence, and believed and practiced those tactics, but saw hatred and violence erupting over and over in a troubled land.

I landed my first full-time professional job, fresh out of graduate school, in an idyllic setting—a beautiful New England college town with a white steepled church on the town green, charming main street, a river with covered bridges, and nearby rolling hills. This setting provided the backdrop for my job as a school psychologist three days a week, and allowed me to work the remaining two days in a small school program housed in a community mental health clinic. I was confronted those two years by rural poverty when I visited students and their families, living in tiny homes in disrepair, sometimes without running water or electricity. But this poverty was hidden in those New England hills, and I could retreat from it as I headed back to our colonial home in the picture-book town.

My privilege continued to charm my life until our whiteness backfired. My husband, on a tenure track position in the college, was stunned to read the college president's memo saying, in effect, that no one other than women and ethnic minorities (the faculty was heavily white male) would be likely to receive tenure in the near future. This was a personal experience with the discrimination that I knew was a common experience for people of color in the United States but not for us whites! How startling to feel that personal qualities, abilities, and performance as a teacher or scholar mattered for nothing. My husband would not be tenured because he was a white male at a time in his institution's history when that was what counted (or, more accurately, didn't count).

I loved my job, our life in small-town New England and the friends we were making. But there were no other possibilities in my husband's field within a geographical radius that would allow us to stay, and my training as a school psychologist would likely make me employable in most large metropolitan areas. So when my husband was offered a position through connections (white privilege?) at the University of Washington, we decided to move to Seattle. I also knew that our "hit–the–wall" experience was far more often throughout our country's history that of people of color than of whites. And I realize, in looking back, that probably the reason I felt some anger and sadness but not rage and despair was once again a result of my white privilege. I could chalk the experience up to a specific situation where we were in the wrong place at the wrong time. But I know that I also felt confident that we would find another situation when my husband's and my professional performance would be evaluated based on our skills and not on the arbitrary criterion of our skin color. This is a confidence that I think many cannot share in our "land of equality." And several years later, after spending time as a full-time mother to our first Seattle baby, another professional door did open to me—college teaching.

My Students—My Teachers

So when I began teaching in 1976 in the Teacher Education Program at Seattle University, I sought to engage prospective teachers in dialogue about diversity and justice. Our curriculum had little multicultural education at that time. After attending a multicultural training sponsored by the Seattle Public Schools, and reading the limited materials I could put my hands on at the time, I designed a portion of the Psychology of Learning course on multicultural education. In my graduate Child Psychology and Learning course, I began tentatively to address these issues with a student presentation on the same topic.

Quickly, my students became my teachers. Three in particular both supported and challenged me on how to include education for diversity in meaningful ways. The experiences I relate are their experiences that, as a white woman, were never mine. But they were powerful to me: they worked their way from the outside in to my heart and mind; they became part of my answer to our president's question, "What grounds your work for justice?" because in a just world, people would not have these experiences of prejudice and racism.

Mako Nakagawa, teacher and later principal in the Seattle Public Schools, and Mae Sasaki, teacher and curriculum specialist, were my teachers. Mako shared with the class some of her experiences growing up as an Asian American in Seattle. The image that I can never forget was the one she shared of a morning ritual in the internment camp where Mako and her family spent several years. At five years old, Mako was marched along with all of her campmates every morning to the spot where the American flag flew. There they began the day, beside the barbed wire fence, reciting the Pledge of Allegiance to the United States of America. "With liberty and justice for all."

Mae was also interned as a young child. Years later, she thought she had dealt with most of the pain and fear left from those early experiences. Then she and her husband were anticipating the birth of their first child. They chose Japanese names for a son or a daughter to honor their roots. The baby arrived, and at the moment of naming, the proud parents could not give the chosen Japanese name. A deep and unconscious fear that the anti-Japanese sentiment and inhuman treatment she had experienced as a child could resurface was too real to take a chance on giving their child a name that could contribute to her being identified as Japanese.

Even as a young child Mae was puzzled by her kindergarten teacher's comment. The teacher looked over the class, with its Asian American, African-American and Caucasian children, and said, "Boys and girls, I want you to know that when I look at this class, you all look just the same to me. I don't see any differences." "Is she blind," Mae thought? The fact that the children's skin colors were decidedly different seemed obvious to Mae. And so the message that Mae took from the teacher was that somehow these differences must be denied; they must not be OK Mae also recalled to the class that when the United States celebrated its bicentennial in 1976, the Seattle phone company published a directory with a collage of faces of people from many racial and ethnic backgrounds. A nice gesture, but Mae noted a problem: here in our city on the Pacific Rim, a city that has benefited over the years from the contributions of Asian Americans, our largest ethnic group, there was not a single Asian American face. "With liberty and justice for all."

Bernal Baca was also my teacher. Bernal was originally a student in my Child Psychology and Learning class while earning a master's degree in counseling, and later a frequent guest speaker in my classes while he was finishing his doctorate in our Doctoral Program in Educational Leadership and directing the Office of Multicultural Education at Yakima Valley Community College. Bernal shared many stories with me and with my classes. Growing up as a Mexican American child in a small Colorado town founded by his ancestors, Bernal felt warmly loved and nurtured by his family. They were open and effusive in their affection for each other and for Bernal. He loved his mother's cooking, her openness; they spoke Spanish at home, so he grew up in a bilingual environment, feeling secure and knowing the world as a good place. But that changed as he started school. "Bernal Carlos Lopez y Baca," Bernal responded proudly on the first day when the teacher asked him his name. "Well, then," the teacher said, as she patted him patronizingly on the head, "we'll just call you 'Bernie.'" Step one in stripping Bernal of the pride in his ethnic identity occurred in this 20-second interchange.

Step two occurred over lunchroom practices. Bernal and his Caucasian friends, in the way of kids everywhere, were intrigued by the foods in each other's lunches. Baloney sandwiches on white bread looked interesting to Bernal, and his friends were intrigued with his tacos and burritos. So they swapped. Until, that is, the white parents learned that their children were eating "dirty Mexican food." So the children were admonished and the swapping stopped. Gradually, over the years and many small incidents, Bernal became ashamed of his Mexican heritage. Once bathed by warmth and love when he walked in town with his mother, who greeted and was greeted by many in her community with hugs, laughter, and rapid speaking in Spanish, Bernal now wanted to hide from these encounters.

By high school, desperate to fit in, Bernal had learned to "buddy up" to the Caucasian crowd, and he began to hang out exclusively with them, a move that boosted his status among the student body. So complete was his rejection at this time of all his heritage that he joined his white friends in using pejorative terms and making fun of the Mexican American students. It was well into his adult years and after much pain, Bernal says, that he was finally able to embrace once again his roots and integrate the disparate parts of his identity.

As we discussed multicultural education in my early classes, I thought I knew what was necessary: to provide a warm, sensitive, inviting classroom environment and to foster the belief among teachers that each child is unique and to be valued as an individual by virtue of her/his humanity. I have been influenced over the years by Carl Rogers and humanistic psychology and education. I believe Rogers' contention that empathy, genuineness and unconditional regard must be present in any relationship as conditions for meaningful growth. What Mako and Mae and Bernal helped me understand—finally—was that this was important but not enough in working with students from diverse racial and ethnic (and I would now add socioeconomic) backgrounds. To teach more effectively, I needed to try to know about my students' cultures, their personal paths, and understand something about self-hate and about stages of ethnic identity and where a given student might be in those stages. Reactions to readings, discussions, to teachers may vary dra-matically from student to student depending upon whether they were in a stage of little ethnic awareness, anger and rejection, self-hate or integration, or self-awareness and love.

Mako and Mae had formed a group of Asian American mothers in Seattle when their own children were beginning school. Wanting to do what they could to prevent having their children experience the hurtful discrimination Mako and Mae experienced as Asian American children, this cadre of committed parents began to work on a curriculum that would help children learn from a young age to value diversity. The result was the "Rainbow Curriculum," one of the earliest multicultural curriculum efforts. My classes were introduced to this curriculum, and later to the Project Reach Curriculum, Gary Howard's multicultural curriculum. Colorful and attractive alphabet cards depicting positive images of children of color adorned the walls in a number of Seattle schools, and teachers were trained to implement the curriculum activities that went along with the cards, activities that gave children hands-on, developmentally appropriate ways of understanding issues of difference.

Third World Encounters

"Solidarity is learned through 'contact' rather than through 'concepts,'" Father Kolvenbach said when speaking of the mandate for Jesuit universities to "educate the whole person of solidarity for the real world. Personal involvement with innocent suffering, with the injustice others suffer, is the catalyst for solidarity which then gives rise to intellectual inquiry and moral reflection." Three of these "contact experiences" in the developing world in recent years have touched me profoundly and will not let go of my heart and mind. The first was a visit to Mexico, the second a six-week stay with the Jesuit community in Kathmandu, Nepal, and the third, a visit to our son during his term with the U.S. Peace Corps in Malawi, in southeast Africa. I continue to reflect on the implications of those experiences.

In 1984 we planned a trip to Mexico with our two children, then ten and thirteen. Mexico City was our first stop. From our hotel in the central part of the city, we looked down on a local market square filled with vendors selling fruits, vegetables and handmade goods of all sorts. Walking around the first night on streets crowded with people and activity, we listened to mariachi bands on street corners, and watched a pantomime artist. Over the next few days we were fascinated by our visits to museums with magnificent ancient artistic and archaeological treasures, to the pyramids outside the city, to many more colorful markets and street performances.

A couple of days into our visit, we got on a city bus. The guidebook had indicated that it was generally a safe route during daytime hours and it was the route that led to our destination. As we rode, the bus filled completely with men; it became very crowded, and we were tightly packed together as we held our children's hands. As we rang the bell to get off the bus, we suddenly found ourselves hemmed in by a group of men—one was trying to cut my purse strap with a knife. In the shuffle, our kids were pushed and we lost their hands; we shouted for help, and it was quickly clear that neither the bus driver nor anyone on the bus was sympathetic to our plight. The door opened and all we could think of was getting our kids and us off together before the driver closed the door. Seeing the door start to close on our children led to a moment of primal fear as I tried to imagine the terror of having them still shut on the bus and us on the outside. When we got them out, it mattered little to me that my husband then realized that his camera had been stolen.

The whole experience was unnerving, and our hearts were pounding hard as we walked back to our hotel. Most alarming, perhaps, was the fact that no one on the bus cared; no one lifted a finger to help and, in fact, people worked together in the attempt to get my purse and the camera. The material value was not trivial for us, but what we also realized was how strong the anti-American feeling was, and the feeling (we assumed, based on other experiences as well) that it was justifiable for those with so little to take from those with, relatively speaking, so much. And I could understand this; how, honestly, could I argue with the logic? Yet I had to reconcile this understanding in my head with the fear and anger I felt. I felt dehumanized, stereotyped, vulnerable and powerless. How could people who had no sense of who we were as people feel justified in robbing us, and treating us—and even our children—in such harsh and uncaring ways. It was a powerful experience of the emotions that I imagine many of the world's people experience over and over again in their lives, and it has stayed with me.

During our remaining days in Mexico, we traveled in a rented car to several other cities, passing through village after village of one-room houses, just five feet back from the road, houses often crowded with people. Barefooted and poorly nourished children played outside, or just sat inside watching the passing cars. When we parked to have lunch or walk around in small towns we passed through, we paid small children "protection money" to watch our cars to see that the tires were not slashed.

We talked on our return of what an eye-opening experience the trip had been for our children, how seeing large-scale poverty and poor living conditions in a third world country was an amazing experience for them—and it was. But I also realized that it was the first time I, too, had direct contact with poverty outside the United States, and it was very different from my intellectual understanding.

February 1, 1995. Steel gray skies. Looking down from the plane, I stared at the massive Himalayas below, glacier-covered and imposing. As we grew closer to Kathmandu, the view was of terraced hillsides above a valley, with the city sprawling at the base. It was my first sabbatical and, thanks to groundwork laid by a colleague on sabbatical the previous year, I was to spend the next six weeks living with the Jesuit community in Kathmandu. It was a wonderful arrangement; they provided me room and board and, in exchange, I did in-service work with the three schools the Jesuits sponsored: an elementary school and secondary school in Kathmandu, and a boarding school in a small village about an hour out of the city.

Although I read in preparation and located the school where I would live on the map, the images formed in advance in my mind of this large city did not match what greeted me. Why should they since I drew on my frame of reference for "cities"? One of the Jesuits greeted me at the airport, a tiny place where I stood in long lines. Then we headed off in the Jesuit community's dusty jeep, probably fifteen years old and with a few non-functioning parts (seat belts, for example), on mostly dirt roads and a few that were paved with lots of potholes. We dodged cows, goats, chickens, malnourished and diseased dogs, bicycles, "tempos" (three-wheeled taxis), buses, trucks and people, past the sprawling squatter settlements lining the Bagmati River, with poles and plastic tarps for shelter, to my home for the coming weeks, a room at St. Xavier's School in Jawalakhel, once the palace of a Nepali king.

New sights, sounds, smells, foods, and experiences bombarded my senses and my mind over the next six weeks. Kathmandu has a beautiful setting in a deep mountain valley surrounded by the highest peaks in the world. But vehicles with no pollution controls (the Nepali government had recently gotten a good price on a large fleet of three-wheeled tempos from the Indian government, which had banned them because they were too polluting) and unchecked smoke belching from the stacks of brick factories have trapped polluted air in the valley, causing a rapidly increasing number of respiratory problems.

A local doctor predicted in a newspaper column that if drastic measures were not taken to curb pollution, virtually the entire population of Kathmandu would suffer respiratory problems within ten years. Exercising by walking the streets and alleys in Kathmandu, my favorite way of getting to know new places, felt like a trade-off between my heart and my lungs. What a privilege it is, I realized, to live in a place with relatively clean air, and how can we possibly complain about paying the costs of pollution control when the necessary technology is available? And how can we allow the poor in our own country to suffer disproportionate health risks similar to those in the Kathmandu Valley by our location of facilities that are known to poison the air around them?

I worked with teachers in one "modern" school, a spacious facility in the heart of Kathmandu where the desktops, chairs, tables, and floors were constantly covered with a layer of dust. The Jesuits wore caps most of the time to keep their hair from being caked with dust from any trip outside. I led a seminar in the country school, with the participating teachers sitting outside on wooden benches because the sun might warm the temperature higher than that in the unheated indoor schoolroom. We wore heavy jackets, hats, and gloves during the day. What an odd experience to move inside the school at one point, to an unpainted room, bare of furniture except for benches, to view a videotape on peer coaching on the single, aged but barely functional VCR available. Here we sat viewing U.S. classrooms in the video, colorful classrooms with computers, gaily decorated walls, TV, desks, tables, cozy chairs for reading, etc. Our supplies included chalk and a small, portable chalkboard carried outside for the day's seminar.

In Kathmandu and the countryside I saw tiny houses with few possessions that may house six to ten people. Many children had few and torn clothes and cast-out thongs for shoes. Teeth were rotting for lack of adequate nutrition and care, stick-thin children and adults, some missing limbs, begged on the streets. One of the Jesuits took me to an orphanage run by nuns from Mother Teresa's Sisters of Charity order. I sucked in my breath when the director opened a door to one of the rooms: it was probably 6 by 10 feet and about fifteen children, ages ranging from a year to probably eight, were playing inside with one adult supervisor sitting on a small bunk knitting. The children ran to us, reaching out for our hands, climbing in our arms, clinging to our legs. They sang a song, took great delight in imitating each other saying "good-bye" as we went out. The space constraints were unbelievable by American standards.

I heard stories of girls raised in orphanages who were "kicked out" at age sixteen with no training or skills to make it in life outside their sheltered walls. Many became easy prey to Indians who enticed the girls to come with them, promising bright futures as actresses in Indian movies; the reality was that this was often, in fact, the invitation to lives of prostitution.

At the school in the country, I worked with a lovely young Nepali teacher. When I talked at one point about a coming trip I planned to Chitwan National Park in the south of Nepal, known for its amazing wild animals, she looked wistfully, sighed and said how lucky I was. "I dream of seeing the Chitwan but it's so expensive that it will be the trip of a lifetime if I can ever go." The trip was about eight hours by bus and I had arranged for three days, with guided safaris and accommodations, for about 100 U.S. dollars.

The Nepali people were overwhelmingly warm, friendly, endearing. I found them to be gentle. In six weeks of being around children and adolescents in schools, and walking daily in the city, I did not see or hear a single unkind word spoken, see an argument or fight. Everywhere, in the city and in the tiny mountain villages I encountered on a four day trek outside Pokhara, older children carried and cared for younger siblings and babies. All of this occurred in a place of overcrowding and material poverty, usually considered breeding grounds for violence. The centrality of both Hindu and Buddhist spirituality had to play a role, I thought.

I left Nepal touched by the gentleness and generosity of many people I met, by the incredible beauty of the country, and haunted by the signs of malnutrition, pollution, deforestation of the mountainsides causing problems with erosion, and huge income gaps between the tiny upper class and enormous lower class. I returned to my comfortable home with all its amenities. I shopped at grocery stores and discount chain warehouse stores that offered a variety of the very latest gadgets or toys that anyone could imagine (and those in Nepal could not possibly imagine), and went out my front door in the mornings taking a deep breath of the beautiful clear morning air as I headed off on my walk around the neighborhood of trim houses and neat yards with well-watered green grasses and lush flowers and shrubbery. How can one possibly reconcile such gross inequities in different parts of the same globe? I still don't know how to answer that question.

"Meager Harvests in Africa Leave Millions at the Edge of Starvation" shouts the headline of the front page of the *New York Times*, June 23, 2002, as I'm writing this. The headline takes me back to August 10, 1997, the day our son, Drew, Peace Corps volunteer in Malawi, met us at the airport in Lilongwe, Malawi. We'd come to see him to try to understand something about his experience since the previous September when he'd begun his volunteer assignment at the Malawi Institute of Education.

The *New York Times* article continues:

> In February, when the food ran out, Ezlina Chambukira started selling her precious possessions one by one. First, her goat. Then an old umbrella. Then two metal plates and a battered pail. When she had nothing left, she started praying for a miracle. For the first time in a decade, severe hunger is sweeping across southern Africa. The United Nations says that two years of erratic weather alternating droughts and floods, coupled with mismanagement of food supplies have left seven million people in six countries at risk of starvation.

> Without adequate food, hundreds of people have died from sicknesses like malaria and cholera that they might otherwise have survived. In February, when many households went without food for a week or more, the European Union found that the number of cases of severe malnutrition identified in local clinics here in Malawi had soared by 80 percent. Tiyankhulanji Chiusiwa, a 20-year-old woman with worried eyes and withered breasts, has gone so long without proper meals that she has stopped producing milk for her baby. He still suckles for comfort, but he is weakening. He is 6 months old, she says, but weights only seven pounds. The people have given a name to the period of biting hardship. They call it the time of "gwagwagwa," the time when "we had absolutely nothing" (*New York Times*, 6/23/02).

I flash back to Malawians who were part of our son's life during his Peace Corps years. What is happening now to Stuart, his cook, and 4 foot 10 inch

William, the "night watchman" who slept much of the night in a hammock in the backyard while armed solely with a whistle tied around his neck as he guarded Drew's house from intruders? Ambivalent about hiring Malawians to perform chores for Drew and his Peace Corps roommate, they were encouraged by the Peace Corps to do so because the monthly wages meant the possibility of food those months for Stuart's and William's families. "Life has been so good since Mr. Drew and Mr. Ty came," Stuart told us daily during our visit.

"Life has been so good." What an amazing statement from a diminutive, large-hearted, good-natured man who had knocked on Drew's door about 6:00 a.m. one Sunday morning shortly after Drew and Ty had arrived in their small village of Malosa. Drew stumbled sleepily to the door to greet Stuart. He had come, he explained, to see if he could borrow enough money, about the equivalent of $6.00 U.S. from Drew because he did not have enough money to buy pine boards to make a coffin for his baby who had died during the night of dehydration from diarrhea. Medical treatment costing mere pennies, more than most can afford, could have treated the dehydration and saved that baby's life. And that story is repeated in village after village throughout Malawi. After getting the money, Stuart invited Drew to come to his village later that morning for the funeral.

So Drew got on his bike to ride to the village of mud huts. He observed sadly as the villagers sang slow and mournful songs, sat without talking for several hours, then brought the coffin out of a hut for the women to kneel around and, after more words and song, carried the coffin to a clump of trees which served as the village graveyard, lowered it into the earth and covered it with mounds of dirt. Drew was the first white person to have been in the village (following a missionary) in 26 years; as he was leaving a stranger came up to thank him for coming, stumbling to find the English to express a human connection: "You have shown us that you are a human being too." In a letter describing this experience to us Drew reflected, "It was astounding to consider how accepted the death of a child can be in the developing world. It was heart rending to see the tattered poverty that permeated even an important ceremony, as not even one of three attendees had shoes." Within three months Stuart arrived at Drew's house on a Monday and reported that a second child had died of malaria over the weekend. "Life has been so good."

In reading Drew's accounts of these experiences, I thought about the emotional toll if I or a friend of mine had lost two children within a three-month period, and it was almost beyond imagining. Was Stuart less caring or attached as a parent? I doubt it very much. But in Malawi the death of children is such a part of daily life that people simply must bury the dead and go on or the entire population would be incapacitated. Drew reported that there was probably, on average, one funeral each week for a staff member at the

Malawi Institute of Education who died presumably, but not usually labeled, of AIDS.

The *New York Times* summary is chilling:

> Over the last two year, severe drought, in between bouts of flooding, has battered the region (southern Africa) once again. This time, the problem is complicated by the high incidence of H.I.V. infection along with the political turmoil in Zimbabwe and mismanagement in Malawi. Without adequate food, hundreds of people have died from sicknesses like malaria and cholera that they might otherwise have survived. In February, when many households went without food for a week or more, the European Union found that the number of cases of severe malnutrition identified in local clinics here in Malawi had soared by 80 percent (*New York Times*, 6/23/02).

But Stuart's babies, and the seven million people in six countries currently at risk of starvation in southern Africa (*New York Times*, 6/23/02), are nameless and faceless to those of us in the developing world. How, I kept asking myself as I wept in my heart at nights in Malawi and upon my return, can one possibly make sense of and respond to such enormous disparities in resources on our planet? I still don't have the answer. People and experiences over many years have touched my heart and raised questions related to discrimination, criminal justice, racism, ecological disaster, global resources. These have been my teachers. I have few answers, and far too often I go on with my life by insulating and distancing myself from these experiences. To absorb completely all the suffering and injustice of the world would be to live, I think, in a state of chronic depression. But to distance oneself completely, and not even attempt to respond in some way, would represent failure to be true to those deepest religious values: "the inherent worth and dignity of every person; justice, equity, and compassion in human relations; the goal of world community with peace, liberty, and justice for all; respect for the interdependent web of all existence of which we are a part" that I profess to guide my life. So I struggle continually, and try to respond in small ways that make some sense to me.

From the Inside Back Out

I began this chapter by describing my commitment to justice as having come "from the outside in." As Gary Howard points out in his book, *We Can't Teach What We Don't Know* (1999), it is particularly crucial for white teachers to be part of the dialogue on issues of race and social justice and diversity precisely because they are, after all, the teachers of most students of color in U.S. schools. Whites need to dialogue on these issues without, as Howard says, having to "rip off their White skin." That means, Howard believes, that we need to "look deeply and critically at the necessary changes and growth we ourselves must achieve if we are to work effectively with the real issues of diversity" (Howard, 1999, p. 3). So in my work I try now to take the experiences that came originally from the outside in and share them back out with my students and colleagues in my school and across the university. An important part of this is a continuing effort to understand my own position as a white. I am impressed by the importance of the concept of "positionality," which elucidates whiteness "as a social construction organizing people into social relations of dominance and oppression, through which some individuals benefit" (Maher & Tetreault, 1997). Let me share several examples of my classroom work.

At the classroom level, education for justice means a number of things. It does mean, I believe, working to create a sense of community in the classroom. All students must feel that their voice is important, that they have a valued place in classroom dialogue even when that voice may be expressing an unpopular view. Easy to embrace in theory, harder to practice when dealing with sensitive issues that stir emotion. But this is critical, I believe, to achieving justice at the classroom level. So in all classes I work at the beginning to get to know the students and to have them get to know each other. This is done through structuring conversations among students the first day of each class, in some cases through having the class collectively develop a "class covenant" that expresses the norms they want to commit to as a group.

It is also done through having students work frequently in groups, with changes in the group composition periodically so that students work with many others in the course. It is done, in one class, by having students read, during the first week, Parker Palmer's article "Community, Conflict and Ways of Knowing" (Palmer, 1987), an article which describes "creative conflict" as a critical ingredient in the search for broader and deeper thinking in real communities and is used as a basis for small group discussion.

My continuing challenge is to recognize that often white classrooms "not only reflect, but also impose, the dominant culture's ideological frameworks" (Maher & Tetreault, 1997). The hope is that with such recognition classrooms "may also function as somewhat sheltered laboratories where those frameworks may be exposed and interrogated. One hope thus lies in students (and professors) becoming authorities for each other as they are explicit about themselves as positioned subjects with respect to an issue or a text (Maher & Tetreault, 1997). Only in community, I believe, can this happen— settings characterized by genuine conflict and dialogue among persons with very different experiences who have developed enough trust to challenge each other in search of deepened truths (Palmer, 1987).

At the curricular level, my commitment means that I search for readings that represent diverse and inclusive voices. In my Child Psychology and Learning class, for example, I became increasingly troubled about the fact that most child development texts, even while attempting to include cross-cultural perspectives, still deal with child development primarily from a Western, white point of view. Where are the other voices? Maher and Tetreault (1997), discussing how assumptions of whiteness can lead to the imposition of certain ways of constructing the world, quote Adrienne Rich:

> When those who have the power to name and to socially construct reality choose not to see you or hear you, whether you are dark-skinned, old, disabled, female, or speak with a different accent or dialect than theirs, when someone with the authority of a teacher, say, described the world and you are not in it, there is a moment of psychic disequilibrium, as if you looked into a mirror and saw nothing (p. 347).

So I added the book, *Children of Color* (Gibbs & Huang, 1991) as a required reading. I provide information and resources to students on ways to advocate for justice on issues affecting children (e.g., provide relevant information from Washington's Children's Alliance on pending legislation related to children). It means reflecting on the justice issues relevant to the content of each course I teach, and including readings and class discussions and our courses and programs that raise these issues—issues of funding disparities in schools, of racism, sexism and discrimination in classrooms, of differential expectations communicated by teachers to women and to students of color, of the effects of the current standardized testing movement on various groups of students of color and low socioeconomic students, of disproportional placement of students of color in special education classrooms, of culturally sensitive assessment measures for school psychologists working with students with limited English proficiency.

Attempting to provide contact, real experiences in addition to reflective reading, I have added an experiential component related to issues of justice in two courses, the Child Psychology and Learning class, and a seminar, "Issues in School Psychology," that I team-teach. One of our challenges is that we are teaching graduate students, most of whom go to school part-time and many of whom hold part- or full-time jobs and have family responsibilities in addition to their graduate studies. How, then, can we realistically provide direct experiences that impact their understanding of justice yet respect the realities of multiple demands on their time? In addition to placing students in field experiences and internships in diverse settings, goals of both programs in which I'm involved, I have tried the following two.

In the Child Psychology and Learning class students visit an agency that serves children or families, write a response and give a small group presentation about the agency, addressing some of the justice issues the visit raised. They also design and participate in an experience with an ethnic or cultural group with which they have little familiarity and, similarly, write up an analysis of their learning from the experience. Both of these experiences are developed to increase contact with the world outside the university walls, and extend student learning beyond the written word.

Issues in School Psychology is a seminar that accompanies students' yearlong full-time internship in a school district in the Puget Sound area. In order to broaden and deepen understanding of the programs/agencies that serve children and families in their internship community, and to gain a broad, ecological/systems perspective on children's needs, students have an option on an assignment (the other option is a research report) that requires that they spend a minimum of fifteen hours with a community program or agency that serves children and/or families in their internship communities. They may spend this time during the summer prior to their internship as a way of learning more about the needs in their community, or during their internship. Following the experiences, participants share in a discussion with their classmates their prepared reflections on a series of questions related to justice. For example, what structural/societal factors contribute to the issues faced by your client population? What systemic barriers do you think exist to seeking help on the part of the clients your agency/program serves? What services or programs do you believe, ideally, a compassionate and just society would offer in response to the issues experienced by your client population?

In both of these courses, students give these experiences high marks for their learning value. Their written and oral reflections often suggest that the experience was eye-opening, often revealing to them an aspect of a culture or of people in their communities of which they had no previous understanding. For the Issues class, some of the students continue to volunteer beyond the hours required to fulfill the course assignment.

Educating for justice also means seeking opportunities to provide special programs that address societal justice issues. Two colleagues and I are currently designing a program that would train school psychologists to work with Latino families in our state, the state's most rapidly growing ethnic group. We will seek grant funding to train two cohort groups, over a four-year period, with an understanding of Latino families and culture, knowledge and skills in culturally responsive assessment, and at least basic proficiency in Spanish so that they might work effectively with Latino students coming to schools with limited English proficiency, and backgrounds that make it very difficult to determine whether language or prior educational experiences or a genuine disability are interfering with the students' learning. This distinction is required by law, but few school psychologists have the understanding and skills to, in fact, make the judgment accurately.

At the broader school and university levels, I have been involved in attempts to examine how we are responding to the part of our mission, as a Jesuit university, to provide our students with a "well-educated solidarity," to help students "learn to perceive, think, judge, choose and act for the rights of others, especially the disadvantaged and the oppressed" (Fr. Kolvenbach, 2000). Such a mission requires rethinking the very nature and role of a university. It means developing a theoretical rationale of social justice as an essential part of higher education; it means, our president suggested, that for a Jesuit university the traditional role of a university as a place for the free search for knowledge is not enough. It remains a critical role, but it is not the search for knowledge for its own sake. In a 21st century Jesuit institution, the search must be for knowledge for the transformation of society. Such a search involves looking at a "university as an educator of students which imparts knowledge about justice, a community where faculty, staff and students treat one another with justice, and a citizen contributing to the common good of the larger society through an ever expanding study of, and advocacy for, justice" (Fernandez, Fitzgerald, & Shefrin, 1999).

At Seattle University, I am a member of the university's Faith and Justice Committee, a group I have co-chaired for the past three years. In response to a national call for Jesuit universities to examine how they live their Jesuit mission of a commitment to justice, this group coordinated a university-wide self-assessment. All schools and units in the universities examined their own mission statements, their curricula, and the ways in which faculty are encouraged to incorporate justice issues in their teaching, research, and faculty development. From there, the agenda for a series of regional and national conferences was shaped. On our own campus, we have developed an annual all-university "Gathering" where faculty, staff and administrators come together to dialogue and plan for ways of making the commitment to justice real in our teaching and our relationships to each other and to the larger community.

As a member of the university's Faith and Justice Committee, I attended a western regional conference in 1999, and then a conference of all U.S. Jesuit universities in 2000 on "Commitment to Justice in Jesuit Higher Education." These groups have begun the ongoing process of dialogue among Jesuit universities on how we can educate our "students to become people of compassion and conscience, as well as intellectual competence, on what research and pedagogy that engage injustice should mean in our world today."

As part of a national process that began in 1998 in which all of the Jesuit universities were asked to conduct a self-study of work they were doing to implement education for justice, each school in our university was asked to submit our own self-study. Out of this process a School of Education Justice Education Task Force formed in an attempt to create opportunities for our own faculty to think and dialogue together about ways of implementing education for justice in our school.

We began in 1999 with a day of "Justice Education Dialogue," which led to the adoption by faculty of an Education for Justice Position Statement that we hope guides our work. We have done common readings on justice-related topics that have formed a theme for the year: Ruby Payne's book, *A Framework for Understanding Poverty,* and a guest speaker on the Living Wage Movement in Washington helped to frame a focus on economic justice in 2001. James Bank's article, "The Social Construction of Difference and the Quest for Educational Equality," and a guest speaker on "Globalization and Africa" helped with our focus on racism and global issues in 2001–02. And members of the faculty and staff engaged in a community service project with reflections afterwards that have led to a commitment to an attempt to find meaningful ongoing involvement in the wider community in ways that address issues of societal justice.

Finally, as part of a sabbatical next year, a colleague and I explored the development of a new course; or alternative set of experiences, focused on justice and diversity that would potentially be part of a core requirement for all graduate students in all programs in the School of Education. Scary? Yes. Challenging? Yes. We anticipate there will be much controversy about content, fundamental and important questions about the meaning of "education for justice," about "whose justice," about how to address the topic in ways that are meaningful across a diverse set of programs and students of a wide variety of ages and stages of adult development, and about how to make room in program curricula for such content.

"Is my goal to affect many broadly or a few deeply?" a colleague asked. It is a hard question to answer, and I think my answer is "both." As educators we never know, I believe, what it is that we do that may impact a student and we sometimes learn years later about something that a student, took away from a course. I cannot *make* students learn or do anything and it would be presumptuous to think otherwise. But I can choose subjects, plan course readings and choose pedagogies that will promote either concern or complacency about the great justice issues facing our world. And maybe, just maybe, one or two or a number of students will leave a course or leave Seattle University with a deepened commitment to justice in our world. So what I can do is keep raising the issues, engaging in dialogue, and supporting in whatever ways I can student and faculty steps toward justice. I choose to do so because my parental upbringing, my religious convictions, my life experiences and those of my students who were my teachers call for nothing less, and I do so in the belief that it may bring us closer to making real the challenge posed by Fr. Kolvenbach: preparing students for the promotion of justice in an unjustly suffering world.

References

Fernandez, M., Fitzgerald, P., & Shefrin, H. (1999). *The integration of justice into the life of the university: Justice as an academic subject, as a research interest, and as a communal practice at Santa Clara University.* Unpublished manuscript.

Gibbs, J. T., & Huang, L. N. (Eds.). (1991). *Children of color: Psychological interventions with minority youth.* San Francisco: Jossey-Bass.

Howard, G. (1999). *We can't teach what we don't know: White teachers, multiracial schools.* New York: Teachers College Press.

Kolvenbach, P-H, S. J. (2000, October). *The service of faith and the promotion of justice in American Jesuit higher education.* Paper presented at the meeting on commitment to justice in Jesuit higher education, Santa Clara University.

Maher, F., & Tetreault, M. K. (1997). Learning in the dark: How assumptions of Whiteness shape classroom knowledge. *Harvard Educational Review, 67*(2), 321–349.

McIntosh, P. (2001). White privilege: Unpacking the invisible knapsack. In P. S. Rothenberg (Ed.), *Race, class, and gender in the United States: An integrated study* (pp. 163–168). New York: Worth.

Meager harvests in Africa leave millions at the edge of starvation. (2002, July 23). *The New York Times,* p. A, 1.

Palmer, P. (1987). Community, conflict, and ways of knowing. *Change,* Sept./Oct., 20-25.

Smith, L. (1949). *Killers of the dream.* New York: W.W. Norton & Co.

Thompson, B. (1997). Home work: Anti-racism activism and the meaning of Whiteness. In M. Fine, L. Weis, L. C. Powell, & M. Wong (Eds.), *Off-White: Readings on race, power, and society* (pp. 354–366). New York: Routledge.

Weinstein, G., & Fantini, M. D. (Eds.). (1970). *Toward humanistic education: A curriculum of affect.* New York: Praeger.

CHAPTER THREE
A Professor, Not a Porter

Lawrence Y. Matsuda

During my career in education, I have been a teacher, counselor, administrator, professor and volunteer working on social justice issues. In 1969 I started the first Asian American history course in the state at Sharples Junior High School in Seattle. In the early 1970s, I was active in the civil rights movement on behalf of Asian Americans and later served as a counselor in the University of Washington's Educational Opportunity Program. As an administrator, I worked for the State Office of Education in Equal Educational Opportunity Programs in the late 70s and I headed the bilingual programs and desegregation programs in the 80s and 90s for the Seattle Public Schools. In between, I was a consultant and K-8/middle school principal in the Seattle Public Schools. As a volunteer and president of the University of Washington Alumni Association in 1996, I started the Multicultural Alumni Partnership, an award-winning partnership that provides scholarships for minority students. Currently, I am finishing a visiting professor assignment in the College of Education at Seattle University, teaching counselors and teachers to become school administrators.

Social justice is rooted firmly in my life experiences and relationships. Being a minority in a white society is an issue I cannot escape. Recently I rented a luggage cart at Sea-Tac Airport in Seattle to pick up my wife's luggage at the United Airlines' carousel. While I was looking, a tall middle-aged white male approached me and pointed to his luggage on the carousel. He said, "My bag is over there." Showing no emotion, I turned and responded, "I am a professor, not a porter. I am afraid you'll have to pick-up your own baggage."

Regardless of my professional accomplishments, training or status, being an Asian American in a white society has meant being mistaken for: a waiter instead of a customer in a Chinese restaurant, a porter at the airport, a shoeshine person at a hotel, a foreigner from Japan, a Korean immigrant and countless others. It makes me angry to deal with racial stereotypes that are insensitive, personally annoying and insulting. Although I handle each situation differently, I found any response, no response, any exchange or any reply makes me feel debased as a human being. I wonder, "Why even bother?"

I have experienced almost all the Asian racist remarks, ethnic slurs, insults or well-meaning comments that effectively separate me from the larger white society in the United States. My blood pressure rises, triggering the adrenaline rush, especially when the offender feels he or she has delivered an insult so creative that surely I must have never heard it before. Nevertheless, my personal racial issues are: How can I channel my anger to creative endeavors that are positive, and how can that anger and energy be used for the betterment of the human family at large? I feel strongly that how one handles the anger in response to racism is the key to having a healthy life and being a productive citizen.

From the point of view of my career, these feelings generate the following questions: How have these experiences shaped my identity? My teaching style? My perceived purpose in life and my career in education? Some of these questions will be answered but most will raise more fundamental questions like: What do you believe? What do you value most? What can you do?

What do you believe? Based on my experiences and evidence in the public domain, I believe that racism permeates U.S. institutions as a cultural norm. We do not have to look far to find a class action discrimination suit against a major American corporation and/or government entity like the FBI, which was recently sued for discriminatory practices in promoting agents. In the late 1960s, Dr. Reed M. Powell surveyed American corporations and found that "like hires and promotes like." In other words, CEOs hire people like themselves in relation to race, religion and socioeconomic background. Over the years, I was hoping to see changes in this pattern but to a large degree change has been slow.

In addition, profiling or selecting individuals based on predetermined physical, racial and other characteristics is just another bureaucratic strategy invented to make racial discrimination more palatable to the larger community. Believing racism is institutionalized presents two divergent paths for me as a minority. The first path leads to changing the system. The second path is to become invisible and to accept the notion that I may be mistaken for a porter, waiter, or shoeshine person for years to come.

In choosing the path of change, I recognize that the concept of social justice could be construed as just another manipulative tool of the larger society that gives hope to minorities for a better life. In this way "social justice" is an opiate for the poor and disenfranchised people, similar to religion as described by Karl Marx in Russia before the revolution. Social justice gives the disenfranchised hope that fairness and justice can prevail. But above all, social justice efforts provide minorities a reason to buy in and to not seek alternative means outside of the system. Social justice can serve as a tool to placate and maintain the status quo. It also can provide a false sense of comfort by shifting the responsibility to the courts, the U.S. government, the state or even the church.

In the case of the Japanese Americans during World War II, the U.S. government, Supreme Court, news media, some chambers of commerce, military, some social clubs and many others conspired to deny Japanese American citizens their constitutional rights. It was a complete breakdown of the justice system. The Japanese American experience, therefore, under-scores the need to be vigilant and to make justice the responsibility of each individual citizen and not to delegate his or her involvement away to an in-herently racist system. This is especially relevant today given the events of September 11, 2001, and the subsequent actions of the U.S. government to detain Muslim Americans without due process.[1]

In addition, since bureaucratic systems are largely dumb by design, they operate under rules, linear processes and regulations that are often not ques-tioned by the implementers. Most are patterned after the Newtonian machine model where each piece has a function operating in isolation toward a de-sired end that fulfills a larger purpose. In such an environment workers are more prone to see their work in isolation and not as a part of the integrated whole. As an agent of change my goal is to turn the rules of the bureaucracy against itself for the good of the disenfranchised. Promoting the adoption of laws and rules was one method that forced systems to implement regulations that support justice. In this way, the concept of social justice became embed-ded and was therefore more authentic and less of an opiate.

What do you value most? I value working on behalf of the disenfran-chised because it gives me an opportunity to correct discriminatory practices that I experienced. I believe that by helping those in need, all people benefit. Hopefully, my work will make society better so that stereotypes and dis-crimination will not fetter my son and his children. Ideally, in his lifetime, he will have opportunities to fully explore his potential. As a father, I hope in my heart that things will be better for my son, but I have cautioned him about the pitfalls of being a minority in a white society. His task, then, is to find his own path and own truth. As I work on behalf of others, my social justice work benefits me as well. It gives me a sense of satisfaction and purpose. But the work also humbles me in that what I accomplished was not done alone but with many people helping.

Although I have taken leadership roles and can claim credit for institu-tional changes, I recognize it was a confluence of many events, activities, people and coincidences that worked on my behalf to accomplish objectives that changed systems. That said, I recognize, too, that when those events

---

[1] Please see a *Brief Historical Sketch of the Japanese in America* on page 74.

converged, I was trained, prepared, confident and ready. Powerful forces were with me to the point that I became the vehicle and not the cause.

The coming of the forces can best be described in metaphysical terms. When my intentions were clear and focused, I felt like I was in a zone where my thoughts acted as a magnet. Through a series of meaningful coincidences, I was drawn into the unfolding of important events.

What can you do? Even though I am pessimistic in regard to social justice in this society, I continue to work for it. Writers like Michael Fullan suggest that one should regard problems as your friends. I have always contended if you do this, you will have many friends. But I developed a corollary to Fullan which is "if you can take problems and use them to motivate you to positive action, you will never be without motivation."

Freud once said words to the effect that that which is not true is only truth standing on its head. Our task is to find that which is not true and to turn it right side up. My contributions to that effort and to social justice have been as small as a donation to a scholarship fund, or a lecture to a large group, or mentoring students.

My contributions also include being a role model and storyteller telling the story so that America does not forget and repeat past mistakes. But above all, I try to live my life with dignity and show kindness to those who have been placed in my path.

Ironically, one never can predict the future benefits of a kind act. For as I consciously teach about social justice and watch as the words seemingly fall on deaf ears, I am reminded of an old saying that a teacher will appear when the lesson is needed.

Hopefully, my efforts will have laid the groundwork for the appropriate lesson and the coming of the teacher when students are ready.

Early Years

In 1951, Justice wore a black mask, ten-gallon hat and rode a white palomino named Silver before television came to our house in Seattle. Each week from the Motorola cabinet radio the Lone Ranger sprang forth, bringing bad men to justice, righting wrongs and fighting for those who were treated unfairly. Because the masked man was not someone we ever saw, it was easy for me as a child to imagine myself riding a white horse in a world where right was right and wrong was wrong.

The fact that my mother, father, grandparents and entire family were incarcerated in American concentration camps in Idaho during World War II along with approximately 110,000 other Japanese and Japanese Americans without a crime and due process was in my consciousness for as long as I could remember. The evacuation and internment came up at every family gathering: birthday parties, Christmases, Thanksgivings, weddings and funerals. It was impossible to ignore the experience at the Minidoka Relocation Center Block 26 annual reunions and the Hiroshima Kenjinki summer picnics in the 1950s. Oftentimes the camp stories would begin with a simple statement from my mother like "We used to have a piano. It was an expensive piano which we had to give up because we only had one week to pack everything into one suitcase."

The following describes the Minidoka Relocation Center in Hunt, Idaho (Takami, 1998):

> Hunt, Idaho, is situated on one of the great volcanic plains of the world, a vast expanse of land spreading toward low-lying mountains in the north and southwest and to rolling hills at the edge of the Snake River Valley. Prior to the Second World War, much of the area was barren desert. The land was settled as a part of the federal homesteading project in the early 1900s, but by 1932, it was abandoned because of harsh conditions. An arid climate and forbidding terrain—layers of lava rock topped with powdery soil—combined to make the plains inhospitable to life other than a scattering of sagebrush, rattlesnakes and scorpions (p.11).

After the evacuation, our family shared a house with the Shiraishi family by the Presbyterian Church near Chinatown. Later when my father got a job as a handyman at the Earl Hotel, we were able to move out and settle nearby on Lane Street. My mother used to joke that because they could not find a place in which to live on the outside when the war was ending, they stayed in camp until it closed and the government kicked them out. Ironically, they were forced to leave their homes and to live behind barbed wire for four years. Then, my family was forced by the same government to leave captivity and return to Seattle without having a real home to return to.

The first house I remember was a two-story rental with artificial brick siding. The address was 921 Lane Street and our phone number was Main 2911. My grandfather and grandmother on my mother's side lived upstairs. My parents, older brother Alan and I lived on the first floor. Mr. Pasqualli lived in the basement.

The neighborhood was composed of five working-class families, three of which were Japanese. There were low-rise office buildings, a sheet metal manufacturing company, tire warehouse and glove factory nearby. Next door were the landlords, Mr. and Mrs. Merlino, first-generation immigrants from Italy. Mr. Merlino ran a successful olive oil business and Mrs. Merlino took care of the house and raised chickens in their front yard. Every morning a rooster crowed in our semi-industrial/quasi-residential neighborhood.

The Merlinos had high turnover among housekeepers because of the demanding schedule. But there was one housekeeper who stayed the longest. I will always remember Anna. She had dark hair and was physically strong with coal dark eyes. Her disheveled hair accentuated the fierceness about her. She spoke with a thick accent and looked like a medieval charwoman or scullery maid who was angry at everyone. One summer day Anna came up to us children in the front yard. We were frightened by her presence and her closeness. "Come and look at my tattoo," she said. Anna pushed up her sleeve. We were expecting to see a beautiful picture or something colorful. Instead, we saw a long series of numbers neatly tattooed in black ink. The stark appearance of the numbers conveyed a powerful presence on her skin. Anna survived the German concentration camps and the tattoo was a reminder of her strength. There were so many numbers representing so many people.

The tattoo's plainness and horror was not lost on us children. We knew Anna's camps were different from our camps because my parents didn't have tattoos. To us this meant that our camps were better. We were more "normal" because our parents were not branded. We, however, did not give Anna's experience much thought because we were safe and secure in Seattle. We were in our own quiet enclave insulated from the larger society. Our minister, lawyer, dentist, doctor, funeral director, insurance salesperson, grocer, florist and milk delivery person were all Japanese. As a result, it was only natural that I imagined the masked man, the Lone Ranger, was also Japanese.

It was the summer of 1951 when my Uncle Kenji returned from Anderson Dam and a construction job somewhere in Idaho to live upstairs between jobs. He bought a television set as a gift to the house. It had a huge four-foot wooden cabinet housing a six-inch black-and-white Westinghouse screen. It was the first television in our small neighborhood and it drew children from all over. We would all sit in a semicircle on the worn linoleum floor with all eyes fixed on the miniature screen. Often we would eat snacks like at the movies. I remember once when the Hodge brothers came over. They wore their Sunday best and had their hair slicked down and the smell of fragrant bath soap billowed from them. We had never seen them so clean and fresh like newly laundered sheets. Their cleanliness did not, however, affect the way they ate the watermelon that night. Their faces required frequent mopping as the melon slices were devoured beyond the pulp and beyond the rind to the green skin. Almost everything was gone except the seeds, which were spit out on newspaper laid on the floor for that purpose.

The television not only brought our friends, but it also brought knowledge that the radio could not. Television altered my image of the Lone Ranger. He was a huge masked man sitting on a gigantic white horse. He spoke with a deep voice, wore a tasseled shirt, black gloves and carried two pearl-handled six-shooters. He exuded confidence and was like no one I had ever seen in my life. He did not wear a ten-gallon white hat as I imagined and above all, he never could be Japanese. But I still could pretend, even though it would be a harder image to visualize.

The other series we watched was titled "Victory at Sea," which was a documentary about America's naval victory against Japan. It had a beautiful Richard Rogers musical orchestral score that was as haunting as waves rolling in the Pacific and it had disturbing images of an enemy that looked like me. This enemy was a defeated foe machine-gunned out of palm trees and flamed out of caves. The Japanese captured were paraded around at bayonet point wearing dirty loincloths with arms raised in the air. We cheered for the victorious Americans and winced because the enemy looked like us.

That same year in September, I started kindergarten at Bailey Gatzert Elementary School. It was a short walk up the hill past the clay bank, City Produce Company and the red apartments. My friends told me if the teacher asks you to stand and tell where you were born I was to say "Seattle." Last year the first Japanese child said "Hunt, Idaho" for a birthplace, as did the second, third, fourth, fifth, sixth and seventh. By the time the fourth Japanese child gave the same response, the non-Japanese classmates snickered, looking beyond the other white and black faces in the row anticipating what the next Japanese child would say. The activity took on the feel of a children's game as laughter greeted the fifth, sixth and seventh Japanese child because everyone predicted their response. No one, not even the teacher, bothered to ask why so many were born in the Idaho desert during the war. We, however, began to arrive at our own answer. We were not part of the "one nation, indivisible," but we belonged to the one nation, visibly invisible.

Being Invisible

This concept of invisibility became more apparent in Miss Waterhouse's kindergarten class where we played with big blocks, marched to music, learned our colors, alphabet and the Pledge of Allegiance. I remember the line "with liberty and justice for all." I learned justice from the Lone Ranger, and because of the evacuation, I knew justice was not for all. We had no tattoos like Anna, but we were marked by the slant of our eyes and skin color just as permanently as Anna was marked. This was a turning point in my life. There were two Americas and we lived in one with less justice.

I especially remember the feeling of alienation learning the flag salute, knowing what happened to my family. I searched the room looking to see if anyone else had doubts or was hesitant. To my dismay, all the other students were unwavering in their recitals. I asked myself, "Was I the only one in the whole room who could not believe?" I recall the feeling of betrayal and resentment toward the flag. I also felt the shame of not being a real American because the words did not apply to me. Nevertheless, every morning for years during the flag salute I held the secret quietly in my heart about being from another America.

In my slice of America, my parents spoke a mixture of Japanese and English at home. Naturally in grade school, I had some confusion about Basic English vocabulary. I remember one lesson where the teacher was talking about using a funnel as part of a demonstration. Naturally, I was familiar with a funnel, but I knew it by its Japanese name. I raised my hand to tell the teacher she was not holding a funnel. Wasn't it a *jougo*? Fortunately, she never called on me and I was saved the embarrassment. What this meant was that I had to take great care in class because I could use the wrong words, thinking they were English when in reality they were not. It also worked in reverse. My mother would say "high tone ne" mixing Japanese and English and speaking in a Japanese manner. The translation meant "isn't it classy or high tone?" For years I thought "high tone" was Japanese until I saw it written as a brand label on the "HyTone" writing tablet in the variety store. The "Hy" spelling was a corruption of English, but the sound was correct.

Because of this potential confusion with words, I would take an extra mental step which was to ask myself whether I was speaking or thinking in English or Japanese. Sometimes this process made it appear that I was not listening or paying attention when in fact, I was in a quasi-translation mode. My lesson was to take great care to understand the conversation and circumstances so that misunderstandings did not occur. My next lesson, however, dealt with context and whom to identify with in a World War II movie.

Turning Point

I was a fairly average junior high school boy concerned about image, fun, good hair, friends and girls. It was one of those summer Seattle days in late August when nothing was happening. Many of my friends were on vacation out of town and there were not enough kids for a baseball game. The berry-picking seasons were over and we were loafing, waiting for summer to end and school to begin.

I was the youngest and shortest of the group and all of my friends were at least a grade level above me. Trying to fight boredom, a group of us decided to take the bus downtown to see a movie. Needless to say, we must have looked rather peculiar to the general public. There were five of us. All were Japanese Americans and dressed alike with the same hairstyles. While downtown, we spent time looking in department store windows and checking out the mirrors, primping to find the ultimate look of cool. I used Dixie Peach Pomade hair grease to create a high pompadour. Those of us who could sported long Elvis sideburns. Unfortunately, I was not mature enough to grow more than wispy sideburns. Rather than pick a specific movie, we read the movie poster ads outside the theatre and the titles on the marquees until we found a show we liked.

One day, my friends and I decided on a grade B war movie about World War II in the Pacific. There was the usual violence, with soldiers blown up by mines and tossed into the air. It was such a low-budget film that the same sequences were repeated and the audience was expected to believe it was a different soldier falling out of a palm tree even though we had just witnessed the same shot minutes before. Part of the plot involved the capture of about four or five white female American army nurses on some steamy South Pacific Island by the Japanese. The nurses had the mandatory torn blouses and dirt on their faces to emphasize their ruggedness as well as their sexuality and beauty.

I was engrossed in the movie even though the enemy soldiers were Japanese and the actors who played them were not. There was one especially memorable scene where the captive nurses had a meeting in their makeshift barracks. The head nurse said, "I would rather kill myself than let those Japs touch me." I was thinking, "I could understand that." I was anxious for them and hoped they got rescued before they had to do anything drastic. Then I heard Freddy's voice in the dark theatre balcony. "Let's get out of here," he said. "Why?" I asked. "We just paid to get in here!" Freddy said that he couldn't watch this insulting trash. Freddy stood up to leave, but the group hesitated for a second. I was thinking about the loss of the hard-earned admission fee. Then, without saying a word, we all stood and left. Deep down we realized that for most of the audience, it was entertainment but for us, it was a personal statement about our potential futures in a white society.

The movie image supported the assertion that from the 1800s until World War II, the Japanese male in the United States was viewed as a person of low moral character who was sexually aggressive (Ogawa, 1971). Japanese men were to be regarded as a threat to white women and the purity of the white race. This was the phenomenon we had just witnessed on the movie screen and the attitude we would encounter when we left our community and crossed the borders into the larger society. Since we clearly looked the part, there was no way to remove the burden of the stereotype. On the other hand, the Japanese female—based on the wartime occupation experiences of GIs—was feminine and refined. She was also cultured and could even be considered for marriage and as a mother of non-Japanese children.

With the growing prominence of Japan after the war, the Japanese American male stereotype began to shift from the prewar sexually aggressive image to the emasculated "lover of gardens and caretaker of nature" (Ogawa, 1971). This change made it more acceptable for the Japanese male to date and marry a white woman and not be regarded as a credible threat to white male sexuality and dominance.

In effect, the Japanese American male was rewarded for passive behavior. The underlying concept was the less visible as a man, the more acceptable in society. In addition, the Asian male images in the media at the time were of the villainous and/or sinister Asian male. As a result, as children we had many role models for being crooks and bad men.

The war with the Japanese continued for years after 1945 in the movies and on television. After World War II, it was the Korean War, with the same slant-eyed enemy followed by another 20 more years of killing "Gooks" in Vietnam. I was secretly relieved when President Bush Senior fought the Gulf War and the enemy no longer looked like me.

As I grew into young adulthood and ventured out of the confines of the Japanese community, I felt the sting and indignity of being different. I felt like a counterfeit bill that was worth less in the eyes of the larger society. I feared trying to pass and being called on my differences even though my differences were obvious and visible.

This was a paradox.

Someone physically different fearing that he would be called on his difference. It was foolish to think I could hide. Because of my last name, I was even identifiable on paper as Japanese.

Asian Identity

Inevitably, my fears of being different were realized. Whether it was the other soldiers in boot camp at Fort Polk, Louisiana, who insisted that they dated my sister during the Vietnam War, or when service was denied at a local Seattle restaurant, or when racial slurs were cast by a group of teenagers driving by telling me to go back to where I came from and the unmistakable "hate stare" that screams "who in the hell do you think you are, boy?" it always felt the same. When a well-meaning acquaintance asked me if I knew his best friend who was Japanese, the pain resurfaced for me.

I was confused and began to become guarded and suspicious when I met new people. I would hold back and wait to see how they reacted. If it was negative, I withdrew. If it was positive, I was cautious. In the process a distinct stammer appeared in my speech and I began to develop an ability to see myself as a third person. There was a distance developing between me and my physical self. It was a great talent for a photographer but not for a young ethnic minority who was trying to find his way in a white society. I needed to change my perspective before I detached. I pondered acting more like a white person and less like an Asian. I hated the idea of feeling like a counterfeit bill. I wanted to be acceptable, at least like an Eisenhower dollar coin. Its monetary value was accepted but the appeal was not mainstream.

As I was dealing with identity issues, the sentiment and attitudes toward Japanese Americans improved as Japan became an industrial power and ally. During the 1960s and 70s, the Japanese in America were touted as the "model minority" by several national publications. This dubious honor not only recognized the hard work of Japanese in America, but it also indicated how much "conformity" was valued as a method to prove worth and gain acceptance. Phrases like "do not rock the boat" were common. The reasoning was that the Japanese had earned some level of acceptance, and calling attention to ourselves would jeopardize our gains. Another underlying reason was that the Japanese were incarcerated without cause and/or crime, imagine what would happen if some in the community actually gave the government cause to act? The conclusion was that everyone would be rounded up again. There was a strong fear that the evacuation would happen again and that all would be lost again.

Conformity was a powerful community cultural value that brought stability. It discouraged individuality and drawing attention to oneself or the community. The outcome mimicked Ellison's concept in his book *Invisible Man* where the African American hero was invisible in the larger society. Bill Hosokawa's book *Nisei* (second-generation Japanese): *The Quiet American*, published in 1969, was hailed as a landmark book that described the Horatio Algier–like story of the Japanese in America. Immediately there was controversy about the "Quiet American" subtitle, which reinforced the stereotype of being passive and stoic.

The "model minority" concept at first blush appeared to be a compliment but was used by the larger society to discourage militant ethnic minorities to fight for equality while encouraging them to behave—"Why can't you be like them (Japanese Americans)?" As expected, this comparison of Japanese to other ethnic minorities created ill feelings and distrust. This comparison was especially ironic considering the Japanese were still suffering the effects of the evacuation. Weglyn (Shimabukuro, 2001) writes:

The recovery of Japanese Americans has been good to remarkable, the rejection and social isolation of the war years have left scars which have not entirely disappeared. A bitter evacuation legacy shared by ex-inmates in varying degrees is a psychic damage which the Nisei describe as "castration," a deep consciousness of personal inferiority, a proclivity to non-communication and inarticulateness, evidenced in a shying away from exposure which might subject them to further hurt (p. 3).

In addition, the model minority concept was used by some of the whites to encourage conformity among young Japanese Americans. As a beginning teacher, I recall when a young Japanese American ninth grade student cut a hole in the American flag and paraded down the school halls in protest of the Vietnam War. Some of my white colleagues asked me to speak to him because he was not a credit to the race. I was angry that they asked me this. I disagreed with his actions, but I refused to take him aside and talk sense into him because I felt he had every right to act in a manner unbefitting the Asian stereotype if he wished. I thought, why should he be held to a different standard than his white-protesting peers?

The Civil Rights Movement

As part of the social movements for equality in the 1960s and 1970s, groups of second-and third-generation Japanese Americans became involved in the civil rights movement. They defined themselves not only as Japanese Americans, but as Asian Americans. Still others became active using the Japanese American Citizens League (JACL) organization. The Seattle chapter of the JACL spearheaded the campaign for redress and reparations for the evacuation and incarceration of the Japanese during World War II.

Within this framework, the concept of justice became a dilemma since much of my true ethnic self was denied. It was difficult to encourage students to be true to themselves when, as a teacher, I had not fully resolved my own identity as a minority. Although this quest for identity is an ongoing process and continues today, in the 1970s I felt a growing need to embrace my heritage and to be accepted as a person. It was, however, Malcolm X who set me on a different path that turned me away from focusing on the larger society's approval.

The Autobiography of Malcolm X reframed my experiences and clarified how racism operates in America. He spoke of self-hate among minorities and how it dehumanizes and limits potential. I identified with his teachings and realized that I shared a common experience with other nonwhites in America. This was not just a Japanese phenomenon, but instead, was part of the majority's plan to make sure that we stayed in our place. There were two opposing Asian stereotypes that served the same purpose of limiting and controlling.

The first stereotype was that we were hardworking, and the second was that we were sly and sneaky. If we worked hard and were not a threat to the larger society, we were an acceptable and colorful addition as long as we lived under the power lines, near the railroad tracks, on the rocky seacoast, or in ethnic ghettos. As soon as we competed against businesses owned by the majority, we became "sly, sneaky and inscrutable." The "inscrutable" was the most devastating since it fostered suspicion and distrust no matter how sincere the motives. Without trust, building meaningful relationships becomes an almost insurmountable task given the existing racial and cultural differences. The outcome was that the stereotype helped to drive Asians away from the larger society and back into their own communities.

I interpreted Malcolm X's teaching to mean stereotypes can restrict but they can also liberate. His thinking led me to consider using the white man's stereotypes to my advantage. I reasoned that if it served my goals, I could be inscrutable to win an advantage. If I had a talent, it was because it was genetic and part of my heritage. I couldn't help it if difficult tasks were easy because I was programmed to be hardworking and pay attention to details. I had no choice but to succeed. The message was clear to the competition. If people wanted to compete with me, I would tell them they were up against all of my inscrutable ancestors and 10,000 years of breeding. Malcolm X provided an interesting perspective to my dilemma.

I was inspired by Malcolm X's words but try as I might, I could not bring myself to embrace more stereotypes. I was on a quest for truth and this was a dead end. Instead, I drew strength from my Japanese heritage. Japan was a small island nation with limited resources that suffered earthquakes, famine and typhoons. As a result, there was a sense that balance was important. The Japanese custom was if someone shared food with you, it was impolite not to give something back in return. Using this frame of reference, there was no balance in accepting and perpetuating your own stereotypes. Balance came from dispelling the myths with truth. In spite of Malcolm X, I concluded that the ends did not justify the means. Instead, I reasoned that the means and end should both be beyond reproach if the outcome of justice is to last and to become a harmonious and balanced part of the whole.

As a junior high school teacher, the revelation of balance led me to my principal, Tom Sheehan. He was Irish American Catholic with a reputation as an advocate for racial equality. He encouraged me to start an Asian American history course, and with his assistance, I developed the first Asian American history course in the state. Since written materials were almost nonexistent, I looked to the community for resources, especially guest speakers. It was at that time that I heard about Reverend Katagiri.

Nineteen sixty-nine was a year of cosmic proportions for me. Reverend Mineo Katagiri, a United Church of Christ minister, called a public meeting for all interested Asians willing to volunteer and contribute to racial equality. He was motivated by the murder of Edwin Pratt, a black civil rights activist in Seattle. Katagiri was a Japanese American from Hawaii. He was short in stature and was in his late 40s. He wore glasses, a mustache and goatee. He did not look like a hero, but I thought with some imagination he could be the Japanese Lone Ranger.

The Reverend set forth the dream which was the creation of the Asian Coalition for Equality (ACE). He advocated joining the struggle for civil rights with our black, Hispanic and Native American brothers and sisters. He energized us to demand opportunities to contribute more fully to the tapestry of American society.

As a coalition of Asians, we were a vibrant group dedicated to promoting and fostering a more inclusive and democratic society. Simultaneously, we wanted more access to the public institutions and private businesses we had been excluded from based on our ethnicity. We were no longer content to limit our activities to our Chinatowns, Japantowns, Filipino or other ethnic enclaves. The time had come to unite the various individual Asian ethnic groups. We would no longer respond to the larger society's label of "Oriental." Instead, "Asians" defined us as a new breed, an identity not burdened with the passive and submissive history of "Oriental."

I listened carefully to the way the Reverend talked.

He spoke about dreams and about challenges. He spoke of equality, brotherhood, sisterhood and social justice. At that moment, I decided that I must learn to speak the language of leaders like Katagiri. I must not only speak in visionary terms, but more importantly, I wanted to learn the language of the bureaucrats. In order to push for change, I must be able to think and speak like the people in power. Coming from a family where Japanese was spoken in the home, I understood the power of language, how it excludes those who do not understand it, and how it draws together and unites people who speak it. Language would be my tool to open doors that heretofore had been closed.

I was excited to become a part of the social revolution and eager to take action and make a difference. I understood racism in the United States and the white society based on Malcolm X. I was impatient, cocky and outspoken. I was no longer reserved in manner because I had a cause which served a common good: justice for Asians in America. At the ACE meeting I met two individuals my age. We three were young, recent college graduates who had something to prove. One was John Eng, an accountant by trade who just returned from the Peace Corps in Nepal. He missed the last three years of social changes and was trying to catch up with the social activism movement in the Asian community. He looked out of place. I will never forget my first impression of John.

John wore wire-rimmed glasses, a white shirt, tie and black suit. He spoke with a British accent and would say "Vee" instead of "We." "Who is this guy," I thought, who said, 'Vee should do this and vee should do that'?" "How does he come off with this attitude wearing a black suit and tie?" Immediately we argued and I found him clearly annoying. Later, when John and I became friends, he confessed that he found me to be an arrogant and argumentative S.O.B.

The other person was Tony Ogilivie, a Filipino American teacher at Blanchet High School. He was 5'10" tall, wore dark glasses and sported a Fu Manchu. He spoke quickly and gesticulated in a very animated fashion. Sometimes he spoke so fast the words couldn't escape fast enough. It was like his body was full of pent-up energy that needed to be spent. Tony was one of the few people who could smoke three cigarettes at once and not be aware of it.

The first meeting of ACE was heady. Katagiri knew important people including the governor and mayor. We were in the big time, but unlike the billing, no action was taken at the meeting since no issues arose that were deemed substantial. Tony mentioned that the University of Washington's Special Education Program (SEP) admitted minorities and disadvantaged whites but not Asians. The ACE steering committee heard the problem but failed to act. At that time, Tony's brother, Alan, was trying to obtain admission to the university but was denied. Tony thought ACE could help.

Making Demands

Later in the summer of 1969, Tony and I met by chance in the cafeteria at the Husky Union Building (HUB) at the University of Washington. Both of us were teachers and we were attending summer quarter to earn additional credits for our certificates. He was still frustrated by the system and hit roadblocks trying to get his brother into the university. Rather than discuss it further, we walked over to the SEP and demanded to see the director. On the way we worked ourselves up into an angry and confrontational mood because Tony was tired of being put off. We were determined to get results. When we arrived at the SEP office, the secretary told us the director was out of town and would not return for a week. We postured and hung around the

SEP office. Standing there losing momentum by the second, we had no choice but to leave quietly and somewhat sheepishly. The disappointment and embarrassment only made us angrier. We had a brief taste of confrontation with the secretary and enjoyed the rush. As a matter of pride, we vowed to get Tony's brother in with or without ACE's support.

Because the SEP application deadlines were approaching, Tony and I drafted a list of demands for the University of Washington that included:

1. a commitment by the SEP to recruit Filipino and needy Asian students;
2. changing the SEP brochure to include Filipino and needy Asian students;
3. hiring recruiters for Filipino and needy Asian students;
4. hiring an Asian counselor in the future.

The emphasis was on "needy" Asian American students because the SEP was established for "needy" students and included African American, white students from a poverty background, Hispanics and Native Americans and not Asians because they were well represented already as a group on campus. Tony took the lead in the confrontation and I helped with the planning. We invited the media, ACE membership and other interested groups.

I remember the morning of July 11, 1969, vividly. Tony and I were waiting in the HUB for Tony's girlfriend and a friend named Woody. We hoped that others would join us there and that we four would not be alone. We scanned the cafeteria to find others to follow or friends to appear but no one else showed. The time had come and we walked to the Administration Building, talking about last-minute contingencies and the possibility of being turned away empty handed. We could threaten violence and a demonstration, but if the director knew we were really schoolteachers attending summer quarter, how seriously would he take us? We strategized and worried about things no longer in our control. We worried that no press would come and that our major event would be like a tree falling in the forest with no one to hear. Above all, we wanted our ACE supporters to be there. It seemed like we were sleepwalking across campus and that it took forever to reach the Administration Building. We were alert, with our hearts pounding and our muscles tense, as we entered the building. As we climbed the stairs, we were surprised and relieved to see reporters from the *U.W. Daily*, the *Filipino Forum*, a radio reporter from *KIRO News*, and a coalition of 20 people including black, Asian and Hispanic students. The size of the group took Dr. Evans, the director, by surprise. As a result, the meeting was moved from his office to a large conference room. We had the advantage of surprising him with the media and a coalition of angry minorities. Dr. Evans agreed to all of our demands and we were ecstatic but unsure of what to do next. Immediately, the radio reporter interviewed Tony and asked countless questions. We were glowing in our fifteen minutes of fame as demonstrators and activists. Aside from our success that day, what we wanted to know was when the radio interview would be aired so that we could run home and listen.

After the confrontation, the SEP changed its policies to admit Asians based on our rhetoric and hard data. When Dr. Evans agreed, he challenged us to find applicants. Tony and I were the first recruiters and Tony's brother, Alan, was our first applicant. In the short time remaining before the admissions deadline, we found fifteen applicants. We visited pool halls, churches, teen hangouts, bowling alleys, restaurants, nightclubs and the International District for Asian students. Alan was the first of several thousand Asians who entered and graduated from the University of Washington through the SEP. The SEP later became the Educational Opportunity Program (EOP) in the Office of Minority Affairs and still exists today.

Learning the System

A side benefit of being a part-time employee of the university was that I learned the university system and the language of the bureaucracy. I was fascinated with how rules could be used to benefit and deny. To my surprise, rules could be appealed and in some cases, exceptions could be made. I quickly learned to assess whether a rule was an absolute rule or whether it could be bent. It was an education in dealing with large impersonal systems, a skill that I was to use in future encounters with institutions on behalf of social justice issues.

In 1970, such an opportunity presented itself. I was invited to help develop a Japanese American history exhibit for the University of Washington's Museum of History and Industry. Mr. Tomio Moriguchi, a member of JACL and a successful businessman, chaired the first meeting of the committee. I was the youngest in the group but I had credibility based upon my experiences as an Asian American history instructor in the Seattle Schools and Seattle Community College. The budget was $600 for the exhibit and at our first meeting we discussed several issues. I recommended the name "Pride and the Shame." There was some discussion about the references to "pride" and "shame" in the context of the exhibit, and I sensed some opposition. I responded that the pride was our patriotism and the heroics of the 442nd all-Japanese Regimental Combat team and the 100th Battalion fighting in Italy and France during World War II. The shame was the shame of the evacuation and incarceration. I thought if that does not capture our story, then what does? The juxtaposition of pride and shame embodied the irony of the Japanese American experience, and it opened the conversation for both the positive and negative.

To my surprise, the group accepted the name as the title of the exhibit. In the meeting I explained the name came from a CBS Walter Cronkite documentary about the Japanese in America titled: *Nisei: The Pride and the Shame*. None of the other members saw the Cronkite special. Even though the name was not original, no objections were stated so it remained. I also contributed photos of the Minidoka Relocation Center and other family memorabilia. My junior high school students from the Asian American history class constructed a somewhat scale model of the camp barracks, guard towers and barbed wire fences that were to be included. The exhibit opened in July of 1970 and ran until September. It was such a success that parts were reconfigured into a traveling exhibit accompanied by a panel of speakers. By 1975, over 100,000 people had seen the Pride and the Shame. Judge Charles Smith, Washington State Supreme Court justice (Shimabukuro, 2001) writes:

> [Pride and Shame] was the first time we in the larger community had an opportunity to see, through this photographic exhibit, what actually happened. This was, I think, the beginning of a conscious awareness, especially of non-Asians and also many Asians. The younger generations of Asians/Japanese [Americans] were not fully aware of what happened during the Second World War (p. 4).

According to Moriguchi (Shimabukuro, 2001), the Pride and Shame project kindled awareness about redress. It energized the community to organize, lobby and publicly demonstrate. The Seattle Chapter of the JACL went on to lead the redress and reparations movement. The approximately 20-year campaign resulted in the passage of the 1988 *Civil Liberties Act,* which authorized $20,000 in reparations for all living Japanese Americans incarcerated during World War II, a letter of apology and grant funds for educational projects. On August 10, 1988, President Ronald Reagan signed the act in the White House. It culminated in an unbelievable victory for the supporters and advocates of reparations and the Japanese community. It was years later that I understood the larger implications of the Pride and Shame exhibit as a catalyst for change and my role in its beginnings.

Resolution at One Level

My commitment to social justice is best reflected by a story about my uncle Shizuo who died in 1995. During the war, he was an interpreter in the Pacific theatre in military intelligence. After the war, he worked as a translator for the Central Intelligence Agency. Uncle wanted to be buried next to his mother and father, Toyojiro and Toku Yamada, in Seattle. His daughter Pam sent his ashes by mail from Virginia. Shizuo was always a very happy-go-lucky fellow with a huge grin and a distinctive laugh. When he and my mother got together, all I could remember was the sound of laughter. We set the date to have his remains buried, but his package must have gotten mixed up in the third-class mail because it took him a long time to cross the country. Finally, the box with the urn arrived before the ceremony. I remember it was raining and we walked to the tented grave site at Washelli's Resthaven Cemetery.

This section of Washelli's had headstones with names like Wong, Suzuki, Yamada, Yamamoto, and so on. I saw one marker with the name "Moore." I wondered what white person would be buried here with all these Asians. Years later, on Memorial Day, I saw the Moore family placing flowers on the grave. The Moores were African Americans and were not token whites in this section.

I realized then that this was the minority section and as such, it was another ethnic ghetto. Ironically, my thoughts were that I was born in a Japanese ghetto (the relocation camp) and that I would be buried near my parents in a largely Asian ghetto in Resthaven. "Ghetto to ghetto," like dust to dust, I thought. At first it bothered me but then I concluded that what really mattered was not where one was born or where one was buried, but what one did with his or her life in that short time between. At that time, I decided to rededicate myself to make the United States a more just place so that future minorities would have opportunities to escape the visible and invisible ghettos of white society. To ease my mind and reflect the irony of my existence, I wrote my own epitaph for an empty grave marker at Resthaven:

Lawrence Y. Matsuda Ph.D.

Born 3-1-45 Minidoka Relocation Center
Block 26 Hunt, Idaho
Died 20__
Ashes in Hiroshima and Ashes at Point No Point,
Washington

Ain't nobody home here.

This epitaph is a symbolic escape toward my own individuality and away from the stereotypes and restrictions of the larger society. It is also a reminder of my life's work to make a difference for others by my remembering the past and telling my story.

Day of Remembrance

In 1978 the Japanese American community of Seattle organized "A Day of Remembrance," which was a day of education and celebration at the former Camp Harmony evacuation site located at the Puyallup Fair grounds in Puyallup, Washington, some 30 miles south of Seattle. A caravan of cars from Seattle and a program was planned to remember the injustice of the evacuation. Dignitaries and elected officials spoke and a potluck lunch followed. I consciously chose not to attend because my parents and relatives were forced to live on the fairgrounds in 1942. For this reason, I vowed never to visit the Puyallup Fair even though it was the largest annual fair in the state. Shimabukuro (2001) writes about the Day of Remembrance:

> The turnout surprised participants and organizers alike. More than 2,000 people had come to Sick's Stadium [in Seattle] to gather. Sam Shoji, at the wheel of the first civilian vehicle in the caravan to Puyallup, said that the sight of everyone driving down the freeway was nothing short of "awesome." Sherry Kinoshita agreed: "I never dreamed of the extent to which the community would turn out for the event. The endless caravan of cars, two-miles long, winding down the freeway with lights on and police escorts, was one of the most impressive sights I can recall" (p. 48).

My first visit to the fair came two years later in 1980 when I accompanied a group of bilingual students. Although the circumstances were different, there were some striking similarities to the Day of Remembrance. As the administrator of Bilingual Programs in the Seattle Schools, the teachers of the Sharples bilingual center school invited me to the fair. It was impossible to refuse especially since it was a request from teachers/staff for the students. This was the first time most of the Laotian and Vietnamese students attended the fair, and it was a first time for me as well. It was a rainy September morning when all 200 students and teachers were loaded on the yellow buses. The translators gave the students instructions and informed them about the exhibits and when to be back at the bus loading zone.

As we drove to Puyallup, the rains increased and it became a downpour. The students sat without emotion and looked at the rain and traffic hydroplaning across the highway. I, however, was panicking. "What kind of experience would this be for them?" I thought. They won't be able to see or do a thing. I remember the bus caravan winding down the hill from the town of Milton off the freeway to the Puyallup Valley and seeing a bright ray of sunshine in the middle of the storm clouds. It was actually sunny in that small patch of land occupied by the fair.

"It was meant to be," I thought.

These children came too far and suffered too much coming from war-torn Vietnam, Laos and Cambodia to be denied a day at the fair. I knew then that I was meant to be working on behalf of these students. They had faith that all would be well and it was. It was energizing to be with them and to be a part of their journey in America. It also was an affirmation to me that I should continue to work for those who did not have all the privileges of most Americans. Finally, it was a homecoming for me, my own private Day of Remembrance without the dignitaries, politicians and speakers. I recall a sense of peace and calm that settled over me as we boarded the bus to return to school. I sat down and gazed out of the window. We left the sunny valley and drove up the hill into the dark skies and rain above.

The bilingual students suffered through war, abandonment by the United States, time spent in camps, loss of loved ones and a difficult transition to Seattle. Yet, in spite of this entire trauma, they appeared to be happy, eager and sincere people who wanted a part of the American Dream. Some of their experiences paralleled mine to a degree when I was a child after World War II. As a youngster, however, I was powerless to implement any changes or advocate for justice. Thirty-some years later as an adult, I had a rare second-chance opportunity to make a difference when I successfully testified in the Superior Court of Washington on behalf of bilingual education.

Over the last 20 years, the Seattle School District has experienced a steady growth in the number and diversity of bilingual students attending Seattle schools. Currently, there are approximately 6,000 bilingual students or about 8 percent of the district's population. In addition, there are over 80 different languages and dialects represented. Historically, Washington state has been committed to providing everyone an education. In 1895 the state passed what was then called the "Barefoot School Boy Law," which guaranteed every child a basic education. But the law assumed everyone spoke English.

As the bilingual programs coordinator for the Seattle Schools in the late 1970s and early 1980s, I headed an education community that worked to develop an educationally appropriate service model related to unique individual ethnic group needs. As I reflect back on my bilingual work experience, it marked a significant turning point not only in the lives of bilingual children, but in my own life as well. By advocating for these students, I gained self-knowledge, confidence and a renewed dedication to pursuing issues of equity in education. It also provided an opportunity to resolve and confront some of my own ethnic identity issues in the social justice arena as a Japanese American in a white society.

The district's non-English-speaking population exploded from approximately 900 in 1976 to 2,700 by 1979. This growth occurred at a time of district declining enrollments. To complicate matters, about 30 to 40 percent of the new students were not literate in their home language and most never attended school. Not only did they not speak using their native languages, but many had never used a bathroom before and most were suffering from culture shock. It was like they came off a 747 jetliner leaving an eighteenth century rural existence to arrive in the American urban 20th century in a matter of hours.

As the bilingual population increased, I began a grant writing campaign and generated one grant every month until 165 program staff were funded by thirteen different grant and funding sources. To accommodate the transition of the students to the schools, I spearheaded the development of a Bilingual Orientation Center in 1981. This was a stand-alone school where all the newcomers attended to learn basic survival English and school routines.

At the end of each semester, typically 150 to 200 students were exited from the orientation center to bilingual programs in the regular schools. There they received English as a Second Language instruction, Basic Skills instruction and mainstreaming in regular classes. As of the 2002-2003 school year, this program is still in existence.

In 1983 I was summoned to testify before the Washington State Superior Court on behalf of bilingual education. The day before, Mr. Mike Hoge, the Seattle School District attorney, prepared me for the testimony. His attitude was upbeat and enthusiastic. Mike called me the "star" witness, so I felt the pressure of everyone's expectations. I took the stand alone and explained how, with the fall of Saigon, the numbers of bilingual Cambodian, Laotian and Vietnamese students increased over the last three years.

To help my testimony, I visualized the first day of school for an eight-year-old bilingual student. I experienced the excitement and anticipation of all the new things in my third grade classroom. I imagined that my parents just arrived in America from Southeast Asia, Russia, Africa, Central or South America or any one of a hundred foreign countries. I could not speak one word of English and neither did my parents. My clothes were different, my food was different and I could not read English, but I wanted to make friends and to be a success. The school doors opened and I walked in with great fear and trepidation.

My court testimony went well and the general feedback was positive. The defense asked some informational questions but did not challenge my data or information during the cross-examination. Several weeks later, Mike

Hoge called and congratulated me regarding the win. The victory meant that bilingual programs would now be funded through direct and stable state allocations in the future. It was a landmark decision and I played a key role. Years later, I would ask myself how was it that I became a part of this major event that impacted thousands and thousands of lives over the past nineteen-plus years?

One Conclusion for Now

I am no longer the child who listened to the Lone Ranger, nor am I the young activist confronting bureaucratic institutions. I have grown to become a teacher who has accepted the challenge of contributing an Asian American perspective to issues of diversity, equity and justice. Currently, I bring that perspective to my instruction as a visiting professor in the College of Education at Seattle University, promoting the development of future school principals and leaders.

I also am a writer telling the story of a largely invisible minority that suffered an injustice perpetrated by their own government. It is a story that has relevance today after the effects of September 11, 2001, on America and Muslim Americans. September 11th and its impact only underscore the need for sensitivity, justice and ethical leadership in America. As an advocate and teacher for social justice, it is very easy to slip into a perspective of righteous indignation or virtuous anger and to see the world as an "us verses them" proposition. When these thoughts surface, I remind myself that people of many races helped, contributed and supported my efforts to increase equity. They brought resources, advice, moral support, fellowship and guidance. It is a mistake to think that all whites are nonsupporters just as it is a mistake to think that all minorities, Asian Americans or Japanese Americans value equality in the same manner that I do.

As I reflect on my desire for creating change over the years, one of my conclusions is that getting involved in the system and creating change can be effective. It, however, is very much like the school which regresses when the strong principal leaves. Instead, leadership may actually be a major role of artists and writers. Telling the story and letting others walk in your shoes to experience a situation through your eyes may be the best formula for change. Telling people to change and giving them alternatives denies them the opportunity to experience the problem and to address it in their own manner. Living the problem through an author or artist's creative work could be the most powerful impetus for change because it fosters understanding and empathy rather than prefabricated alternatives and solutions. When touching someone's heart generates change, that change may be worth more than all the rules, laws and policies a bureaucracy can generate.

A Brief Historical Sketch of the Japanese in America

The Japanese immigrated to the United States in the late 1800s, primarily to the territories of Hawaii and Alaska and the West Coast of the United States. They supplied labor for agriculture, fishing, forestry, railroads and other industries. As with other nonwhites on the West Coast, they encountered the overriding attitude from the larger white society that they could not be assimilated. A 1910 Asiatic Exclusion League bulletin stated the Japanese were so un-American that "we cannot assimilate them without injury to ourselves" (Ogawa, 1971, p. 10). The major criterion was embodied in the question, "Would you want your daughter to marry one?"

For the separation of the races, several mechanisms existed. Laws were passed to create separation. For example, approximately a dozen states prohibited intermarriage. Japanese (noncitizens) were not permitted to own land in certain states, and Japanese aliens did not have the right to earn citizenship until after World War II.

The negative effects of the stereotypes and mistrust, combined with the attack on Pearl Harbor and the declaration of war with Japan in 1942, resulted in Americans of Japanese descent being viewed as potential enemies of the state. In response, 110,000 were evacuated and incarcerated into relocation centers under Presidential Executive Order 9066 for the duration of the war. Some called the centers surrounded by barbed wire and guard towers concentration camps, but they were not Nazi death camps. Nevertheless, Japanese and Japanese Americans were removed from their homes and incarcerated without due process and without having committed a crime. Lives were destroyed and hearts were broken.

After the war, the status of Japanese in America rose. The 442nd Regimental Combat Team and the 100th Battalion composed of Japanese Americans from the camps and Hawaii fought valiantly in Europe and became the most decorated group in the European theatre.

Japan's status improved and so did that of the Japanese in America.

References

Ellison, R. (1995). *Invisible man*. New York: Vintage Books.
Grosskopf, B. (1999). *Forgive your parents, heal yourself*. New York: The Free Press.

Hosokawa, B. (1969). *Nisei: The quiet Americans*. New York: William Morrow and Company, Inc.

Ogawa, D. (1971). *From Japs to Japanese: The evolution of Japanese-American stereotypes*. Berkeley, California: McCutchan Publishing Corporation.

Shimabukuro, R. (2001). *Born in Seattle: The campaign for Japanese American redress*. Seattle: University of Washington Press.

Takami, D. (1998). *Divided destiny: A history of Japanese Americans in Seattle*. Seattle: University of Washington Press.

X. M., (1969). *The Autobiography of Malcolm X*. New York: Random House.

CHAPTER FOUR
Portray Me in Silence: Teaching for Justice

Althe Allen

Writing my doctoral dissertation gave me an opportunity to explore my career in education, as a teacher, principal and district-level administrator. It also gave me an opportunity to examine my own personal story, my life and my relationship with "that place called school," and my desire as an educator to find a sense of justice in the midst of it all. The writing process became a vehicle for finding truth and knowledge, and a vehicle for finding a better understanding of my desire to help students, teachers and others struggling with isolation and despair to mend themselves, and possibly to carve a place where they could better give of their whole selves and possibly better belong.

I intended to explore my career in education, my love for challenging students, and my need to provide them with a place. I wanted to understand why young people in despair intrigued me, why I am drawn to children who experience pain, alienation, and hopelessness, and how we may serve a purpose for one another. Additionally, I was in search of the ways in which my students gained resilience, how they found a sense of self, a purpose, and a place. I hoped to discover the ways in which schools could help these students heal and overcome.

My writing began, then, as a reflection and examination of my life as an educator. I intended to explore the ways in which my students experienced alienation and conducted their personal search for self. I planned to study their experiences with schooling, examine how and the extent to which they realized a sense of belonging, and to determine how they might experience greater belonging and happiness in the future.

What I discovered was that my life as an educator frequently confounded me. I moved through most days with determination and ease, sometimes failing to realize the significance of my work. An occupation of service allowed me to emerge as an individual and to find my place in the world while helping others find theirs. In the quietest moments I would reflect. I felt powerful emotion as I acknowledged those young people I was able to reach and who, in turn, touched my heart and prompted me to wrestle with my soul. At the same time, however, I was empty. It is in the silence that I struggled to hear my voice and in the darkness that my face appeared to me. During those moments, I could hardly see myself. I was curious but afraid to confront my purpose.

I frequently "went against the grain" and struggled to change a system that I found too often stressed conformity, obedience and punishment as opposed to possibility and hope. I wanted to empower others to confront the process of silencing that occurs in many schools; I wanted them to hear that passions and dreams may be reality and that we have the chance to choose a different ending for our life. At the same time, I wrestled with my own doubts and searched for clues into who I am and how I became myself. As I sought my own purpose, I realized that many of my students' emotions were familiar to me. I remembered that in my life I had often felt silenced and insignificant, empty and alone. I struggled to understand myself and my place in the world as I sensed they do. I felt alienation and loneliness and acted out of anger and fear.

While I began my journey exploring the reasons why I find the greatest satisfaction when working with the most needy students, I ended it knowing that I was one of them. Where I was often amazed at my ability to "touch" them and their ability to "touch" me, I now know that I am significant. Where I once wondered at my readiness to endure the turmoil, pain, and anger that dominate their lives, I now understand that profound loss prepared me. I am now sure that we serve a purpose for one another and that there are ways in which my life paralleled theirs, ways in which I have experienced and sought many of the same things, ways in which I can serve them better.

Like my students, I have felt bored, worthless, and rejected. Scars on my soul and heart remind me that I was different. When young, I suffered silently, afraid to admit those differences and my pain. Although my successes in school often masked my loss, I nonetheless struggled. Like many of my students, I sought validation, worthiness, significance and concealment in all that I did. As a child I fought to find my place, my power and my voice without being seen. I share these students' sorrows and I can identify with their desire to be heard without making a sound.

These students remind me of myself, suffering silently and alienating themselves from others. In schools, many have the capacity to excel yet feel loneliness, isolation and despair. Their suffering goes unrecognized, perhaps avoided. In writing my autobiography, I sought to understand why I chose a different path, why my years as an educator have been consumed with passions that have to do with creating a place filled with peace, respect and justice. What factors contributed to my concern for the least advantaged? When did I learn that teaching for justice means teaching others to find the power of their voice and a way to tell their story? In what ways did I attempt to move my students toward a more just place? In my life, how did I move there as well?

Experience

We all teach what we need to learn.

During my work as an educator, whose experience includes years of working in residential facilities for children, I learned I often felt silenced in life and in school. In my own schooling, I felt suffocated by the entanglement of narrow hallways, a prescribed curriculum and format of delivery. The isolation of "tracking" and a daily schedule that fragmented courses into bits and pieces of knowledge did not help me to know. Regurgitating answers for standardized tests, upon which all student achievement was based, introduced little difficulty and in fact, brought comfort.

A sadness filled my first teaching experience. I was held captive by the clock, the bells and a cold, impersonal structure that silenced me and made me feel insignificant.

Like the students I observe today, I felt that the louder I spoke, the less I was heard in a school that was results driven, standardized and without care. As an outsider inside the traditional school setting, I felt power in the choices that I made. I sensed power to lift students who grapple with distrust, inadequacy and hopelessness.

I understand that as these young people struggle to overcome pain, they often disappear on large school campuses. It is not uncommon for them to succeed yet remain invisible, to feel alone and earn labels such as "bright" but "apathetic" or "disruptive" in their effort to be seen. I know that they have felt shame in classrooms because I have seen it. I know, too, that they have felt fear; their eyes tell me. I have observed them being embarrassed, ridiculed and scorned. I have watched them on campus, recognized yet forlorn and estranged from the activity in which others participate. On the outside, looking in, they seem lost.

Experience tells me that if placed in a small, nurturing environment, surrounded by caring, interested adults, the aforementioned students would overcome. I know that when others care, students who are alone, distrustful and angry can nonetheless find their voice, speak and disrupt the silence. I see beyond their eyes. Silent, cold with anger and pain, we find self-knowledge and hope. Not strangers, we understand each other's healing and despair. It is with these people that I am one: nearly comfortable as an educator and person; it is together that we participate in self-discovery.

Reflections of Leadership

The day begins as most others; however, for the first time in a long time, our southwestern morning sky is gray; a storm is coming in from the west and I am invigorated as I walk out the door. I take in my surroundings and find that I am shaped by them; I enjoy this day's scent and the dampness I feel on my skin and I easily remember a childhood sensation of cold, wet rain against my face.

It is this strong emotion that pulls me in the daily struggles of being an educational leader. Once, as the new director of alternative education for a large school district, I encountered many challenges, challenges that forced me to balance my academic knowledge with my emotion, my creativity and my pursuit of social justice. Oftentimes, the scales were tipped and I left wondering if I made the right decisions, if I moved in the right direction and if I did the best thing for the students.

On this Monday as I drive to work, I look beyond the dark skies and imagine the dawn as it appears to my students. I wonder how many of them can relish in the mornings, breathe deeply the air and feel it give form to their spirit. I know that for many of them Mondays are difficult; they have spent weekends in homes that are filled with anger, sadness and chaos. Some have been torn between the different households of their parents and others have not been home at all. I anticipate absences, especially with the weather. The walk and wait at a bus stop may be too cold for some without coats, too strenuous for those who haven't had a nourishing breakfast and too disheartening for those who find no success in a classroom.

I worry about one of my runaways, wonder where she is, how she survived the weekend, whether or not she'll make it to school. I am saddened knowing another child has spent days in the hospital after an overdose and remind myself to call her mother. Almost immediately my academic training intrudes. My to-do list plays out as I drive: call the hospital; phone parents regarding absences; put in a third request for counseling services for my students; follow up on the facility possibilities; find out where the textbooks are; check on the delivery of desks; get an updated student roster (I fear we're already full); make site visits. The list continues and carries me to the threshold of my office. I smile because in spite of the chaos and the daily struggles, I love what I do.

As I retrieve my phone messages my list grows longer: the planning committee needs my "numbers," they're thinking about selling our facility. "How many students will that displace?" I'm needed at an afternoon administrative meeting to plan next year's calendar. Would I handle the revision of our district handbook this year? Could I put together a report including our student profile, achievement thus far and program goals (as soon as possible)? An angry parent wonders why no one at the "main office" knows where her daughter is supposed to attend school after being placed in "alternative education" last week. Is this the place? Not for a tenth grader, I think to myself. We don't have room.

Last Friday I visited the middle/high school classroom. Twenty-two students sat in a circle, shoulders almost touching, as their teacher passed out achievement awards. For some, the small handmade ribbon worth two bonus points was the first award received in school. My emotions were bittersweet. Sadly, I wondered how they had been overlooked all these years. Didn't anyone notice those smiles? The subtle ways they cared for one another? Their curiosity and determination? Happily, I watched as some shared comments of pride. I grinned as they applauded one another. I felt warmth as I watched them carefully place their ribbon under the protection of their binder cover, displaying a token of recognition.

> Last Friday Andy asked me: When are we going to get more classrooms here? As if to say, we're prepared to stay! Yeah, when are we going to get our desks and stuff? We don't even have a place to play ball or anything. When are we going to get a school? Last Friday the room was silent as twenty-two students waited for me to answer.

In the middle of central office requests, a message from a teacher informs me that it's 58 degrees in the classroom this morning, a student has written about suicide and there's no response from the counseling center. Another student will be returning after a two-week "lock up." Should he sign another behavioral contract? Is there anything I could do before the students arrive at 9 a.m.? I discover that the counseling center has not received "approval" to serve our students; I am told to inform the parents that services are available through community outreach. I phone building services only to be told that the facility is too old to simply switch from air conditioning to heat. Getting heat today is a major task and once it's on, it's on. The other tenants in the building won't be happy; therefore, I'm told that the system will not be switched this early in the year. "Savage inequalities."

I pack my things in a bag and leave the office for the school site. Driving in the rain, I worry about where the kids will eat lunch; usually it's outside on the picnic table but today that is impossible. They'll have to spend all six and a half hours in the room, which is difficult for 22 students who need, more than most, to move, stretch and experience fresh air and activity. I am concerned about the lack of heat; how can we educate these kids if their basic needs are not first met? I struggle, knowing that the facility is inadequate yet feel that without this one room, my students would not have a place. I am frustrated with the constant pressure that I face, the constant tension between what I know is important and what I am forced to accept. I have dutifully met the program expectations for the adults. Procedures and policies are in place, yet I am unable to provide that which is most important for the students: the symbols (facility, resources and materials) that tell them that they are important, worthwhile, and that they have value and meaning to "us."

I pull into the school drive and realize I haven't resolved the issues of heat, facility limitations and today's weather in time: the students have arrived. I watch them from my car. They're sitting together on the picnic tables outside their classroom door. They've got jackets on (they'll need them inside); the rain is drizzling off their shoulders and they're smiling, laughing and sharing stories. I watch a group of students who appear comfortable with one another, accepting, caring. I notice the teacher, sitting among them, her hand on a young girl's back as she initiates their movement into class. They follow her, like little ducks in a row, courteously holding the door for one another, sharing nods of recognition, these kids who were sent away from traditional schools.

I watch the door close behind them and I sit for a while, unable to move since I don't have the answers. I can't give them the facility that they need and deserve; I can't provide the money that we must have for resources; I can't remove the challenges and hardships that they and their families will face. On this rainy Monday morning I can only contribute to what I just observed: a sense of community, a sense of belonging, a sense of "place" that is not dependent upon four walls, desks, chairs or even books. I can provide support for a teacher who has fostered this; a teacher who brings spirit, courage and hope to a group of young people who are in desperate need of care, honor and justice; a teacher who builds her day around relationships, feelings and individual needs; who develops her lessons with the students and creatively engages them in their learning. I can offer my own spirit, my perseverance and pursuit for what is just.

tears
dance
in your eyes

[com]passion
made visible

students have
moved you—
experiences
are shaping
you
I recognize
the form—
feel its
weight—
know of its
power

I have danced

this dance
and
continue
to become
dizzied
by its
[e] motion

I have to remind myself that I have accepted the paradox of my role as an educational leader, understanding that at times, I am torn between institutional practices and my own values. As a leader it is my responsibility to face the tension that this creates and to remain in motion, cultivating action, trying to make a difference. Finally, I move out of the car, into the rain and into a classroom where kids are listening to a story; a story about hope, courage and the ability to survive injustices that are not their fault.

I remember my own days of teaching "at risk" youth, of having to build lessons upon the unique lives of my students and around the daily situations that presented themselves to us:

impromptu lesson

I bring to the classroom
stuffed animals
intending to donate them—
have you donate them—
to the children

forgetting that you—
young teens
were robbed of a
childhood—

the ability to
play
pretend
imagine

a different world
clumsily deposited
in a cardboard box
furry creatures
call to you
from the back of our room

I notice
your stolen glances
each of you—

curious
needful
cautious
waiting for the first
to dare
to play

you are patient

it doesn't take long
for someone
to grab the
purple spotted dog
carelessly
and toss her

carefully
watching our reactions

it doesn't take long
for each one of you
to touch—
feel—
experience
comfort
in the memory
perhaps created—
of childhood

innocence

an escape
from your
harsh realities

you smile
and I say nothing
realizing
you need this
more than
our math lesson
today

The Teacher

My entrance into the world of teaching contrasts with the years that followed. At 20 years old, idealistic and eager, I found myself at the threshold

of a modern, suburban high school, set amidst the hills of upstate New York. Upstate New York in September is perhaps one of my favorite places to be. The crisp air smells of a mixture of hot apple cider and firewood; the wind is just cool enough to leave its marks on your cheeks, and the memories of first days of school never seem to dissipate. My first days as a new teacher are no exception; I remember them vividly. They have not disappeared amidst all the memories that follow.

Recalling that first day now, I smile, thinking how naïve I was, how anxious to begin a career that would allow me to enjoy my love of literature and give me the opportunity to share that love with young people. I looked up at the vast entrance to the school, admiring its façade, a bit envious that my own private high school seemed so small and insignificant in comparison. Even as a boarding school, its facility and landscape could not compare to this one. I had always felt cheated out of the education that I thought a large suburban high school would have offered.

Now, as a teacher, I looked out over this campus, the buildings that stretched across the landscape, and the words of Winston Churchill echoed in my mind: "We shape our buildings and they shape us." How on earth would I give form and spirit and voice to all of this? I inhaled and began to ascend the stairs. I exhaled slowly as I crossed the entrance and felt the cold, brisk air whip across my face. Churchill's quote is one that on that day, seemed only trivia. A lost tidbit of some history course that made its presence known in what I thought was a moment reflective of my academic nature, symbolic of "The Teacher." Instead, I now know that it holds much more truth than I imagined and that it has gained significance throughout my years in education. I recall it each time I enter a new school building and I listen closely for the voices that give each structure shape.

On that day, hundreds of students gathered in the commons, lingered in the hallways, excitedly trying to cram two months' worth of stories into a few moments before the starting bell. How fondly I remembered my own first days, my crisply ironed outfits, new notebooks, decorated lockers and the anticipation of rekindled friendships. As a teacher, I had to smile. Those days seemed long gone yet the scents of fall and of the first days of school lingered. The students around me looked and sounded much like we did as teenagers. They were loud and anxious and spirited. It was startling to me, though, how much they all looked alike.

In those first months, I was swept up in the pressure to follow the prescribed curriculum, use only the number of days that were allotted for each piece of literature and prepare the students for the standardized tests that were to come. My classroom was orderly and my students respectful. Most of them attended each day and were prepared, eager participants. They shared stories of their summer trips abroad, weekend jaunts to the coast and tales of football games and dances. They were model students; I was the model teacher and together, we experienced success.

Being the "model teacher" was important to me. It followed logically from my need to be the "model student," "model child," and "model daughter." In my life I had longed for the approval of others.

It is the first grade. Our desks are neatly aligned in rows; the room is silent; sunlight streams through the windows. I hear only the teacher's footsteps, the hum of the fluorescent lights. I am distracted. I want to look outside but know that I must keep still, sit straight, and focus on the task that is in front of me. I straighten the skirt of my uniform and sit even taller in my seat. I have that familiar feeling of uneasiness, fear. My stomach hurts. I wish I could be at home.

The teacher's hips brush my desk as she walks up our aisle. I feel her presence; I feel her quickly gaze over my shoulder, making sure that I am writing my letters. I do so diligently, wishing though, that I could read my *Little House on the Prairie* book. Reading is much more fun than writing these letters over and over.

The teacher stops at the desk in front of me. She grabs the fat green pencil from John's hand, correcting his form, sternly telling him how to hold it properly. He lowers his head. John is quiet and shy. His face reddens as the teacher scolds him. My stomach churns. I feel sorry for him. I don't ever want to be him, though. I want to be perfect. I check to make sure I'm holding my pencil the right way. The teacher takes John's and returns with a different one. This one has a rubber grip. Putting her hand over his, she molds his fingers to the pencil. Her directions become muffled. All I can hear are my own thoughts: "I don't want to be different. I don't ever want to be singled out like John."

In the midst of the ivy-league-bound juniors and seniors whom I taught, there were others who reminded me of John. They were quiet, more subdued students who often lowered their heads when spoken to, who didn't share many stories or attend many football games or come prepared each day. These students were different. They seemed lost, forlorn, estranged from the activity that filled those walls. They came to my class, though, sat in the back of the room and silently observed. As I performed, I felt them watching me, as if they could see through me, and that grade-school fear was ever present. What did they think of me? Did they like me? Did they think I was smart enough? As I regurgitated information I had so carefully learned, I knew I wasn't being the "model teacher" for them. I knew they longed for more, possessed something inside that needed saying, and had opinions, hopes and dreams. I was drawn to them but wasn't sure why.

I began to observe these students each day, in class, in the cafeteria, the hallways, outside (the place they seemed most at ease), away from the confines of the brick and mortar, the stark walls, tiled floors, cold stares. In the fresh air and open space, they breathed—exhaled, as if relieved. It bothered me to think that they would feel relief after leaving my classroom. I wanted them to like my class; I wanted them to experience freedom, to escape their fears. I wanted to be a different teacher for them. I just didn't know how.

So, I watched them. I began to understand some of their silence; I came to know their stories and saw through their masks of apathy. My role as a teacher shifted. I wanted to connect to them. I no longer wanted to "stand and deliver." I wanted to find what they kept inside, and I wanted to bring them out of their hiding places. I began to let them teach me. Many days, even in our silence, we began to communicate.

I watched them read Camus, Sartre, Algren (books that weren't on our reading list) while I dutifully taught Mark Twain and Shakespeare. I spent hours responding to the challenges they presented in their journals, and in time they came to understand me and to trust that I believed in their intelligence.

What went unnoticed in the midst of the pomp and circumstance of traditional high school I found between the pages of dilapidated notebooks. However, the pressure to teach to the top 95 percent and to somehow provide "appropriate" placement for those who were apathetic to the importance of the "All-American High School" was a constant struggle for me. I was torn between wanting to be the perfect teacher and wanting to comfort the scolded child. After a year of trying to make a place for the students who didn't belong, I, too, needed fresh air. I walked out of the building that only months before, I had approached in awe. I descended the stairs and exhaled, noticing that the haze of summer had subdued the colors of the landscape. The crisp freshness of fall had faded, along with my idealism. I headed west to begin again, to pursue my love of literature and a master's degree at Arizona State University.

First Days of School

Two weeks after I arrived in Phoenix, I was drawn back to the world of teaching. Although I had decided that it "wasn't for me," I happened upon a unique opportunity, one which I could not walk away from. I put my master's degree in English literature on hold and found myself, instead, in a refurbished car dealership that served as a school for over one hundred homeless students. As I toured the facility with the personnel director, I felt the warmth of the carpet beneath my feet, heard the muffled sounds of children playing and saw their stories in the drawings that were displayed on the walls. Immediately, as I took in the building, I began to take shape.

I was offered the teaching job on a Wednesday afternoon. The classroom that they hoped to fill with high school students on Monday morning was empty. There were no desks, no books, nor any chalkboards. I asked for the curriculum. "We don't have a prescribed curriculum, but since we will use a block schedule for the high school kids, you'll only have to teach two subjects. So, start with what you know and then we'll go from there."

> Start with what I know? He had to be kidding, I thought. I know how to follow directions; I know how to implement a curriculum. I felt both fear and excitement. Inside welled a sense of creativity that had succumbed to rules long ago. I nervously imagined the possibilities of freedom.

"Two subjects? I'm only certified in English. What else will I teach?"

"History is pretty close to English. Just teach an English and history class. Hopefully, we'll be able to hire another teacher soon."

I couldn't believe what I was hearing. Thus began my career in alternative education. In four days, I created a classroom out of anything I could find. By Sunday I was exhausted. On Monday morning I faced another first day of school.

In August at 6:30 a.m., the heat was already unbearable. I hated it. I parked my car in the only lot and began to move boxes into the classroom. My new, crisply ironed dress began to wilt and the heat emanating from the pavement burned my eyes. I longed for fall and the beginning of school as I remembered it back east. I spent the next hour reviewing my lesson plans and putting the finishing touches on the room. My new paper, pencils and pens were neatly arranged. Always the model student. My class roster, empty for now, was ready and waiting. I felt prepared. The model teacher...

At 7:30 a.m. I stood at the side entrance, waiting anxiously for the first bus to arrive. As a student and teacher, I had always enjoyed the newness of the first day, the excitement of seeing old friends, the feeling of new school clothes and the smell of new books and supplies. Writing this, however, I suddenly recall a very different first day and buried memories began to emerge.

> I stand next to my mother worrying the small white beads of my purse. My cardigan sweater is buttoned to my neck yet I shiver; the September morning air isn't even cold. Butterflies dance in my stomach; this feeling is familiar. It's my first day of kindergarten and I am scared.

> I remember waiting for what seemed like hours, looking up and down the desolate country road, until my mother and I slowly made our way back up the long drive. The bus should have been here by now, I thought. Why did they forget me?

> The classroom door opens and simultaneously a circle of heads turn to watch me enter. The teacher gets up from the rocking chair to greet me; my mother turns to leave. I feel small and lost. Somehow, I am different. I don't like everyone watching me. I hang up my sweater and reluctantly add my purse to the metal hook attached to the cubby that bears my name.

> I am shown to my place on the carpet amidst a group of strangers, and I am self-conscious of their gaze. It's my very first day of school and I don't like it very much.

Standing in the Arizona sun, my anticipation grew as the school bus approached. I could see some of the students and I smiled as I tried to press the wrinkles from my new linen dress. The bus pulled into the drive and stopped. It seemed like minutes before the first pair of feet appeared on the blacktop. Those aren't new sneakers, I thought. Instead, torn tennis shoes emerged, sizes too big for the little girl who donned them. She slowly walked away from the bus, empty-handed, not a notebook or lunchbox in sight. With her eyes cast down, she stood to the side and leaned against the wall. She was small and looked lonely. The other students followed and as I watched each one, my heart sank.

There were no new outfits, new backpacks, lunchboxes or books. There was no sound of laughter or stories of summer vacation. There were no parents to wave good-bye or pass out lunch money. There were no smiles. These kids looked tired, sad and afraid. There was solitude in the multitude, a silence that touched my heart, a silence more powerful than the voices of the hundreds of students I faced the prior year. At that moment, I knew that the lessons I had planned were of no use. This first day was one like no other, and I would have to feel my way through it. I exhaled slowly and opened my arms to embrace the heat of the Arizona sun.

The Chosen

The students I have chosen to work with have given me experiences that have led me back to myself. It wasn't until recently that I began wondering why I had devoted my life to young people in despair, children who experience pain, alienation and hopelessness and who search, almost desperately, for a place. It is through their eyes, their responses to school, that I have slowly begun to uncover myself. I have begun to remember the truth about my life and my pain. It's been 32 years since I came into the world. Born in a suburb of Buffalo, New York, I imagine that September day in 1968 was a dreary one—gray skies, cold temperatures and a wind that chilled one's soul (quite typical for fall in upstate New York).

Fall has always been my favorite season. It is the season that I miss the most, the one I long for in the midst of the Arizona heat. Crisp air and crackling leaves enliven me. Gray skies always serve as the perfect excuse to curl up and read a book. The pastime of my preference has seen me through the dreariest of days. As an only child, I spent a great deal of time with my books. I remember now that some of my childhood school days were spent home in bed, reading. I was curious and imaginative; I was filled with questions and in search of answers which school never seemed to provide. So, I turned to my books and sought solace in their pages. From as early as I can remember, I felt afraid; afraid of what others thought, afraid of being a disappointment, afraid of not being "good enough." There existed within me a deep desire to be recognized by others, validated and made to feel as though I really did exist. I carried with me an emptiness that I couldn't describe. Emotions were entangled so that I couldn't separate one from the other. I went through many days confused and sad. Reading gave me an escape from myself. I could become absorbed in others' emotions so that I didn't have to think of my own. I felt safe in the world of books and could, for a while, avoid my fear.

I experienced the effects of abandonment at birth, separated from my mother and given up for adoption. As an adopted child, I believe that some of my fear existed as early as the day I was born. I believe that my incessant crying throughout infancy was my response to feeling helpless and alone, longing for the mother's touch that I had missed during my first few weeks of life. As a small child I craved attention and constant activity. With age, I developed additional responses and created an identity that masked a sorrow I could neither describe nor identify, carefully constructing walls that allowed me to conquer yet hide from the world. I buried my feelings beneath an "affectionless" nature. My pain and emptiness, warmth and caring remained invisible to others. However, in my quiet rebelliousness one could see the angry protests of a child and a hidden sense of sadness. I've often wondered about my first moments of life. Whose voice did I recognize? Whose scent comforted me? Whom did I reach for? Who held me? It is known that the hours and days following birth are critical for an infant to bond with her mother. I wonder if I experienced that bond. I wonder how long my mother was allowed to hold me (or if she wanted to) before I was taken away, given over to foster parents and left to wait for my adoption.

I know that my adoption did occur two months later. My foster mother cried as she left me with my new family. In the midst of others' extreme happiness, she relinquished me, put me in my mother's arms and with my dark eyes peering out from under my fur-lined hood, she turned and walked away. It must be difficult leaving an infant whom you've cared for and nurtured since birth. I think it must have been difficult also for me to be left. I have carried the fear of abandonment with me through life.

My parents have told me that in those first few weeks I cried and could not be comforted. In fact, according to my mother, I cried for practically the first three years of my life. I've been told that my mother slept in her rocking chair with me in her arms. Any attempt to put me in my crib resulted in screams and sobs. So, we rocked. To this day, I still rock myself to sleep, in my bed, comforting myself as my mother once did. Those moments and years were formative. I know this much is true.

I also know that being "chosen" contributed to the fear I felt as a child. My parents told me over and over again from infancy how they chose me, and how I was special. For that, I am thankful. However, being "chosen" is difficult. As Betty Jean Lifton (1975) says,

> What does it mean to be chosen? To be chosen is to be acted upon, to be passive. It is not to choose. It is a burden to be chosen. Its very specialness isolates one. It can be a very lonely and awesome responsibility being someone else's answer. Where do you connect with the human condition when you are chosen and every one else is born? (p.19)

I don't remember being told I was adopted. I always knew. There wasn't a defining moment in which I learned that I had another set of parents out there. I do remember, however, being told how "special" I was, how I was "chosen." Watching my mother worry about me, always fearful to let me out of her sight, created a great deal of anxiety for me. I felt as though I was her "answer" and that I couldn't disappoint her; I couldn't let her down; she had waited for so long to "get me." This "specialness" sets one apart as "different." I carried this sense of difference with me at all times. I never had a strong sense of place, of my identity, and I know now that this contributed to the way I felt in school. Somehow, others always seemed to have something that I did not. I stood as an outsider—watching—and afraid. As a child, I never felt like I fit in and although I had many advantages, I wasn't satisfied. At times, the advantages made it even worse. Because I didn't have any real problems, all of my sadness seemed to be my fault. I wanted so badly to please others (particularly adults), to gain approval. Therefore, I learned how to obey the rules of school and to be the perfect, chosen child.

Difference

Growing up, unsure of your "true" identity, is difficult at times. I often wonder about the significance of my birth name. Upon my adoption, "Deena Lynn" was quickly changed to "Althe." I wonder if, at the time, I ever even noticed. I wonder if the sound of those new syllables startled me. In school, assignments that centered on family history, names and heritage were frightening. I felt as though I didn't really have a past, one that was really mine. Another adoptee recalls, "I felt I had no self. When you don't know how you were born, you don't exist" (Lifton, 1975, p. 20).

I was given the pieces of my history that my parents knew, pieces from which I formulated my own conclusions. Both of my birth parents were college graduates; therefore, I was intelligent and expected to follow in their footsteps. They must have at least been in their 20s, in my opinion, old enough to get married; therefore, I truly wasn't wanted. My birth mother was an artist; my artistic and creative talent was inherited. I surmise my often-bohemian nature was inherited as well. There's no other explanation. I've guessed that I'm Italian, probably from southern Italy. At other times, how-ever, I've been French, more closely linked to my adoptive parents' heritage. There are times when I'm tired of guessing and I just want to know.

The question of nationality, history and family lineage is the most diffi-cult for me. It still catches me off guard when I'm asked, "What are you?" Quickly, something comes out of my mouth and almost immediately I feel the pangs of guilt, knowing that whatever I said was a lie. Guilt proved to be a major theme in my childhood. I've read that the problem of guilt lies within the heart. In a household established upon fear (that I would be stolen away) and faith (Catholicism mandates it), I grew up distrustful and guilt ridden. My heart was heavy. I knew that my mother's fear that I would be taken and the pain and anguish that that caused her were somehow my fault. I watched her nervousness, adopted it as my own and was frightened by my ability to mean so much to another person. My mere existence caused her great an-guish, I presumed. Therefore, I went easy on her; her fragility demanded it.

Part of her frailty was evident in her ability to blindly accept the doc-trines of the Catholic Church. Those doctrines were a part of my life since birth. Thankfully, I was baptized in the hospital; we have the papers to prove it. My mother got great comfort from knowing that my original sin had been washed away. Thankfully, I was a Catholic and I was made to participate regularly in my religion.

Every Sunday I sat in an old wooden, brown pew with my eyes lowered, knowing that I was not worthy. While the priest was chastising the sinners (I knew I was included), I wondered how all of this came to be. I questioned the "God theory" and realized that my curiosity must be confessed the fol-lowing week. For I did not have "blind faith," and thankfully so; I was re-lieved that I at least had something to tell the priest during confession. When I began to question why I had to tell a man my sins, having been taught that God was there to hear me, I was again chastised. Obviously, I just didn't get it.

Therefore, I didn't understand how I could enter the church as an adult who accepted God and all of the Catholic doctrines. As the only eighth grader in my private Catholic school to refuse her confirmation, I again felt guilt. Strange, though, I felt power, too. The power to choose, to doubt, to question and to finally hold my head high and reject all that had been pre-sented to me was invigorating. Devastating as it was to my parents, I chose to denounce Sunday worship and became the spokesperson for Darwinism.

The power that I felt with that one decision was exhilarating. I remember the day clearly and I remember the shock and pain that I caused my parents. I came to view that power as a form of punishment to them. Thus, a cyclical pattern of guilt and self-imposed punishment began. How could I cause such pain to people who chose me? I felt guilt; without Sunday sermons to chastise me, I chastised myself.

I spent a great deal of time making sure that I was a small speck, lost amidst the brilliance of a northern night sky. I built my walls carefully so that I could hide easily and become invisible to others. I felt constantly torn between my mother's faith and the expectations of humility and the pedestal upon which I stood in her presence. The attention I received for being the only child, the "chosen" adopted child, made me feel uncomfortable. My existence, which seemed so powerful and overwhelming in my family life, frightened me. I wanted nothing but to hide and to disappear and to escape. At the same time, I felt this deep sense of rage and anger that I couldn't express. Expressing such feelings might have jeopardized my place in an adopted family. They remained buried, emerging only in the rebellions that caused my parents pain.

It was always difficult for me to emerge from that desire to retreat and to relate to others. In many ways, I was able to do it and do it successfully. I was a stellar student, involved in all that one could want for a young person. I have continued to be what others would describe as an outgoing, assertive and successful woman. My need to be perfect, to be accepted and to be obedient has served me well. However, as an educator, I found that I couldn't just "go through the motions." Something deep inside pushed me toward students who were cast away, who were different and who did not have a place.

A Beginning

I'm not sure how I knew what to do with the students who sat before me in a refurbished car dealership on a sweltering August morning. Almost intuitively, I knew that the "get to know each other" activities and pretest writing assignments that I had used in New York would not suffice. As the ten students entered my classroom, with their sullen expressions, angry glances and vulgar words, I knew that they saw me as the enemy. I imagined, as I have many times since, that they had experienced humiliation and failure in the schools they left behind. I knew that they had experienced the pain of difference.

I quickly put all that I had learned in my teacher preparation classes away. At the time I thought that I was drawing upon all that I had gained while working in a group home in New York. I had buried too deeply my own memories of hating school, being an outsider and being afraid. Dealing on a daily basis with children who had been removed from their homes as a result of abuse and neglect, I learned that earning their trust takes time.

Unfortunately, that was a lesson that I had yet to learn as well. I couldn't see that I was still unable to trust, that I still didn't feel safe and that I still sought the approval of others. Out of my need for approval, I learned that in order to reach these students, I had to prove to them that I was different, that I would offer them different experiences than other teachers had in the past. I knew that telling them this was not enough. I would have to show them and show them consistently over time. I wanted so badly to reach them.

I am coming to know that I drew upon more than my work in the group home. The skills that I learned there were coupled with something else, a deep desire to serve these children; an empathy for their struggles and a keen insight into their feelings which are rooted in my own life experiences, my own feelings of fear, inferiority and difference. I am beginning to uncover pain that I have hidden beneath educational success but which was always present, always vulnerable in the traditional classroom.

My First Assignment

My first writing assignment was "What is the difference between an effective (good) teacher and an ineffective (bad) teacher?" I explained, "Don't tell me things that I cannot work with. The purpose is so that I know from your point of view, what you want in a teacher. If you tell me that a good teacher is someone who gives a party every day, I can't do anything with that. I want to be a good teacher for you but first I need to know what that means to you. Please take this assignment seriously. Be honest. I will be the only one reading it." Amazingly, the students did this. They worked quietly and intently every single time! I knew that the "tell me what you did on your summer vacation" assignment would be humiliating for them; they would laugh and act out to avoid, at all costs, such a task. Therefore, my standard "first day" writing exercise became their opportunity to tell me what they wanted from me. From here, we would negotiate the terms.

At home, I sat for hours and read their responses, taking copious notes to provide the foundation for the next day's discussion. I presented the common themes that emerged from their writing: a good teacher is someone who cares, someone who listens; a good teacher is someone who explains things and doesn't just write on the board; a good teacher is someone who is nice, who shows respect. Their bad teacher definitions were the opposite. In reading this assignment year after year, I found that individually and collectively, these students perceived many teachers as apathetic, uncaring and disrespectful. I felt embarrassment for my profession and I felt sorrow for the teenagers who had grown to hate school.

I spent those "first weeks" of teaching in such environments desperately trying to give my students a voice. Together we established ground rules based on what they wanted from me as well as what I needed from them. After giving them the opportunity to define an effective teacher, we then defined an "effective student." Again, they told me all the things I would have told them. And in the end, we were so much better off because I didn't have to. During those first days we put our ideas on posters, made contracts, played music, told stories and laughed. The week culminated with another writing assignment: "This assignment is entitled 'Me.' It's going to be all about you. Don't just tell me, 'My name is Javier; I was born in Arizona.' Instead, tell me who you are, what you like, what you hope for and dream about. Tell me who you love and why; tell me what hurts and what brings you joy; describe your life, past, present and future." The room was silent for a few minutes as I saw some looks of fear, a few signs of the distrust that I had worked so hard to dissipate throughout the week. "Yo, Miss!" Carlos was waving his hand. "Yes, Carlos?" "Miss, nobody reads these 'cept you, right?" "That's right," I said as I, too, took a deep breath and sat down to write my story.

I always dreaded the personal writing assignments as a child. I would sit in fear waiting for the teacher to outline the expectations, hoping we would not have to give our family history, make a family tree or talk about our heritage. These were popular writing topics in school, and even most recently in a doctoral course, I was given the choice to do a research paper or a more creative "ethnic roots" essay. Hearing the options, my heart sank and I again felt like the frightened child in grammar school, alone, sitting among classmates with rich histories, extended families and stories to tell. As an adopted child, such assignments filled me with confusion, fear and pangs of guilt.

My adoption was not public knowledge, so my completion of the tasks somehow seemed dishonest to me. Sure, I had stories of growing up; I had a mom and dad but deep inside I couldn't forget the painful reality that I really didn't know who I was or where I came from. Even now, when I'm amidst a group of new people who ask about my heritage I still feel the emptiness of not knowing. I still face the possibility of a life that I will never fully know; I still wonder who I really am and at times I really long for the answers, for truth. Friday was a good day for the "Me" essay since I needed the weekend to not only read all of the students' responses and make comments, but also to make peace with the many stories they shared. Children are brutally honest and forthright when you give them the opportunity to tell their tales. In their writing they shared experiences that I never could have imagined nor would have wanted to encounter. They gave me the insight and the material I needed to better understand their perspectives, to prepare lessons that would incorporate their dreams and honor their life stories.

Only one student's "Me" essay has remained after all of these years, folded in one of my journals. I'm not quite sure how it found its way into my memory box. I didn't choose to save it necessarily because of what this student wrote but instead, because she made such an impression on my heart. She was a striking girl, with long blonde hair, the figure of a model and crisp blue eyes. I recall, however, that she was perhaps one of the most difficult students I had encountered in terms of her attitude and the perseverance with which she maintained it. It took me longer to reach her than it typically did other students, yet in her essay, she shared bits of herself:

"The things I like about myself would be my eyes. I like my body. The things I don't like would be my smile, my hair and my hands. I hope that in the future I will graduate school then go to medical school to be an anesthesiologist. If I cannot become one, I will continue modeling and get my poetry published. I enjoy writing poetry, talking to people…and playing the drums. I am a deep, emotional person. I have a lot of problems that I try to work through by myself which usually isolate me from others…I use [my problems] in my poetry and hang on to my pain that I cannot get off my mind. I make wise decisions and am loyal to family, friends and myself."

One of my greatest teaching triumphs was reaching this student. I had the opportunity to watch her become comfortable with education, to let down her guard and laugh and play like a teenager. I got to see a lot of smiles and she often came to my desk just to talk. During one of our last classes together, she thanked me and told me that I had made a difference to her and that I gave her confidence in school. Only days before the final exam, she was killed in a car accident as she left school. By the time of her death I had lost many students, so the experience was not a new one. However, the same feelings of shock and sorrow never disappear. Perhaps that is how her essay, plucked from the portfolio that would have been returned to her on our last day, found its way into my box of memories.

Recalling that student and her death, I am reminded of the first student I lost. It was my first year in Phoenix, in that dilapidated old car dealership that we made "school." Pouring over my old journals, I found my entry and the newspaper clipping. I remember a boy who had all the outward signs of a juvenile offender and devoted gang member. Reading my entry, I remember how Mario used to saunter in just a few minutes late each day, making his appearance, hair slicked back, wearing brown dickies and tan shirt. He would enter the room quietly and take his seat, becoming part of the class. We used to make guesses at his arrival time each day; it became a ritual for us and we would share knowing glances and smile when he appeared at the door. Mario was killed on a Friday. I had the weekend to prepare for Monday, the waiting and the emptiness at the door and in our hearts. In my journal I wrote excerpts from his essay; I sent the original to his mother.

Now I am proud. So is my family. When I was locked up in adobe I wrote to my mom and I always misspelled all kinds of words and I felt so dumb and embarrassed that I started to cry. Then I started going to school…then I felt proud. Then I was proud because I got my 8th grade diploma, so I thought I was a very smart boy.

Together, my students and I mourned for Mario that Monday morning. We shared stories, remembering a boy who had wanted to turn his life around. We celebrated our dreams and our families and our education. Some students prepared poems for Mario and shared them amidst tears. I smiled at their sensitivity, courage and the sense of community we had formed. I smiled knowing that my students felt safe, knowing that as they joined hands and pledged to continue their education, Mario would be smiling, too. I knew that on that Monday, we made him very proud.

Emotional "Pull"

To empathize with what a child is feeling when
he or she is defenseless, hurt or humiliated
is like suddenly seeing in a mirror the suffering
of one's own childhood

Alice Miller, 1983, p. 177

It has been years since that Monday and sadly, I have encountered many more student deaths. I have also shared in student triumphs, celebrations and accomplishments. As an administrator I try to help my teachers find those small miracles amidst bureaucratic disappointments, student hardships and what they often perceive as their own failure. There are moments when I, too, need reminders of the successes.

It's another Monday and I find stacks of files on my desk and realize that today is the day I've scheduled a number of intake interviews for new students. Without opening each folder, I already know how the referrals will portray each child: disruptive, apathetic, refuses to work, potential for violence, truant. Referral forms are accompanied by a number of suspension forms, discipline logs and attendance reports. (A dismal picture if I chose to look too closely.) Instead, I skim the paperwork, looking for something more substantial: a family profile perhaps, attempted interventions, evidence of counseling support and/or a medical diagnosis. The rest I leave up to the interview itself, understanding that by the time they reach me, parents and the children have had a plethora of negative experiences with school. It is my intent to change that beginning with our first meeting.

It's 8:50 a.m. and I wonder if my 9:00 will even show up. The principal of Billy's last school had to send the resource officer to the home last week to serve the mother with Billy's withdrawal paperwork. She has already called this morning to warn me that they probably wouldn't make it. That's funny; Billy and his mother were actually here on Friday (the day after the withdrawal) to inquire about registering him. Since I had another appointment, I had to have them return today. I'm wondering now if that was a mistake, if I somehow should have fit them in.

At exactly 9:00 the door opens and a small, tired-looking woman enters, her son following closely behind. She smiles, extends her hand, and we introduce ourselves. She quickly asks how long this will take since she's feeling very sick. I assure her I'll do what I can to get them out in 30 minutes and hand her the forms that need to be completed. Together, they sit on the sofa, Billy reading the admissions contract aloud while his mother fills out paperwork. I offer her tea and she says, "That would be nice." I keep myself busy but glance out of my office occasionally to see her working diligently in spite of her constant cough and apparent sickness. It is a cold Arizona morning and beneath layers of clothing Billy's mom shivers.

During the interview Billy is articulate and respectful. His first concern is whether or not we have a band. My heart sinks. "No, we don't have a band. Do you play an instrument?" "Yeah, I play the saxophone." "That's great. Unfortunately, the alternative programs really only focus on the core academic courses. Maybe you could bring your sax in to the class one day and play for everyone." He smiles and nods his head. I know how important such interests are for students, especially those at risk, and for a moment I'm angry that others don't see this as well. Why is it that we take everything away from these kids who struggle the most?

"It's okay," his mom responds. "I promise to get you into some type of music program." A far cry from the disinterested, hostile parent I was told to expect. "That's really important," I add. "You're lucky to have a mom who supports you." Out of the corner of my eye, I see her smile.

As we get to the details of the interview, Billy explains that he was sent to me because he needs help with anger control. He says that he gets upset when the kids make fun of him and then he gets in fights. He knows that he needs to work on math, and his favorite subject is social studies. He's a pleasant boy and demonstrates a willingness to work on his issues. He also surprises me with his ability to recall the details of the admissions contract he read moments before. He knows that there are consequences for his behavior in this program, and we discuss some of those as well as some techniques that he could use when he's feeling upset or angry.

Billy's mom becomes tearful when I describe the uniform policy and explain that it may take a week to get Billy transportation on the bus. "He doesn't have those clothes and I can't get them right now. I don't even have a way to get him to school. We left California in a really bad situation and now we're all alone. (I can only imagine her story…) I don't even have any friends who have a car." I pick up the phone, call my teacher and ask about our latest donations. He tells me that we'll be able to get him a uniform. I give Billy's mom a nod and when I hang up, I assure her that I will call transportation and see what I can do about the bus. "I'd like him in school tomorrow so I think we can make an exception." She smiles and excuses herself for a moment. While she's gone, I ask Billy how they got to my office Friday and this morning. "We walked," he said. "It's not too far." Again, my own heart sinks, partially from sadness for their situation and partially because of the courage this woman has, the perseverance. I wonder if anyone at his other school took the time to hear their story.

As I walk them to the door, I place my hand on their shoulders and thank them for taking the time to come to my office. I now know that it was truly difficult. Billy's mother thanks me and tells me to have a nice day. I hear sincerity in her voice. These are good people who just need a break. I close the door behind them and for a moment I just need to breathe, to take a deep breath and prepare for the interviews that will follow.

Return to the Inward Journey

When I reread the previous section, I wondered why I had included it here. Although the incident wasn't particularly shocking, profound or even that unusual, on the day that it occurred I felt the need to record it. At first glance it seemed rather ordinary and I've thought that it will surely be one of the sections to be omitted in the final draft. However, I believe that its importance lies within my desire to understand why I feel such strong emotion when encountering these daily events.

Billy's mom is a frightened woman; she has been mistreated, abused and feels shame at her inability to provide for her children. She has been judged, probably ridiculed, and has suffered at the hands of others. Similar feelings of pain, unworthiness and fear are so much a part of my being that I experience them all over again as I observe others. Billy hangs his head as we talk, and I know that he, too, has felt ostracized and mistreated. I'm sure that he has faced the taunts and jeers of his classmates and that school is a scary place. I know that as a child, he wants desperately to fit in and yet feels helpless to change his world.

> In my own childhood I feared the scrutiny of others and yet was subjected to it every day. Mornings would arrive and I would cry, begging my mother to stay home with her, attempting to convince her that I was sick so that I could hide from the uncertainty of school. Each day I left home, unsure if the other students would be nice to me or if they would taunt me for my straight A's, call me the teacher's pet, or say mean things about my mother, who taught at our school. With each accolade I received in the elementary grades, my classmates would plant the seed of doubt in my

mind, saying that it must be because my mom was a teacher. I didn't earn the awards; I was given them. As an adult I now know that such taunts are part of childhood; children are cruel to one another; it's all part of growing up. As a child, though, I felt only sadness, fear and insecurity. From as early as I can remember, I was overwhelmed with a sense of being not good enough, of being given things that I didn't deserve, of not fitting in. I carry so much of this with me today that I realize when working with my students and their families that I haven't let go of that pain.

During most of my life I have felt a sense of helplessness. I have doubted my own abilities and have been driven by my insecurities. There are days when I have felt immobilized with fear, the fear of what others think of me, the fear of not being good enough, of never fitting in. Working with other individuals who are in pain and who have felt rejection and fear brings me back to myself. It also gives me an opportunity to help, to feel worthy and of some value. Such self-worth does not yet come from within; I continue to seek security outside of myself. For me, this is frightening.

It is a warm summer day in July. I awake to the sound of birds, the smell of fresh grass and the wooded northern California landscapes. For most 21-year-olds, this would be bliss; living in the guesthouse of a home that sits amidst the hills of Portola Valley, minutes away from Stanford University and San Francisco.

For me, the move from New York to California has brought immense stress. My best friend and I planned this trip as an adventure, an escape from failed college relationships, and an opportunity to begin again. I also sought respite for my health. My insecurities in college had led me back to eating disorders that I had never really learned to control. Months before this move, I had made a vow to myself to get better so I wouldn't have to continue lying and hiding and feeling shame.

The California lifestyle, especially as an au pair for a wealthy, high-profile family, only intensified my insecurities. I plunged even deeper into my disease. On this July morning, when I should have been filled with energy and excitement for a great summer day, I found myself lethargic. My throat had swollen and when I tried to speak, I couldn't. Suddenly, panic set in. I would be discovered. Everyone will know what I do.

I took the day off and went to the doctor's office. In a whisper, I explained that I must have laryngitis; the doctor said, "You know exactly what you have. Your throat is swollen because of the blisters." In that split second the fear returned. I had nowhere to hide. He looked into my eyes and I knew that I had been found. Thus began my journey toward health.

My eating disorder existed since childhood. My mother was a vegetarian. With a boyish figure, she never had to worry about her weight. She had the body that I idolized—a tall frame, narrow hips, and no breasts. My father, on the other hand, always struggled. His weight fluctuated and my mother's health-conscious lifestyle was in direct opposition to his love for sweets, good food and the occasional burger. She was forever trying to instill in him her beliefs for exercise and dieting. He was forever trying to find the occasion to go out for ice cream.

From as early as I can remember, the three of us were on a "diet" so that we could help my dad lose weight. My mom's diets ranged from "the soup diet" during which we ate soup for lunch and dinner (fruit for breakfast) to the grapefruit diet to strict vegetarianism. None of these diets seemed to help my dad, though. He became a "closet eater." Candy bar wrappings, McDonald's bags and doughnut boxes were often found in his car. Upon discovery, my mother would go into a tirade about how we suffered to help him, how if he continued to eat as he did he would die of a heart attack and leave us alone. I would watch my dad nod his head in agreement and vow to change his habits. I stood in the distance, listening—watching—fearing a similar scolding.

As a child, I didn't have a sweet tooth and was somewhat used to the health food that I was served. I remember feeling sorry for my dad and at the same time knowing that my occasional "craving" was bad. I became acutely aware of the importance of food and more than anything I didn't want to disappoint my mother. I grew up feeling that my personality alone was a disappointment to her. She was athletic and tomboyish and frequently commented how she "should have had a boy." She felt that her interests (sports) didn't match mine (hair, nails, make up and looking pretty) and that she wasn't a "good mother" for me. I hated sports and I loved everything that was feminine. My mother would joke that I would kick and scream and throw a fit as a toddler when she tried to put pants on me; I always wanted a dress.

I also remember the times my mother would bring me to the softball field to play catch and how I hated being there. At the same time, I wanted to please her but I just wasn't good at sports. My frustration level was high, my patience low and I know I must not have been the "best student." Here, too, I was self-conscious and I feared not only failure but the disappointment that my mother would feel. After awhile she gave up, writing me off as "a girl" and I was left to my Barbie dolls and make up.

What I did gravitate toward was theatrics and dance. My parents remind me that I loved being the center of attention (I always thought I hated it; I always felt like I wanted to disappear) and was at an early age "a natural actress." I found my athleticism in the art of ballet, jazz and modern dance. I traded all opportunities to play sports for hours in a dance studio. My parents were supportive but inside I felt that it wasn't what my mother would have chosen for me. I felt guilt and freedom and power; I had found something that was mine, that my mother couldn't criticize or "correct" and I cherished it.

My issues with food and self-image were exacerbated by my desire to be a dancer. I felt most free when I was dancing; with my head held high I moved across the floor and felt as though I could be someone else. I worked diligently to master my form, took a variety of classes to broaden my experience and fell in love with performing. When I put on my ballet slippers and took my place at the barre, it was as if I gave myself permission to feel with some intensity; I could have emotion without owning the feelings myself. I was safe.

Dance and agility came naturally to me. I dreamed every little girl's dream of becoming a ballerina. As a child I felt tall and lean. I was taller than the other girls, which gave me a sense of confidence and strength. Physically, this advanced development would come to haunt me as a teen. However, in childhood, I welcomed it. I was able to construct a vertical line with my leg and easily propel myself into the air. For a few hours each day I felt absolutely free as I moved across the floor. I finally existed in my own eyes and I could feel that I existed for others as well.

One day, however, the dance studio changed for me. I suddenly allowed the fear that existed outside its doors to follow me inside. Instead of stepping to the center of the floor, as I always had, I stood in the back of the room, arms folded; shoulders lowered, and leaned against the barre. I dreaded stepping on the scale, fearing that I would be the first to weigh 100 pounds. Insecurity intruded and I became self-consciously aware of my changing body, my hips, my waist and my thighs. Looking in the mirror I no longer resembled the pencil-thin figure that I had been. Suddenly I had shape. Anger, fear and panic welled inside of me. I couldn't be a ballerina looking like this. I began to look around me and envy the girls who had the shape that I lost, the shape that I now desperately wanted. For the first time, I didn't want to dance.

It's after 8:00 p.m. on a school night. I have just come home after a two-hour dance class. As always, dinner is in the refrigerator. "I'm not hungry," I tell my mother. "I already ate something," I lied. I watched for her reaction and was amazed at how easily my deceit was accepted. My stomach rumbled and I looked at my thighs, which seemed to be bulging underneath my pink tights. "I hate them," I thought. "I hate them so much."

Instead of dinner I lay on the floor and began a series of leg lifts. "I have to make them go away. I have to make them skinny again." For an hour I exercised until the hunger subsided. I lowered myself into the bathtub, repulsed by my teenage body. I wanted to look like I used to; I wanted to look like the other thirteen-year-olds; I wanted to look like my mother. I let the hot water run off me and thought, "If only I could cut this all off." I felt angry and desperate.

I made my way quietly to bed where I tossed and turned, unable to think of anything but how fat I felt. I was almost into the triple digits; I couldn't let that happen. "I will not eat," I told myself. "I will get skinny."

My self-consciousness affected my form and my ability in dance. "Open up," my teacher would say as she walked by me. I was "turning in" and was criticized many times. Without having gained an ounce of weight, I felt heavier. My body no longer moved easily; I was paralyzed by fear. I could no longer escape the scrutiny of others as I danced. I felt clumsy, awkward, as if I didn't belong. My dance teachers became like my schoolteachers, people whom I feared. "I do not want to be singled out," I thought. "I do not want to be criticized; I need to regain control." I didn't want to go to auditions and have to remove my sweats; I knew that everyone was critiquing my body and I just wanted to hide. At the same time I wanted desperately to be a dancer. I wanted to be in control and not feel helpless and hopeless in all aspects of my life.

So, I chose to control every morsel that went into my mouth. It began with eating fruit, salads, and skipping dinner. It turned into eating one apple or one orange a day. I began to shed the pounds and my fear was simultaneously mixed with a sense of victory, relief. I loved the feel of clothes hanging off of me; I loved seeing just muscle in my legs, extending my toes above my head and being able to create that straight line that reminded me of myself as a child. At thirteen years old, I didn't want to grow up.

Standing in front of the mirror, I remove my towel to study my body. My stomach is flat and my ribs are showing. My breasts have shrunk and my hipbones protrude. I love to feel them jut up against my clothing. I like to see the clothes hang loosely over me. My muscles appear like strands of rope beneath my skin. I feel strong.

I step on the scales at least three times each day and I look in the mirror to judge how I've changed. Last night my dad pulled me onto his lap to give me a hug. "God, you're bony," he said. I quickly moved away, angry that I might be discovered, angry with my dad for noticing. I wanted to be left alone. I wanted people to stop looking at me. Anorexia eventually contributed to the end of my dancing. At thirteen years old and less than 80 pounds, I couldn't sustain enough energy to see me through my dance classes. My instructor and my parents conferred and I was taken to the hospital. I remember the anger that I felt at everyone around me. I felt betrayed. How dare they rob me of this? I wanted to be self-destructive and refused to open up to anyone. I was silent when asked to talk about my feelings. I gave short, succinct answers that I knew would "get me off the hook." I knew what I had to do and "yes," I could do it. I would go home and I would eat. I would make everyone happy; I would do what they wanted me to do so they would leave me alone. In the process I lied; I shut people out, but eventually, I ate.

I ate enough to keep everyone satisfied and went through high school repeating the same cycle of insecurity and starvation. I tried every over-the-counter diet pill I could find. I cut every portion of what I wanted to eat in half. I didn't eat breakfast, skipped lunches and once in a while dinner, and never ate between meals. Each time I stepped on the scale I felt triumph in even a pound of loss. Every time I looked in the mirror my thighs reminded me that I wasn't quite "there" yet. At the same time my obsession convinced me that I was a terrible person. Each visible rib screamed, "Look at what you're doing! You're slowly killing yourself and you don't even care." It was proof that I was bad.

I never felt that my hundred-pound body was skinny enough, though. Entering college, I continued to obsess about my weight and was mortified when I reached 112 pounds. I often stayed in my room while my suitemates went downstairs for meals. I would sleep to get my mind off food; I hid my self-consciousness and fears. It was there, in college, that I learned to be bulimic. It was difficult to starve myself in front of my friends. After being taunted by them for not eating (which in college was socializing), I learned that I could eat, drink and then simply make it all go away. I felt extreme guilt and a sense of helplessness. I wanted to punish myself for no longer having the "will power" to resist food; I condemned myself as "weak" for not being able to starve. I felt such self-loathing for my loss of control.

> It's my 20th birthday and a group of friends take me to dinner. I weigh 117 pounds and I hate myself. It took every bit of energy I had to come here. I just wanted to stay home and sleep. I was angry with my friends for planning this. Like I really needed more food. They must realize I've gained weight. They should be helping me to stay thin. They probably talk about how much weight I've gained behind my back; I bet they feel sorry for me. I look around the table and wonder who weighs more than me. I miss weighing less than everyone. I miss having people tell me how skinny I am. I measure myself against each woman who walks into the restaurant. "Is she skinnier than me?" I want to ask. "What do I look like?" I wish someone would tell me. I want to know.

At 20 years old, why was I unable to see myself? How did I come to this place? My sense of displacement, sadness and emptiness has seemed to always exist. However, the anger and the punishment and the hatred began. At what point in my life did I begin to fear the world, to punish those around me and to hate myself? From what was I trying to hide and why did I strive for invisibility?

Reflection

When I was finally able to move beyond my adult self and to look deeply into my past, I was struck with the profound sadness, anger and confusion I felt growing up. It was then that I came to realize how much my students and I had in common. I discovered feelings of self-doubt and fear that existed in me as a child, who struggled to overcome abuse, control my world, secure my place. When I looked beyond my rebelliousness as a teenager, the "acting out as a child," I came to know that the feelings of hopelessness and emptiness were born in me as an infant, perhaps even before.

As I have struggled to understand who I am, I have reinterpreted my story and gained new understandings along the way. I have been challenged to come to terms with experiences that have shaped me and to confront fears that have stifled me. For as long as I can remember I have been searching for a way to fill the void that exists within me. It seems like I have always been fighting against a sense of hopelessness that threatened to overwhelm me, a powerlessness that I couldn't quite overcome and yet a need for control that I couldn't escape. Like my students, there are times when I still question and search for ways to validate that there really is a bigger picture and that I can have my place within it. However, since writing my story, I have come to own my past: I know what it feels like to be locked within the confines of needing security yet trying desperately to escape from it; to be a child lost in a woman's body, doubting whether I could ever completely trust and perhaps even love. I know what it feels like to be floating in an abyss, a gaping hole that you cannot see or fill, experiencing loneliness in the midst of others, turning from their love inward, to find you are not there. But I also know what it means to own loss and to turn pain into possibility, to be at the crossroad, the point at which you've reconnected and have begun the true healing that comes with the journey back to the original self and the experience of others. Writing my autobiography has taught me as much. Such has been the process for me. It involved not only writing my narrative, but also my exploration into it. In doing so, I looked beneath the surface of the tale and found emotions that had been deeply buried. The writing, telling and analyzing were therapeutic exercises that brought me back to myself. I discovered a child who was confused, angry and frightened. I found a teenager who rebelliously sought love and attention and a way to secure her place. I found a woman who now knows both of them, who cares deeply and feels passionately. I found a place scarred by loss but a place that led me here, to a place of forgiveness and peace.

Where I was once confused about my desire to work with outcast children, I now understand that my sensitivity and empathy developed because of the loss that I endured. I grew up keenly aware of others' needs, which led me to service. What began as an exploration into what I do, developed into a discovery of who I am.

October, 7:30 in the evening. The outside air is brisk, dried leaves rattle against chilled panes of long sinewy windows. I sit in a large converted factory; bricks pronounce the interior yet dashes of warmth splatter the red mortar and the icy glare of plaster walls. The room is full of activity. Children running, laughing, yelling in anger. I sit mesmerized. I focus on a young woman holding a small girl. They were wrapped in each other's arms, as if survivors of a great disaster. Tears welled and rolled down the woman's cheek. I didn't know who was being comforted. Their union was oblivious to the surrounding chaos. Pure, uncontrived emotion. The woman's heart surfaced and I witnessed it. The small girl and I benefited. She released the child and looked at her. She gazed into her face; silently, she conveyed serenity. My soul smiled. In the midst of turmoil I saw her—peace. I first noticed her heart. It was gorgeous: passionate, unyielding and pure. Her eyes "windows to the soul"—no—gateway to her heart. She saw with emotion and moved with passion. She showed that pain can be comforting. Tears can wet a dry soul. It is quite transparent, Althe. It is the first time I ever saw you.

The heuristic process brought me not only to myself but also to my experience of others. It helped me to know that through my own loss, I am able to connect with others. So often I looked for the reason behind the intense emotion I felt when I experienced those in pain, those who were alone and who longed for a place. It reinforced my belief that when provided a nurturing place, one may find the courage to grow. It taught me that sometimes answers appear in the silence and all of us should have a quiet place to stay. It reminded me that the work I do is important and that profound change occurs when others listen.

What implications does this have for the work that I do, the students I cherish and the others whom I lead? The possibilities are endless. Reaching peace within, I am able to exude peace to others; by engaging in the heuristic process, encountering the power of the autobiography, I can more powerfully advocate a phenomenological approach to the curriculum. I embrace a humane and holistic approach to education, one that emphasizes the lived experiences of our students and promotes an environment which conveys the message that they matter.

We can offer curriculum with emotion at its heart. Such curriculum exists in a culture of caring, listening, sharing and reflection. It exists when a sense of community is created, which evolves when we know who we are and what we are able to do. Such curriculum allows for the development of relationships, characterized by shared values and common activities. Above all, it is our duty to foster inclusiveness, trust, empowerment and commitment. Only then will our students be able to learn well and deeply. I have experienced an awakening that gives me the confidence to know that our reality can be transformed—that what we believe and how we live and what we do in schools can lead to not only personal empowerment, but also social action. We must convey the message to students that they can change their lives; we must provide them with a place that fosters trusting relationships and kindness with one another; perhaps we must even walk alongside them as they journey to themselves.

My search has taught me that I have been pulled toward a career working with children like me. I understand now that my need to work with them may have been to save them from being alone and ultimately, to find myself. I also understand that although I have somewhat been transformed by this process, and have reached a place of peace, my search for self continues.

I have a great deal of hope. Through heuristic inquiry I have been able to own my self, know my truth and see its possibilities. I have traveled painful roads, suffered my own loss and felt sorrow alongside my students and their parents. The ebb and flow of the process continually brought me to myself, to others, and back again. Where I once felt the outsider, I now have companionship. Where I felt fear, I know peace. I feel as though I am at the end of my journey and yet simultaneously at the beginning. It feels somewhat like home.

References

Lifton, B. (1975). *Twice born: Memories of an adopted daughter.* New York: St. Martin's Press.

Miller, A. (1983). *For your own good: Hidden cruelty in child-rearing and the roots of violence.* New York: Farrar, Straus-Giroux.

CHAPTER FIVE

A Story of Complexity: Identity Development, Difference, and Teaching for Social Justice

Jacque Ensign

I have never been satisfied with academic descriptions of different paths of identity development, the paths differing by racial and sexual orientation. I'm now realizing part of that dissatisfaction stems from my experience that identity isn't static but rather, depending on life circumstances and perhaps other reasons, identity is something that is somewhat fluid and may evolve over a lifetime.

For me, this evolving identity has been mostly in terms of race—issues that I've faced in the last decade but that have roots that go back, way back, and depending on my situation at the time, have faded and surfaced and have affected who I am.

As I've explored this aspect of identity and revisited memories of my life experiences, I've been able to see some of the roots of why I am so passionate about helping teachers build on each student's unique background. Exploring my identity has also helped me deal with recent challenges in teaching students different than those I've taught most of my life, students who are different and in some ways similar to me. Experiences in social injustices based on racism, classism, regionalism, and sexism have all influenced who I am, my thoughts about identity, and why I teach for social justice.

My Story

Since this story spans 50 years, the terms in my narrative will change depending on the time period and context I am recalling. My story begins in the segregated South in a family that was actively involved in ending segregation. I come from a long line of social activists: a paternal great-grandmother who came south after the Civil War to teach Latin and Greek to poor students in a Tennessee college; a maternal grandfather who left his coal-mining background to found a church and school in Japan; and parents who took a rural pastorate in North Carolina where my father was a minister active in ending segregation. My fate and the title of this piece are rooted in this background context.

When I was born, a member of my parents' church was alarmed to see my body, which had prominent birthmarks on my legs. My mother was told to keep my legs covered so no one would see that I had "colored blood" in me. I grew up with my parents laughing about this incident and being very supportive of me *not* covering my legs. This was my first experience with my parents including me in their defiance of racist constructs. Far scarier were my experiences in North Carolina in the early 1950s that were related to my father's work for integration. I spent my first six years being guarded from those who might poison or hurt me in retaliation of my father's work. I recall being instructed to never accept cookies or food from anyone except my parents or their close friends and to not go out alone from our rural house. I recall fearfully watching my father from my bedroom window at night when he had to go outside at the same time that dangerous people were in the graveyard next to our house with flashlights. They were parishioners so upset with my father's opposition to segregation that they would not come to the church except to go to the graveyard in the dark of night to tend the flowers at their relatives' graves.

When I was six, my father accepted a position in Virginia to found the first integrated summer camp for children south of the Mason-Dixon Line. My early memories of Virginia involve discriminations and threats my family continued to face over race issues. In third grade, when my elementary school was converted from a school for whites to a school for Negroes due to the changing population of our neighborhood, I had to go to a white school across town, where I was placed in the lowest reading group. I hated school, especially the way my teacher talked down to me. I began to cheat on spelling tests as I thought I couldn't learn the words. When I began to fail and my mother met with my teacher, the teacher responded, "Jacque is doing just fine for a girl from that neighborhood." It took my mother's showing my teacher the book my parents had just written to convince my teacher to let me read with a higher reading group.

I didn't like school with all the repetitive things to do at someone else's bidding, or the way I was treated as a girl in school who had to wear dresses and could only play girls' games. I wanted to be home where I could run, climb trees, wear jeans, play with my Matchbox cars, and dig forts with the boys in the neighborhood.

In the summer, I was the only white child sleeping in tents with the Negro campers who came to our camp. While I was vaguely aware that I was playing a part in breaking a system of segregation, I was more interested in these new friends who let me braid their hair, who combed my hair, and who followed me up trees that we loved to climb together. I recall my family keeping a close watch on anyone coming into camp, as there was concern about problems from the Ku Klux Klan and related people. I remember screaming hysterically and clawing at anyone who would threaten my father, even in jest.

When I was nine, my family moved out of the city to live full-time at the camp sixteen miles outside of Richmond. I recall one of the few times my family went out to eat hamburgers at a drive-in. That night I saw, I think for the first time, water fountains labeled "White" and "Colored" and noticed that there was only one bathroom, with a sign over the door, "Whites Only." Even though I was young and "had" to go to the bathroom, my parents forbade me to use it, saying if Negroes had to wait until they got home, we would too. I recall being incensed that anyone would treat my friends like this and being proud of our family's decision to leave that drive-in.

It was about that time that I became aware that motels on our annual trip to Florida were for whites only. I remember being upset when my father explained that one reason we stopped before dark on those trips was for safety. While we could check into a motel for the night, Negroes who were driving long distances could not, and so they sometimes fell asleep at the wheel, endangering themselves and others on the road. He explained that until segregation could really be ended, Negro drivers would either have to continue to risk their lives or not take the long car trips that our family could enjoy.

While I was more aware of the effects of race than many young white children at that time, there were many ways in which I was blind to the effects. I recall passing the Negro kids waiting for their bus to take them to their school and not questioning where their school was or what it was like. It wasn't until I became a professor of education that I searched for their school and saw how far away and poorly equipped it had been compared to mine. I do recall my mother telling us that her schools in Philadelphia were not segregated, but the message there seemed to include more than the black and white issue since she also stressed that her schools honored the Jewish holidays as well as the Christian holidays whereas my school only honored the Christian holidays. I know I was totally unaware of how I was able to walk into stores and libraries and be respected, and unaware how that respect I had been afforded had something to do with the white color of my skin.

The year Virginia schools were to be integrated for the first time, my parents decided to send me back to Richmond to attend junior and senior high school. This meant I would be crossing two school districts that were segregated to attend an integrated school. When forced to integrate the schools, Virginia used a Pupil Placement Board to control applications of students wanting to attend schools outside their neighborhoods. It was a thinly disguised way of controlling what races could attend what schools. When my application was received at the Pupil Placement Board, prominent members of that board visited my parents. I was an exception, as my application was for me as a white child to be placed into an integrated school rather than away from one. My parents were urged to "not ruin this child's education and future success in life by sending her to a school with Negroes." My parents persisted and my application was approved. It was probably actions like this that led my parents to instruct us children not to talk much on the telephone or say any details about our family on the telephone since there was a high likelihood that our phone was being tapped. When we received my junior high class picture, my mother was incensed when she noticed that all the black students' faces had been bleached out to not be as obviously black. I still have the photo, a stark reminder of how uncomfortable southern culture was with race.

When I was sixteen, my Chinese boyfriend and I were walking in a park in Tennessee, holding hands, when we were stopped and I was told, "Get away from this monkey. We are in the Ku Klux Klan and we'll be watching." From then on, we realized we had to be very careful about showing affection in public. As much as I knew about history and desegregation, I was shocked and scared to think that these KKK members considered some people to be inhuman and that they would try to control my love life.

After high school, it wasn't until the 1990s that race played an obvious role in my life again. In 1994, I was divorced and entering my life as an academic in higher education. I had a partner who had lived much of his adult life in Africa and who in the United States was considered black. When I tried to bring him to a family reunion, I had race thrown in my face in a way I'd never experienced before. I was told, through interpreters for one of my relatives, that this man was using me as a "white trophy" to be successful in OUR society. I asked how this could even be considered, since by OUR standards, he was more successful than I—he was a graduate of Princeton and Harvard, had been a diplomat of the United States, and a professor at two tier-one re-search universities. I was told that details such as these were his lies to get me to like him (never mind that I had been at Princeton and Harvard reunions with him and had attended government symposia to which he was an invited speaker). For the first time in my life, I had to recognize that I had overtly racist relatives and that the relatives with whom I felt the most acceptance and rapport were on his side of the family, not mine. For the first time in my life, I also began to really reexamine my own identity as it related to race and ethnicity, for now I could no longer accept that I was only a part of those who considered themselves to be white. I am writing this a decade after this event and realize that this is an identity issue about which it has taken me years to be able to come to some degree of understanding and ease in explaining to myself and to others. Identifying as white and black, as I do now, has not been an easy concept to acknowledge or to explain to others. In hopes that I can convey a bit of the complexity I've faced in wrestling with this aspect of my own cultural identity, I'll attempt to explain.

I began to see racial discrimination in ways I'd never before experienced. Take racial profiling, for example. As I stood by unexamined, my partner was repeatedly checked by authorities at airports and when driving in white areas. He had to whisper reminders to me to keep quiet during these checks, as he knew that protesting would only make matters worse. I began to understand some of the sources of seething anger and distrust of police that people of color often have, and the accompanying feelings of powerlessness to overcome such humiliation. Not only did I see that in others, I began to feel it in myself.

For the first time in my life, I began to experience confusion over my racial identity. Having flown to Connecticut for an interview for an academic position, I was anxiously awaiting being met by members of my search committee. What I never suspected was how confused the search committee would be upon meeting me. What I didn't know was that they had thought they had a great minority hire when they saw my application. Since my name is spelled, "Jacque," until they heard my woman's voice when they called to arrange my interview, they assumed I was male, and because it did not have an S, they figured it was an Anglicized version of "Jacques" and therefore I must be originally from Quebec. They were sure I was black because most of my publications were in the area of black education, I had taught a course on Brown v. Board of Education, and I was from the South. The search committee was expecting to meet a black woman academic, resulting in the following fiasco when they came to meet me in the hotel for my interview. At the scheduled hour, I heard a very friendly greeting behind me in the lobby, "Well, Dr. Ensign, we are so happy to meet you." I also heard a very baffled reply from a black woman walking out of the lobby, "I'm sorry, I am not who you think I am." I immediately replied, "I'm Jacque Ensign," and turned to face two confused middle-aged white men who were on the search committee. Until meeting me, they did not know the color of my skin.

This isn't the end of it though. A few months later, I was in an African American Studies Program session about the one-drop rule and the decisions being made about how people could identify themselves on the 2000 Census (whether they could check off more than one box or not and what the legal ramifications of that would be). The audience was all shades of colors from light skinned to very dark. Partway through the lecture, the speaker, a woman who was as light skinned as I am but who clearly identified as black, stopped and said, "This can get so ponderous that we can forget it can also be humorous. Does anyone have a funny story to tell about race?" I told my story of the search committee meeting me. The questions and comments that followed made it evident that members of the audience perceived that skin is not the sole determining factor in racial identity and that they considered me to be more than the color of my skin.

Until the family reunion described above, I had never questioned my own identity as it related to race. Now I had another powerful experience to add to that, and I found I really had to examine my identity. The sense of belonging that I experienced in the black community had deeper roots than I'd realized. I was now becoming aware of the commonality of some experiences and ways of thinking that bound me to blacks and of how I was often recognized by strangers as well as close friends in the black community as somehow a member, not just a visitor. My partner and I had previously discussed how in much of his life he has operated within the white community—educationally, professionally, and personally. We had discussed how he is treated as black in the United States on the basis of his skin color, and yet how he is treated as something other than black elsewhere, a sign of how he is black as well as white. In ways, he and I were each experiencing variations in what it is to be black and white, and not solely white and black, in our lives.

Defining my identity is a struggle that for me is not resolved. I've wrestled with how much my identity is chosen, how much I have a "right" to it, how much it is defined by my experiences, and how much my identity is legitimate. Certainly my early life experiences were not entirely chosen by me. Beginning in adolescence, though, I have been an active agent, particularly in terms of intimate relationships, and where I have lived and worked. I know others who have had similar experiences who have never identified as anything other than with one race. For many years this was true for me, too, but in this last decade, I've felt driven to acknowledge an identity that is more complex. I realize some may pass me off as a wanna be, yet the longer I've wrestled with this, the more I've felt I have no choice if I'm to be honest. I have never experienced an absence of being white, whereas I have experienced an absence of black. In the last decade, I have realized that I feel out of place when I do not have both races present in my life. This became most clear after I'd moved to Seattle and wondered what felt wrong. Diversity of race was not as apparent as I'd known in East Coast cities. Having lived in the Northeast for just a short period of time, I found my new community in Seattle was strikingly less diverse when compared to my urban Connecticut experience where I had long-term relationships with people of very different backgrounds and ways of living. This forced me to realize how key both races are to my identity. I had flashbacks to descriptions from others living in unfamiliar surroundings in which they felt they had to shut off a part of themselves to adjust. Their descriptions mirrored my experiences and helped me to see that I had to find ways to support the other parts of my identity that were not being fed in my present circumstances.

I struggle against labels and categories while writing this. I find they describe some of my experiences, yet I find labels and categories for race to be constricting, too. I believe that labels and categories essentialize what I have found to be more and more complex about race. I have been privileged by my skin color, and yet I do not identify only as white since there are ways in which I feel as much black as white. Because of the difficulties of explaining such crossing of mainstream-defined boundaries of race, I hesitate to use labels to define myself. Instead, I want to do the same for others, to "get on with the show" of social justice in which people are celebrated and supported for all of their individual complexity. I find a quote of Johnetta Cole's helpful as I struggle with the problems of using labels: "We are for difference: for respecting difference, for allowing difference, for encouraging difference, until difference no longer makes a difference."

My preference for using labels and categories sparingly is echoed by some cultural theorists writing about race, as well as by some anthropologists and queer theorists writing about sexuality. Jacques Derrida's writings about borders and border crossings make use of a concept he calls an aporia: the enigma of borders that really do not exist but which we have to treat as possible in order to deal with them in society. I take from Derrida's writing that to advocate for changes in how society treats those who differ from the mythical norm of white/male/middle-class/heterosexual, one must treat these categories as possible while also working against the essentializing of these categories. In their work on border crossings, Henry Giroux and Peter McLaren argue for the importance of decentering whiteness and privilege in efforts to further the cause of non-essentializing differences and of recognizing that identities are always in flux.

Those writers who have wrestled with their own lives that cross borders (be they racial or sexual or class borders) I find most helpful in describing my own experiences and leanings toward minimizing the use of labels. Anthony Appiah asks that we not focus on labels that constrict people to fixed expectations but instead, that we see people for all their complexities. According to Appiah, ethnoracial identities "risk becoming the obsessive focus, the be-all and end-all, of the lives of those who identify with them. They lead people to forget that their individual identities are complex and multifarious" (Appiah in Appiah & Gutmann, 1996, p. 103). Johnetta Cole and Beverly Guy-Sheftall describe the flexibility of gender constructs in some non-Western and non-dominant cultures. They cite the work of Gloria Wekker, an Afro-Surinamese anthropologist, and her stance on labels for sexual orientation, "Wekker...avoids language that would attribute a homosexual *identity* to these women, most of whom are mothers and single heads of their own households. Wekker does not, therefore, use Western labels such as heterosexual, homosexual, or bisexual in her analysis" (Cole & Guy-Sheftall, 2003,

p. 164). Queer theorists argue against essentializing sexuality and gender by categories, preferring to recognize their complexity. They have a problem with categories since this perpetuates heterosexist ways of thinking about sexuality that place people into exclusive categories. Audre Lorde argues against focusing on one label as a definition of who someone is, contending that it is important to keep all the parts of one's identity, embracing the contradictions in those parts (in her case: woman, feminist, lesbian, black) and not focusing on only one. If one focuses on any one part, "you become acquired or bought by that particular essence of yourself. Only by learning to live in harmony with your contradictions can you keep it all afloat." (Hammond, 1981, quoting Lorde).

I'm torn about the use of labels, especially since I am speaking as a white-skinned woman who has privileges in this society. I realize that the use of labels can be positive as well as negative, since as long as racism, classism, and sexism exist in our society, labels become a way of talking about those discriminations to reduce injustice, just as they can be used to exclude according to differences. I realize that my wanting to not use labels can have opposite results from my intentions and hurt the very people I want to support. So, I use the labels when I name problems that need to be addressed for social justice, and I try not to use them when I'm trying to accentuate the unique humanity of individuals, including myself. For instance, when I write about inequities in schools serving different racial or economic groups of students, I use labels. When I am describing individuals, I try to not use labels in order to avoid expectations and assumptions being placed upon them. I want to honor individuals for their complexity, just as I want to be seen for mine.

Effects on My Profession

What has been the effect of my life experiences on my profession? I have always felt different than those around me. For most of my life, I've dealt with feeling different by being strongly independent and not really wanting to fit in. I now realize that by being complex, I have no one niche where I can feel I belong. I have searched for people like me and for how I'd find them. Perhaps in teaching those whom I have taught, I've found a home in differentness. Perhaps with those with whom I have been intimate, I've found other homes in differentness. I am not sure. What I do know is that these complex and sometimes confusing feelings of differentness have fueled my passion for helping others as well as my passion for teaching for social justice.

Acknowledging the different facets of my identity and acting on them has caused added problems for me. They serve to isolate me from the very groups who might have harbored me. I can be praised for championing one cause but then be suspected as a traitor for not fighting hard and exclusively enough for another. I confuse those who do not understand why I also am championing another, seemingly contrary cause. It may seem to be one thing to work for quality education for young black children, and another to work for quality education of poor white children. Both of these relate directly to who I am; my own complex identity and both are causes with which I have engaged.

Having experienced discrimination based on where I lived and who my parents were, my teaching from its earliest days has been with students who are outsiders in society. For fifteen years, I taught in an all-white extremely poor rural Appalachian area, working with economically poor children in public schools, and then founding and teaching in the first preschool in the mountain county in which we lived. During most of those years, my family lived well below the poverty line—a consternation at times for me but in retrospect, a powerful learning experience to begin to fathom a tiny bit of what those in poverty face. For several years, we lived without running water and one year without electricity, learning how hard it is to keep clean when the only place in the house that ever got above freezing was next to the wood heating stove.

We learned what it is to have that stove catch the house on fire and nearly consume everything we owned. We learned what it is like to lie in bed and to see snow come through the cracks in the wall when the wind howled outside. We learned how much food one has to eat just to keep warm when you are without warm housing. We also learned the power and kindness of neighbors who came to put out our house fire, and who shared their wealth of knowledge of living with simple means. We learned how difficult it is to keep antibiotics for your infant when you have no refrigeration. I recall the pain of embarrassment in paying for groceries with food stamps and how I decided I'd raise more of our food and forego store food rather than go through that humiliation again. Yet, even at the time, I realized many of my neighbors did not have that choice as they did not have enough land or the health and skills we did to farm.

It was during this time when we were living way below the poverty line, after I'd quit teaching in the public schools to raise our young children, that a secretary from the local school bitterly said to me, "Well, some of us have to work for a living." I wanted to argue my case—we were not rich kids living a carefree life—but I said nothing. After all, there was a sense in which we were different as we didn't feel forced to work for someone else—we knew our educational backgrounds would allow us the option to have jobs if we wanted them. We chose to live a subsistence lifestyle while knowing we could later choose to live differently. But her words stung and still echo in my head 25 years later, reminding me of what poor parents and children face too frequently in schools and how some can choose and others cannot choose to cross borders. It has also led me to try hard to never do things in my classrooms that would "mark" those who have less choice and money.

Our three children were born in this Appalachian county and spent much of their preadolescence there. I recall taking them to a hot dog stand one day and the person serving us saying to me about my children, "They aren't from here." I assured her they were born and had lived all their lives there, and she assured me they weren't "from here" as they didn't talk or eat like other people from there. It was then that I realized my own children were being called the term I'd heard others use about us when we first moved to Appalachia— "foreigner"—and that no matter what, my children would always be treated as different and not really as part of society there. Later, moving to a more cosmopolitan university town outside of Appalachia, we realized how much more easily our children "fit" in our new community, even though we weren't originally "from there."

After I got my doctorate and began my career in teacher education in Connecticut, I taught in urban elementary schools one day a week so I could better understand the needs of those students we were preparing our teachers to teach. My classroom in one school had plastic over the bulletin board to protect it from water dripping through the ceiling when it rained. We had little paper to use, so we made ample use of the chalkboard instead. Economically, in terms of material supplies and buildings as well as the socioeconomic level of the students, the schools were quite similar to those in which I had taught in Appalachia 20 years earlier. In both cases, I watched as children turned on to learning when I took time to learn about them so that I could connect what I was teaching to their own lived experiences. It was when I treated them as the unique individuals they were, rather than somehow simple and deficient, that they thrived. I am now in Seattle, a city of wealth compared to any other place where I've lived or taught. But within that apparent wealth are the hidden students, those who are perceived as different from the norm and who are hurting in schools. I now work with preservice teachers who are more affluent than those I've previously taught, and this has posed a major challenge for me. I have to bridge to them in ways I've not had to with less affluent preservice teachers. I'm finding I need to help them bridge from their life experiences to those experiences of students who are not thriving in school. I can't re-create what poverty really feels like, or what discrimination based on race or poverty feels like, though that sometimes feels like what is needed. What I can do is to hope they understand that students who are poor, students whose parents are not heterosexual or conventionally married, students who themselves are gay or lesbian or bisexual or transsexual, and students of color have much to teach us about ourselves and our world if we will listen. Most of all, I need to teach my preservice teachers that students who are different can thrive in schools that build on the students' experiences and interests. Until I can hear my preservice teachers question what role perceptions about differences play in why some students are struggling, I will not rest easy.

I find that teaching about the complexity of differences to privileged preservice teachers isn't easy. Frankly, I am scared. I realize these teachers will be leaders in schools and our society, and I'm afraid I won't be able to move them far enough for them to really fight for social justice. I am afraid they will settle into comfortable schools with students like them and ignore the injustices in our society. I'm afraid I'll be whitewashed, afraid I'll learn to cater to the privileged by using feel-good teaching that is comfortable to my preservice teachers and that doesn't challenge them to examine their perceptions about differences and learn to do something proactive about that. I'm afraid my students and my colleagues may not understand why my passion for teaching for social justice is so important to me. I'm afraid I'll not fit in enough to be heard. I'm afraid I'll get so used to the comforts of privilege that I'll learn to teach without worrying about persons who are different or even remembering that I, too, am different.

And yet, I stay and gladly. Despite the challenges I face in working with my preservice teachers, there is a support base from the university in its mission statement for justice, and colleagues who really do care and support me to pursue my passions, including urging me to write this chapter. Besides, facing this hurdle has challenged me to apply what I have done well in K-12 classrooms. Instead of looking at my preservice teachers' privileged life experiences as only deficits in their ability to relate to disenfranchised students, I have realized that once again I need to apply what has worked in other situations—get to know my students as complex individuals and work from what is unique in their own experiences. Just as I do not want to be written off as "another white woman education professor" but rather seen and supported for the complexity of my own identity, so too do I need to afford my own students that consideration.

After completing most of this chapter just prior to the beginning of a term with a new cohort, I looked at my students, all of whom are able to attend this private university as full-time students, and most of whom have white skin. Recalling my own challenges in not feeling safe for the complexity of who I am, I took another look at my students and realized I knew very little about who these students really are. I looked at my course plans and the number of students and realized I had work to do. As I write this over a month later, I now see far more in my students and I hope, likewise, that they see far more in me. Here are some things I have done to move beyond the objectification of people to personalization in my teaching.

Rather than a transmission model of teaching in which students receive knowledge from professors, I am using more of a gift exchange model in which there is an exchange within a community in which all of us are learners and all are teachers. I've done this in a number of ways. The first day of class, students write a letter to me in which they describe how they learn as well as note interests and areas of our course in which they already have expertise. This lets me draw on their expertise and interests throughout the course. I structure class sessions so that there is time for students to share ideas and questions with each other in small groups as well as with the entire class. In this way, I get to know more of my students than I would in a transmission model of teaching, and they get to know each other more. While some students share themselves readily in class, those who do not I invite to my office to tell me about themselves. At the end of each class session, students write notes to me and before the next session, I have written a short response to each. Without those notes, I would not have known who had just been reunited with a loved one the day before, or whose child was sick last night, or who felt deeply about a portion of our class that day. I still miss getting to know some, but at least I'm getting to know many. My intention in all of this is to establish lines of communication and a caring community, to reach their hearts as well as their minds.

As a class, we analyze every course session for how it affected them as learners, and periodically we take time for class members (professor as well as students) to share this with the entire class. This has helped them see how differently people interpret and react to the same experiences and has helped them to see ways they can structure their own teaching to include more students.

Whenever possible, I have personalized assignments. I've urged students to pursue their own interests through some of our assignments, and even when writing lesson plans, to choose topics of interest to them as a way of sharing some of their interests in their own teaching. Students work in cooperative groups all term for discussions, thereby learning not only cooperative group skills, but also forming a trusting support community of peers. I ask them to periodically share with their group how they are learning and what the group can do to enhance their experience. When they did this at midterm, several students were teary-eyed and wrote in their response journals how powerful it was to feel comfortable to share with their group and really feel heard. I have always advocated for personalizing our teaching, though until I wrote this chapter, I had not done so with this depth of exposure of my own identity. I have finally taken the risk of telling my students this story of my identity journey, and in doing so, have discovered a new level of depth in what students are now sharing with me and with their classmates. In personalizing my teaching, I have learned how complex my students' identities are

and how varied their backgrounds and interests are. The longer we are together, the more we learn of each other and of ourselves and the more interesting class sessions become. Even grading papers, the bane of my workload,
can be intriguing when I'm reading their personalized assignments.

I'm realizing teaching for social justice takes time, and that different
people are on different timelines and agendas, often due to their own experiences. Some need my support to help them move to a level of awareness,
whereas others need my support in moving from awareness to social action.
My challenge is to find more effective ways to help these teachers teach for
social justice. I tend to want it all to happen quickly, as I'm tired of seeing
another wave of students and teachers not thriving in our schools.

What keeps me going? I, like pre-collegiate teachers who teach for social
justice, can't do it alone for very long and so need support. At every university I've worked, I've found some supportive colleagues. For support from
teacher educators, I've usually relied on distant educators, reading their writings in journals, books, and e-mails, and talking with them at conferences. I
have learned that other teacher educators teaching mainstream middle-to up-
per-class students are expressing similar fears and challenges in their work
for social justice. In the past few years, I have been an invited panelist at
several major conferences. In each, the focus has been on dominant–culture
preservice teachers' resistance to diversity and social justice. A book, *Preparing Prospective Mathematics and Science Teachers to Teach for Diversity: Promising Strategies for Transformative Action*, being published by
Erlbaum, is an outgrowth of our panel at the American Educational Research
Association annual meeting in 2001. Our panel at the American Educational
Studies Association annual meeting in 2002 was titled, "Preparing Teachers
for Working with Diverse Students: Moving beyond Awareness to Practice."
And our invited presentation for the 2003 American Anthropological Association annual meeting is titled, "Multicultural Pedagogy: From Resistance to
Integration in Pre-Service Teacher Education." Through these conferences in
which we share experiences and strategies, we as teacher educators are finding ways to support each other in continuing our work for social justice.
Though challenged by geographical distance, some of us are also making
plans for holding periodic salons to talk about teaching for social justice as a
way to talk frankly and deeply about issues we face and to provide some
needed support for each other.

Recently, I've found it immensely helpful to observe and meet with other
concerned teacher educators by visiting their teacher education programs and
seeing them in action. It is through seeing and hearing what other teacher
educators are experiencing and doing that I find support as well as renewed
determination to "keep on keeping on." And as is true for any teacher, it is
my former students who really keep me going. I'm heartened when a former

preservice teacher tells me of all the varieties of family configurations in his class and how comfortable all these parents appear to be in working with the school. I'm heartened when a former preservice teacher calls me to ask for advice on what to do in her school where the students who have been failing in most of their middle school courses are black males. These students have been struggling for years in schools, and here is a teacher who notices and is intent on doing something about it.

References

Appiah, K. A., & Gutmann, A. (1996). *Color conscious: The political morality of race.* Princeton, New Jersey: Princeton University Press.

Cole, J. B., & Guy-Sheftall, B. (2003). *Gender talk: The struggle for women's equality in African American communities.* New York: Ballantine Books.

Derrida, J. (1979). Living on borderlines. In Bloom, H., deMan, Paul, Derrida, J., Hartman, G, & Miller, J. H .(Eds.). *De-construction and criticism.* New York: Continuum.

Derrida, J. (1993). *Aporias.* Dutoit, T. (trans). Stanford, California: Stanford University Press.

Giroux, H.,(1992). *Border crossings: Cultural workers and the politics of education.* New York: Routledge.

Hammond, C. M. (1981). Audre Lorde: Interview. *Denver Quarterly* 16.1, 10–27.

McLaren, P. (1995). Border disputes: Multicultural narrative, Rasquachismo, and critical pedagogy in postmodern America. *Critical pedagogy and predatory culture: Oppositional politics in a postmodern era.* New York: Routledge.

CHAPTER SIX

The Guardian of the Dream: A Journey through Attention Deficit Hyperactivity Disorder to the Other Side of Me

(Unpublished Dissertation)

Katherine Nell McNeil

Growing up is not easy for anyone. It is a time when our lived experiences form our concept of "self." I never liked my "self." Many times I have tried to run away or hide but it never did any good because I was still there and so was the hurt and pain. I could say that I just got used to a hurtful life, but that would be a lie. However, not understanding how to change my life, I just lived. I lived a pretend life.

I pretended I didn't care when I had no friends. I pretended it didn't hurt when the other kids called me "monkey." I pretended it didn't matter when I was stood up for a date. I pretended it didn't hurt when my peers called me a "whore" as I walked through the halls at school. I pretended it didn't matter that I could not remember my multiplication tables. I pretended it didn't matter when teachers told me that I was lazy and unmotivated. I pretended it didn't matter when the counselors told me that people like me didn't go to college. So I just pretended, day in and day out.

For many years I thought my negative life experiences were due to a number of other forces. I thought it was in part due to my family being poor or because my parents were divorced. I thought it was because my father walked out on my mother and their eight children. I thought it was because my father was a drunk. I thought it was because of the never-ending verbal and physical abuse at the hands of my father and mother. I thought it was because my mother was so extremely mentally ill that I had to step into her shoes and become the parent. I thought it was because I didn't wear the right clothes. For years I asked myself, why? Why didn't I have friends? Why didn't I have dates like the other girls? Why couldn't I understand math? Why couldn't I remember something as simple as multiplication tables? Why couldn't I remember the rules of grammar, something as simple as remembering where the apostrophe goes when you have a possessive? For years, I thought this was just how life was supposed to be. I thought my life would change as soon as I graduated and entered the world of adulthood.

How wrong I was.

I thought if I married all these things would change. I thought if I had a child all these things would change. I then thought if I divorced all these things would change. I thought if I married again things would change. I thought all these things would change if I had another child. But no matter what I did, nothing changed. I still could not keep friends. I still could not write a paragraph or do my multiplication tables. I still did not like my "self." As the years went on, the hurt and frustration with life were increasingly expressed through outbursts and fits of anger. Anger, rage, and tears so bad they made my head hurt for hours. It hurt my heart for days. Why couldn't I just get it right? Why couldn't I just get life right so I didn't hurt?

Memory Lost: ADHD

All my life I have known I was different. I was different because of the way I acted and behaved. The greatest discovery for now is finding there are others like me, others who have experienced the pain, isolation, and failure that go with Attention Deficit Hyperactive Disorder (ADHD) and Learning Disorders (LD). Others who like me have become successful adults. My memory problems stem from my severe ADHD. This disability affects both long-and short-term memory. There are periods in my past over which I have no recollection. There are years in which even if I look at photos, it is as though I were not present. It is hard for me to understand this, much less to explain it. But there is one thing that has never been lost or forgotten. That is how painful my school experience was.

A Beginning

Many teachers, at one time or another, are confronted with the challenge of teaching a student with a serious behavioral and/or emotional disorder. I tackle this challenge every day. I am a special education teacher and behavioral specialist for middle school students with severe behavioral disorders. One factor that I believe has contributed to my success stands in my ability to identify with my students, a skill that results from my overcoming many of the same disabilities that my students face. Another factor relates to my cultural heritage. I am a Choctaw/Cherokee Indian by birth, and my work with some of the most challenging students in my school district is part of my commitment to honor my culture through my actions. My experiences are relevant to all teachers, I believe. Writing about my experiences is also relevant to understanding me.

Family and Time Spent in School: The Early Years

My parents named me Mary Katherine, a name that I came to hate and later changed in my adult life. I am the oldest of eight children. Mine was a matriarchal family. Its matriarch was Nellie Irene Hill, my mother's mother. While I remember occasional visits with my father's family, all family events were celebrated mainly with my mother's side of the family. My father worked in a factory, building wood molds for ceramic sinks and toilets. My mother was educated as a dental assistant but became a full-time mother. My father was born with a congenital eye defect and due to failing eyesight, was forced to quit his job when I was in eighth grade.

I remember I loved the walk to school. "Mommy, what smells so good?" I asked. "Mary, see those big trees? They are pepper trees, and you'll never forget their smell." As we walked I wondered what school would be like. I can see the swings now. The two kindergarten rooms are separated from the rest of the school. The school had a fence around it. We walked through the gate. I tugged at my mother's arm. "Hurry, Mommy, I want to see my teacher."

We walked through the door and I could not believe all the kids. I started to run off. My mother quickly caught me by the arm. "Mary, please stay here with me until I can meet your teacher." My mother soon got her turn to introduce herself to the teacher. "Hello, this is my daughter, Mary," she said. I looked up at her and said, "Hi, can I have my name tag so I can play?" She smiled and pinned a green name tag to my dress. Her hair was black and short. Her face was so beautiful.

I looked at my mother. She had this sad look in her eyes, one that I had never seen before. I let go of her hand. She bent over and snuggled my neck and kissed me good-bye. I couldn't run around the room fast enough. There were so many new things. Bright colors surrounded me. New smells tickled my nose. I ran so quickly to the swings. "Hey, Susan, I can swing up to the sky," I yelled. Susan sang back, "No you can't. No you can't." Our skyward flight was broken by the sound of the large bell our teacher was ringing. Only now do I understand how the cryptic comment on my report card was a sign of things to come. My teacher wrote, "Mary has been carried away by her enthusiasm at times, but has shown growth this year."

I hated first grade. My dad had prepared me by saying that the nuns would "take care of me if I was bad." I was so scared the first day of school. I no longer could wear anything I wanted. No. Now I had to wear a plaid uniform with a white blouse, navy blue sweater, and a plaid beanie. Sister Rose Mary was my teacher. I have three distinct memories from that year.

The first was how my dad made sure I studied and memorized my spelling words. I would bring home my list of words and each night we would sit down at the table so he could "help" me memorize them. He was less than patient with my performance, so to get me to focus, he would bring his belt to the table. If I misspelled a word, he would hit the table with it and threaten to use the belt on me if I didn't start spelling the words right. Needless to say, I got all As that year in spelling, but not in the years after that.

The second memory I have was that art was a big thing in class. The teacher would always pick out the "best" projects and display them. No matter how hard I tried, I never measured up in art. In the teacher's eyes I never had anything "good" enough, and my grades in art reflected this.

My last memory about first grade was the fact the classroom was crowded. Recently, I counted how many classmates I had in my school photo for that year. There were 50 of us! Fifty kids and one teacher! No wonder the room was crowded. One day Sister Rose Mary was fed up with students dropping their pencils on the floor. I guess it was making a lot of noise. She said the next student who dropped a pencil would get swats with the pointer. Well, as I colored, my desk wiggled. My pencil flew out of the indentation on my desk and clattered to the linoleum.

Sister Rose Mary glared at me and called me to the front of the classroom. She held my left wrist and took her pointer. She hit my backside three times. I can't tell you if it was hard or not. I don't remember. But I do remember that I was small and petite in size, even to this day. I remember the hurt I felt, the shame, and all over a pencil being dropped on the floor. I told my mom and she told my dad. My dad said I deserved what I got. How could any little child deserve to be hit by a big person? And why didn't my mom and dad do anything to protect me if they loved me?

It didn't take long before I learned I couldn't get anything right in school. The kids picked and poked fun at me. No matter how hard I tried, I never made it on the honor roll. Every time report cards came out, the parish priest came to hand them out. He would call your name, stare at the report card and either smile and hand you an honor roll certificate, or stare at it and shake his head and say you needed to do better. When I look at the report card now to see my grades, I find I had a C+ in music. I received Cs in penmanship, art, math, health, P.E., conduct and effort. Funny, I don't ever remember health class. I was in the school choir and participated in all the P.E. classes. It is sad that my art projects were not up to whatever standard was set. This is probably why I hate art to this day.

All of this led me to start hating school, hating teachers, hating my peers. Why bother if nothing I did was "right"?Well, there was one place that was safe for me where what I did was accepted. Here I drew magnificent pictures and got As in art. In this special classroom the other students liked to be with me. I could teach them what I knew. I was good in this school. This was my school held away from others in the privacy of my bedroom. It was a place where I played, teaching my stuffed animals for hours.

With each grade it became noticeable that I continued to have problems: problems with peers, academics, and my behavior. My grades slipped more and more; more Cs and a few Ds. However, fewer checkmarks on the behavior part of the report card. I remember hating one of the weekly activities that our teacher made us do. I hated playing spelling bee. The game was fashioned after baseball. Every week we would get our words, study them, and the day before the test the class would choose teams. Of course no one wanted me, so I was usually picked last. The words were split into three categories based on how difficult they were to spell. The easiest words were singles. The more difficult words were divided into doubles and home runs. The students would spend a half hour competing to spell more words right than the other team. The team that scored the most runs got candy. My spelling has always been atrocious and this just added to the embarrassment and harassment from my peers. I even resorted to cheating just to get them off my back. Well, I got caught and it just made matters worse.

My report card sums up sixth grade. The same teacher as last year, but my grades dive again and there is a checkmark in just about every square under desirable habits and attitudes. A checkmark denotes that improvement is needed. According to my sixth grade report card, I did not obey promptly and willingly. I did not acknowledge my mistakes and improve my behavior. I did not work or play well with others. I did not conform to school regulations when I was not supervised. I was not courteous in my speech and manner. I did not accept responsibility. I did not respect private and public property. Furthermore, I did not listen to or follow directions. I did not begin my work promptly. I did not complete my work on time, and I did not produce work that was of quality and that measured up to my ability. I did not observe simple health rules and did not observe traffic and safety rules, whatever that means. I wasn't doing any good with my peers, either. When I went to a Camp Fire Girls'campout, my peers put toothpaste in my shoes, hid from me, and all I wanted was to go home.

Seventh grade was my last year at Catholic school. My report card got worse. My conduct and effort stunk, and the event I remember most was Valentine's Day, 1968. In previous years our teachers gave us dittoed lists with the students' names included. We decorated bags and taped them to the sides of our desks, but in seventh grade more and more students started discussing who they were going to send valentines to.

I overheard these conversations and was hurt that my name started coming up as one of those whom the students were not going to send a valentine to. On one occasion, I asked why I was not going to get a valentine. The student snickered and said that he didn't like me. The students also urged one another not to send me valentines, too, or they would no longer be welcome in each other's groups.

I had this sad feeling that I would be the only one in the class with only a couple of valentines in my bag. So I decided I could hide this situation from others if I sent valentines to myself. Well, I took all the extra cards from my brothers and sisters and did just that. But I did not sign any names. All this so I would get some. That morning everyone trooped in and put their valentines in a big decorated box. Later that afternoon we had a class party and two individuals took the big box and started up and down the aisles placing the treasured valentines into the decorated bags.

Well, it backfired. When the students around me started noticing that I was getting just as many valentines as they were, they demanded to know who I got them from. Someone yelled out, "Who sent her some? I thought I told you all not to." Those around him reaffirmed that they had not sent any to me. He then grabbed a couple out of my hands and started looking at the backs to see what names were written on them. Discovering none, he just smirked, "You sent all these to yourself, didn't you?" I tried my best to deny it and not listen to them. It hurt but I pretended not to hear the comments and that it didn't matter because at home other pressing things were happening.

My father was forced to quit his job due to his failing eyesight. My mother had been ill and slept a lot. It would not be until I was in my late teens that I would understand the depth of my mother's illness. My father's drinking increased and my mother fought a battle of depression and mental illness. The family now had to rely on welfare and disability payments for a living. I remember there was a constant battle for survival due to the appearance of the lack of money. My father was responsible for all of the household finances. Many times during the year, extended family members would get together and buy shoes and make clothing for me and my brothers and sisters.

Eighth grade was my first year in public school. I didn't realize at the time that there was no money to continue sending us to Catholic school. We were on welfare but I did not know what that was. Since I no longer had to wear a uniform, I needed school clothes desperately. The school had a dress code and we had to wear dresses or skirts; no pants. Grandma Nellie made me a few dresses and my father took me shopping for shoes. All I wanted was a pair of shoes that would look nice with my dresses. What he bought me was a pair of all white-saddle oxfords. I cried. I threatened to go to school barefoot, but on the first day of school I tried my best to hide my feet and the dreaded shoes. I ended up going to a garage sale and buying a pair of shoes that were too big for me. I stuffed the toe of them with toilet paper so they would stay on. In my mind they were better than the dreaded shoes and they only cost me a quarter. So I wore them, day after day.

Public junior high did not turn out as I thought it would. The kids were just as mean, if not meaner. Things were really not any different than they were at Catholic school. I had the same academic difficulties as before. The only success that I remember was in science. I finally had a teacher whom I didn't drive crazy. My memories are hazy, but I think my science teacher was an older gentleman. He introduced me to the world of science fairs. My first science fair project, "The Effects of Heat, Light, and Cold on Crystals," won first place in my grade level division. I remember him as a supportive teacher, but I still remember having trouble with the class content. All the tests involved memorization of the material but it just did not happen for me. But no matter how I relished these small periods of positive times, they were short lived because of what was going on at home with my family and what continued to happen in high school.

High School

The household rocked with change in my freshman year of high school. My father's drinking had gotten to a dangerous point, and my mother finally kicked him out and she filed for a divorce. It was only after he left that my mother found out he had been hiding money from the family for his future. Still my mom did her best to both raise eight children on what the state provided and to fight her battle with severe depression.

During this period of time I remember the hunger, as it was an ever-present part of my life. Having a boyfriend usually ensured that some meals would be bought for me, and this did help. However, just about this time the Federal Free Lunch Program was initiated in school across the country. My mom asked me to bring home the form because she knew that we needed to eat. I brought home the form, she filled it out, and I took it back. I thought at least now I could get some food. I went and waited in line with the other students who were buying their lunch. When I got up to the front of the line I told them my name was on a list. The lunch lady just stared at me, asked me my name, and checked over her list. As soon as she found my name, she handed me a red lunch ticket. I thought that was strange. The few times I had money to buy lunch the tickets were yellow. I asked her why I didn't get a yellow ticket. Now, understand by that time I was holding up the lunch line and the kids in back of me were not being the least bit patient. She told me loud enough so the other kids heard. Free lunch tickets are red, and the ones that are paid for are yellow. Well, there it was out in the open. Separate…singled out again. Everyone knew that I couldn't afford to buy lunch, and it opened up the avenue for kids to tease me that somehow I was getting something they weren't and I didn't deserve it.

Well, it did not take me long to solve that problem. I was not going to take that red ticket for lunch. I'd just as soon go hungry than to stand there and have everyone know that I was poor and different. My solution: there were so many kids that just left their trays and plates on the tables in the cafeteria when they were done. The cafeteria ladies did not clean up until well after the lunch bell rang. I sat at a table pretending to study. Actually, I was eyeing the tables checking out what was left and where. As soon as all the kids left, I went by the tables and took what had been left. There were plates where nothing was touched. So I ate what others left behind and in my eyes solved the lunch ticket and hunger issues.

Painfully I became aware that I was not to join student groups. My choice was to either hide in the girls' bathroom, which turned out to be a real mistake the first time I got beat up, or to stand painfully alone by my locker. Later, I ended up devising a plan that put me right in the middle of the quad on my terms. I figured out how long it took me to walk to school to be the first one there. The rest was easy. Once I found this out, I parked myself and my books on the lunch table in the middle of the other group's territory.

I know now that peers are important in how a student views him or herself, and I was no different then. I longed to be part of the group of kids that were from the right part of town. They had the clothes, makeup, the friends, the family, and the money. I knew I did not belong. I also thought that if I just could find a boyfriend, that I would also be loved and accepted. I liked a senior. That was until I found out that he said some things that made others whisper and laugh at me.

Academics were another area where I became a pretender. My high school report card denotes an overall 2.0 GPA, but when you separate out core classes from electives a disturbing pattern appears. My core class average was a dismal 1.3. My overall GPA was 2.0, but only because of electives such as choir and woodshop.

I remember all too well the stinging remarks from teachers who told me that I was unmotivated, lazy, and stupid. I always wanted to learn math, English, and all other core classes, but found these subjects confusing. No matter how hard I tried I always had difficulty with memorization and the basic concepts. Furthermore, I found the demands of home, school, and a part-time job overwhelming.

My mother always told me that I should go on to college. This proved to be a paradox to me. It seemed like everyone around me was making plans to attend college but I did not even know where to start. My mother had few ideas of where I could get the help and information that I needed. Money?

None. College where? I went to my school counselors and they told me that my grades were not high enough to go to college. They insinuated that kids on welfare didn't go to college. One counselor even made the comment, "Just wait and you'll be married before you know it." All I got out of that conversation was that I was too poor and stupid to go to college.

I persisted, intent on proving I was smart enough to go to college. My counselor said I would need to take the SAT. He told me that I would need it to get into any college. The school paid the fee and helped me fill out the paperwork. On that Saturday, like many other seniors, I showed up for the test. I sat down and opened up the test booklet. The reading was not too difficult. Then I moved on to the word analogies. Most of the words I did not understand, and I did not understand what they wanted: a duck is to water as a hat is to what—who cares, I thought.

Then I got to the math part of the SAT. I stared blankly at a page filled with math problems that I had no idea how to do. In my mind I heard the voice of my math teacher clearly, "lack of interest, boys, immaturity...". I realized that there were only two problems that I knew how to do. So I closed the booklet and walked out. I thought to myself, "Maybe they were right. I will never go to college because I am just not smart enough." As I walked home I thought, "Well, I guess that I am as stupid and dumb as they think I am. How could I ever go to college if I don't even know what is on that test or how to do my multiplication tables? I guess it is time to stop pretending that I will ever go to college."

To graduate from high school, I needed to get though basic math for credit. All I ever wanted to do was to understand and pass algebra. It had been this way for years, but no matter how hard I tried, I just never got the concepts. No matter how hard I tried, I could not remember my multiplication facts—the 6, 7, 8, and 9s. Year after year I tried but just when I thought I was on the verge of remembering them, the information was gone. I tried adding to multiply and it worked. I counted on my fingers, and that worked also. But my teachers admonished me for doing this, even if it worked. So I dropped out of algebra for the third time with an F. This meant that I would not qualify for college because I did not have the level of math needed.

My math teacher made sure I understood his frustration with me and penned this in my high school annual:

> I'm beginning to think it's useless—two years now! The reasons: lack of interest, boys, immaturity—to name a few. I surely hope you find yourself for it's a shame that such ability is going to waste. I sincerely hope and wish for you a successful future.
> Best Wishes R. S.

Just like many other teachers, he would say that if I just tried harder, just spent more time studying, just applied myself, just concentrated, just... I heard it before. I thought I was stupid, or I would have gotten it by now or at least that was what the teachers said. My inability to act in a way that was acceptable to other students caused major problems for me in school. Students called me weird, stupid and a creep. Pages of my yearbook are filled with writings with sexual overtones. One drawing in my school yearbook is of a character with long hair and glasses. It says, "Mary this is your life and if you are smart you would kill yourself you stupid [scratched out but readable] slut.

Junior College

It took many years of encouragement by my husband to convince me to go to college. I always declined and said that I was just not smart enough. Finally, he gave me an ultimatum: "Get a job or go to college." I had experienced far too many failures being fired from numerous jobs, so I decided to try school. I was 33 when I took my first college class. I was so afraid that I would fail and failure hurts so badly. I didn't want to disappoint my husband and I didn't want to appear stupid.

However, somewhere inside I always felt I was a lot smarter than everyone said I was. But I really could not write, spell, or do math. I also had a difficult time verbally expressing myself when under stress. And above all, the behaviors I displayed and had displayed all my life continued to place me outside of what was acceptable in most social situations. It was not easy and there were many things that I had to start over in. But two years later I had successfully struggled my way to an A.A. degree.

During junior college I met the first teacher that I really respected and looked up to. She challenged me, laughed at and with me, and saw my potential. I took two European history classes with her. During that time, and because of her encouragement, I started to discover that if I tried hard enough, I could be anything I set my heart on. I told her that someday I would come back and find her, but only after I achieved my doctorate. From that time on I have remained in contact with her and updated her on my progress toward that goal. She remains encouraging and supportive to this day. However, another incident from this time remains burned in my memory.

I took an English class on Shakespeare. I struggled through the material and the assignments. The only other exposure that I had to his works was during high school, and I failed that part of the class. I tried and tried. I did the reading and took the tests and thought I did well enough to squeak by with a C. However, when I received my grades, the professor had given me an F. The professor refused to talk to me, so I went to the college administration to find out what I could do. They showed me the papers that I could fill out to challenge the grade. This would lead to a meeting between the professor, an administrator, and me.

The professor just glared at me during the meeting. She told me that my grade stood. She accused me of cheating on my final. I made an attempt to find out how I was supposed to have cheated. She then stood up, put her hands on the table, leaned across towards me, and growled, "You know what your problem is? You are only half as smart as you think you are." The look on her face was one of utter contempt. I looked at the administrator to see if she was going to intervene or do something, but she just sat there with her hands folded and a smirk on her face. She then asked me if I had anything further to say. I just shook my head, got up, and walked out the door. That phrase just continued running through my mind, "only half as smart as you think you are." Despite the F she gave me, I retook the class at another junior college, received an A, and subsequently graduated from that junior college in 1990.

A Fresh Start and a New Name

When our family moved back to Washington, I thought a name change could be a new beginning. I also hoped that somehow I could escape from the old me. I had always loved my middle name of Katherine, and Larry always called me by this name. I just decided from that point on I was NOT the person I was previously. I wanted so badly to be someone who was successful in all aspects of life. I thought by giving myself a new name it could be a start. I took my middle name as my first name. Out of respect and honor I took Nell, the first name of my grandmother and also my mother's middle name, as my middle name. It seems rather ironic but it would take five years before I felt strong enough to make the connection to my Native American culture. During that time, I would read the words that my best friend Scott Kayla Morrison (1997) wrote that explained why I changed my name. She wrote,

> Names for American Indian people can be adopted, discarded, changed, modified, personalized, and forgotten, over the course of a person's life. The name on a birth certificate may not be the name you are known throughout your life. The name your family calls you may not be the name your non-Indian friends and co-workers call you. Names are often changed throughout the cycles of a person's life. And that is how it should be. Your relationship with the universe changes over time as you grow and mature. These steps must be recognized somehow, and a change of name is one visible way. A voluntary name change signifies the choices a person has over his or her own life (p. 88).

Initially, I changed my name hoping to escape the old me. However, after years of reflection and rereading Scott's words, I understand that I was going through one of the first major changes in my life. I was trying to become who I really was: the other side of me.

The Other Side of Me

My new beginning gave way to the desire to continue my education. I applied to the University of Washington and was accepted under their Equal Opportunity Program. My program of study was American History, and for two years I struggled to get through. I hated going to school where I would read and forget what I read two seconds later. I hated teachers giving me the glare when I asked too many questions or talked too much. But in June 1992 I became the first member of my family to graduate from college when I walked across the stage at the University of Washington. So was I through with school? No. Go figure. I decided I needed to be a teacher.

I continued on my education journey and encountered many more problems. In January of 1993 I was accepted to a teacher education program and in October of 1993 I was asked to leave. My behaviors and problems with the course work were the reasons. In my heart I knew that teaching was all I wanted to do in life, but I believed the individuals in charge who maintained I would never have the skills to teach. After this experience I thought I was better off in the business world. However, the more I tried to resist the pull of becoming a teacher, the more circumstances would bring me back into teaching. I found myself applying for and accepting a job working with a first grader with behavior disorders.

The Keeper of the Dream

This first grader was filled with anger and hurt. This little guy had wreaked havoc since he enrolled in school the previous October. He threatened students with scissors, dumped over desks and chairs, and turned the classroom into chaos. It was my job to work one-on-one with him in his classroom and to keep him under control so the teacher could teach the class.

I had no previous training working with this student population. But something inside of me instinctively knew what to do. I set boundaries, praised and rewarded his appropriate behavior, loved him despite the times when he kicked me, bit me, and yelled at me when I made him go for a walk to calm down. By the end of the year, there was a wonderful turnaround and he was able to experience a level of success that escaped him before.

He was not the only student during this time. I became a student also in many ways. This little boy taught me so many things as did the teacher with whom I worked. She told me I had gifts. She saw them at times when I did not. She encouraged me to somehow get my teaching credential finished because I belonged in the classroom. She knew of my past and what others said about me becoming a teacher. But nonetheless, she never stopped telling me that somewhere there was a classroom that needed me in it, and she was right. It was during this time and despite the pain that a memory was unlocked. It was so vivid I saw it in such detail that I was able to reproduce the memory in a watercolor at a later date. The memory was of a little girl pretending she was a teacher. She stood in front of an easel in a room that is vaguely recognizable. The little girl has her back to me. She has long hair. She is writing on the blackboard. She is giving homework to a group of dolls and stuffed animals.

I start to see things that are familiar. I see a chest of drawers to the left of the easel. I notice the roof slopes to the right. To the left of the chest of drawers is a door which is open, and outside is a hallway. To the left of the door is another door which is open and appears to be a closet. I can also hear the little girl. She speaks with such conviction and determination in her voice. She tells her class that school is over and erases the board then folds up the easel. She picks it up and walks over to the closet and sets it in the back. She backs out of the closet, shuts the door, and then turns around.

This is the first time I see her face. She is smiling. There is something very familiar about her. She walks over to the dolls and stuffed animals that had been her students and starts to pick them up and put them on a small table beside the dresser. She is talking to them about making sure they do their homework by tomorrow. The little girl is me. But how can this be? How can someone pretend to be or play something I so desperately despised?

During that year my supervising teacher gave me her heart figuratively but at the end of the school year she gave it to me literally. As a gift from her and the students, she gave me a beautiful crystal heart dish. I keep the card to this day because it sums up her faith in me. Inside she wrote:

Dear Katherine,

Each time you look at this gift, may it remind you of the hearts you have touched this year. You have made a difference in so many ways. Thank you for all you have given us.

Fondly,
Blanche

Master in Education Program and the Diagnosis of ADHD

I started finding small successes in my adult life that escaped me in the past. In 1995, I decided to get a Master in Education degree. Go figure. Most individuals would have given up by this time. Despite having a wonderful advisor, I had difficulties immediately. It was just so hard to understand concepts and to remember what I had read.

I found myself knocking on the door of the director of Disabled Student Services. I always knew I had a learning disability. Don't ask me how, but I just knew that no matter how hard I tried, there were things I could not do for a variety of reasons. She asked me a number of questions about my educational history and my family and personal life.

After more than an hour, she said it was her professional opinion that my difficulties both personally and educationally could stem from learning disabilities. I was urged to seek testing, for potential learning disabilities. I knew I needed the testing but my husband and I had no insurance and I was making only $8.50 an hour. It seemed like another insurmountable barrier placed in my path.

I picked up a phone book and started calling psychologists. I asked two questions: how soon could I get an appointment and how much was a consultation. The results were not good: they all wanted too much money. So I just went on with my life, if you can call it that. I wanted to do better in school but no matter how hard I tried to get things right, it just didn't happen. I just could not get anything right.

It wasn't long before I found myself looking at the phone book again. I kept wondering why I should even bother since no one was going to take me —a person with no insurance or way to pay to be seen. I don't remember the events surrounding how I found Dr. Bee or ended up with an appointment with her, but I ended up securing a one-hour consultation with her later that week. During that hour she asked me what brought me to her. I related to her the difficulties that I was having in grad school and I thought I had always had a learning disability. I hated school and always struggled in it, but I wanted to succeed in my master's program. She took my family history and asked me to return for testing the following week. I thanked her for her time but also told her that I did not have insurance or the money to pay her. She just smiled and said that she would work with me on a sliding scale. For the first time in a long time I felt maybe, just maybe, there might be an answer to why I was the way I was.

The following week I spent two hours taking a series of tests. I remember how stupid I felt taking them and how frustrated I was when I could not answer a basic question. After it was all over, Dr. Bee said that she would have the results in one week. The week went by so slowly but there I was sitting there on the other side of Dr. Bee's desk. She told me the results of the tests showed that I indeed had several learning disabilities. Dr. Bee found I had significant discrepancies in mathematics, written language, and spelling abilities. She also found that I had difficulties with my auditory and spoken processes. I asked her if this is why I had never been able to memorize my multiplication tables. She said that was a possibility. She explained that with this diagnosis, I would be able to get help through Disabled Student Services at school. I would still be responsible for all the required work, but she felt that my academic success would be increased if I had additional time to do papers and projects. I would need someone to help proofread my papers and help me work through the corrections. I could benefit from using a laptop to take notes, or use a tape recorder. I would need to use a calculator for math. The results explained that my problems were not due to any cognitive deficits. Based on the test data, I had the intellectual capacity to succeed.

I left her office with the papers in hand. For the first time I felt that I was not stupid or dumb, as some had made me to believe in the past, and as I had come to believe here in the present. She also felt that it would be a good idea in the future to do a comprehensive neuropsychological evaluation. It was her opinion that there may be other issues that could only be addressed through this type of evaluation. I told her that I would consider it.

With the help of Disabled Student Services, my academics improved somewhat. The additional time with regard to projects helped the most, but there was a larger issue that remained. I continued having problems that I could not describe. I continued to experience failure socially. I began to spiral downward mentally. This was not the first time this had happened to me. In the past I would find my way out. However, this time was different. I found myself at the lowest of the low. Life had become so painful that all I wanted was off this world to a place where I did not hurt anymore. Internal pain had become a daily part of my life. I found myself unable to rationally discuss problems at home with my husband. I had always followed a set pattern of behaviors when frustrated, mad, or unable to get my point across or heard.

These behaviors included yelling, crying, throwing things, and saying hurtful and hateful things to displace what I perceived as hurt coming my direction and always ended with indescribable pain in my head. I had now hit bottom. No matter how hard I tried, I could not get anything in life right. I felt I had two choices: find someone to help me or take my life to stop the pain. So back to Dr. Bee's office I went. Dr. Bee explained that the testing would take two days. Two weeks later I returned for the test results. She asked me if I had any idea of what might be causing my difficulties. With a laugh I told her, "You are going to tell me I have ADHD." She looked kind of stunned but she simply said, "Yes, the testing shows that you have severe ADHD."

Well, there it was. It had a name, a description, and a set of behaviors. It had been a part of my life each and every day. It explained so much, yet so little. Dr. Bee recommended that I would most likely respond well to Ritalin. She asked me if I would consider it. I said yes, anything that would help me become "normal"—like any other person. I signed a release of information and she called my family physician and discussed with him her findings. He agreed to start me on Ritalin.

I was apprehensive about the medication and so was my husband. What would it do to me? After I had the prescription filled, I let it lie on the seat of my car for a week. I finally decided that if I really had severe ADHD that this might be the help I needed, and it was just sitting there. So, I started taking it and keeping the doctor appointments that went with finding the right level for my body. With the diagnoses of four specific learning disabilities and severe ADHD, part of the answers to my inability to be successful in school and life was revealed. I still wondered if, after all these years, I could learn social skills.

The one profound memory that I have when I started taking my meds was when Fall Quarter, 1995, started. I had been on meds for about four weeks and had achieved a fairly stable level. I showed up for class, sat down, and listened, fascinated by the dialogue. I was entranced with the exchange of thoughts, ideas, and background on youths at risk. Before I knew it, two hours had passed and the class was over. As I put my books in my backpack, my professor asked if I could stay so she could speak with me. I said sure. She asked me if I was OK. I told her that I was fine. She asked me if I was having a problem with her class. I said no, I loved her class.

These questions perplexed me. I asked her why she thought something was wrong. She said that I had said nothing during class. I was perfectly quiet for the entire two hours. This in itself amazed me. I had never been able to remain quiet. It was as if I was driven to talk. If I did not get out my thoughts, I would end up forgetting what I needed to say. This was not the situation that night. As I thought about what she said, it dawned on me that it was the first time in my life that I had been able to listen. Yes, listen. Just sit there and take in what was being said. I then told her that I had just spent the last two hours listening. She gave me a strange look. I just giggled. I told her about my diagnosis and that I had started taking meds a month earlier. I told her that I did not even realize that I had not said a single word. I was truly amazed that I had been able to do something as simple as listening.

Success

The drive to get back into the classroom gnawed at my insides. The successes I was experiencing gave way to strength that I had never felt before. I started calling all of the colleges in my area to inquire about how I could transfer the classes I had already completed into their programs.

Well, no school wanted to have anything to do with me. As a last resort, I called our state's Office of the Superintendent of Public Instruction (OSPI). To make a long story short, after meetings and phone calls, they put me in touch with Heritage College. OSPI felt that this small college out on the Yakima Reservation would be the one place where a student like me could achieve my dream. I made the call, met with education staff, and was accepted on the Wednesday before classes started on that following Monday. All of this happened so rapidly. I approached my school principal to see if I could stay on at my job, working Mondays and Fridays for the two weeks left in the year. I really did not want to leave my students. But the principal felt that I needed to resign, and also that I would most likely be happier at a school that had more diversity. So much for tact. So I resigned my position and started the next journey in my life.

Every Tuesday morning I set out and drove two hours to Toppenish and lived with a family until Thursday night when I turned around and drove two hours home. This was what it was like from June 6, 1999, to July 22, 1999. Many people thought I was just plain crazy for doing this. But for me, there was never a question.

I did it because it was supposed to be.

Finally a Teacher

Two weeks before I finished my classes at Heritage College, I sent out a flood of résumés to see if there was any interest in me. It did not take long to get a bite. One afternoon between classes at Heritage, I received a call. It was the principal at Northwood Junior High School. He wanted to know if I was available for an interview. I did my best to suppress my joy, eagerness, enthusiasm, and delight at his invitation. I calmly told him that I was available. He said "great" and told me he looked forward to talking with me. I hung up the phone and started dancing with excitement. Finally, after all these years I was nearing the goal I had dreamed of for years.

Larry was as excited as I was. He took me to the interview. We ended up at the wrong school and I felt panic that I would miss my first interview. But I called, and got the correct directions and it was not long before Larry kissed me on the cheek, told me to kick butt, and I walked with my head high into the building.

For the next hour and a half I answered questions from the school princi-pal and the two other special education staff. I laid out my dream of a pro-gram where students would achieve academic and behavioral excellence through the use of technology.

I did not hide anything.

I explained my disabilities, my gifts. I told them about my dream and commitment to these students. I acknowledged the difficulties students would bring to my program, but that I honestly believed that I could be effec-tive in exiting them from special education. It was no holds barred. I wanted these educators to know who I was and what I stood for. I wanted them to see the desire in my heart and feel my commitment to teach. They listened, asked questions, smiled, and finally thanked me. The principal then showed me around the beautiful school. He told me about the history of the school. As we reached the front door, he told me that he would make a decision by the following Thursday. I smiled, shook his hand, and left.

Larry was waiting for me in the car. I got in and just smiled. He looked at me and said, "You did OK, didn't you?" I smiled and said, "Yeah, I did well. Now let's go eat." Whether I got the job or not, I knew then and there I was a teacher. It was simply a matter of time before I had a classroom.

The following Thursday, July 22, 1999, I obtained my teaching creden-tial from Heritage College. I had a certificate that I could present to school districts which demonstrated that I had indeed fulfilled the requirements to be a teacher. Later that afternoon I received a phone call. It was the school principal. I was pleasantly surprised. He wanted to know if I was interested in joining the staff at Northwood. It was all I could do to temper my enthusi-asm and get out the word, yes. He then congratulated me and told me he would see me the following week.

I had achieved the dream.

Everyday Is Filled with Wonder

They come to me broken and battered, their spirit unable to see their true value and self-worth. They are fragile, bound together only by the survival instincts that enable them to face school and me one day at a time. These young men and women arrive at my classroom door dealing with pain and failure. But all of these kids share one thing: they are so fragile. What is left of their spirit reminds me of a precious but fragile heirloom that has been dropped so many times that the glue barely holds it together any more. They come to me. Or have they been sent to me? I have been entrusted with their fragile spirit. Me! I hold this spirit this life in my hands. Scary yet awesome. Someone feels that I can be trusted with his or her frailty. I will do every-thing in my power to protect them until they are strong again.

Not only must I educate but also nurture and strengthen. These young men and women have endured things in their lives that no child should have to endure. They are at times in their lives when they should be carefree and growing up. Instead, they try to make meaning of a world where they attempt to mask and hide their pain behind an array of outrageous, inappropriate, and sometimes dangerous behaviors.

They know they are not wanted in mainstream classrooms. They get this message loud and clear. Many of their behaviors serve to deal with the pain and failure that they are experiencing inside and outside of school. And oh, the pain.

Their Stories

He was in seventh grade when he came. John had been in self-contained classrooms since first grade. Teachers always wrote about his behaviors. They had a hard time working with him. In the fourth grade, he started refusing to do many of his assignments and had a hard time writing, and his behaviors became worse. When he came to me, he was like a wild animal. Working with him I have been bitten, hit, kicked, and called every name in the book. But that is nothing to what he has endured. Sometime in his past his mother's boyfriend had physically and sexually abused him. After watching him for six months, I realized that his academic and social difficulties were coming from some cognitive deficit.

I pleaded for months to have him retested. Finally, the school psychologist agreed. The test results were as I had suspected—he is mildly mentally retarded. His behaviors stemmed from his frustration in being truly unable to grasp the concepts teachers, each year, were demanding he learn. Pain in and out of school and unable to cope in either world. Did I lower my standards and expectations? No. He works for excellence at his true level. I accept nothing but his best. It took him a year and a half to trust my staff and me—to really believe it when I told him there was nothing he could do to make me hate him.

Howard was the classic ADHD student. At fifteen, he had been in special education for seven years. When he came into my program two years ago, the smart money in school said he'd never make it out of Special Ed before the year's end. I had little evidence to counter this argument. He had all the classic ADHD behaviors that included being impatient, argumentative, and distrustful. I refused to give up. There were brief intervals when he was able to control himself and focus on his studies. He seemed bright and capable. These times were rare. To complicate matters, his home life was tumultuous. As he became increasingly technology savvy, he demonstrated much more capability than had been previously expected.

One of the most surprising changes was his ability to multitask. He could conduct online research, compose the first draft of a research report, and help other students at the same time. It was as if all the energy that had been expressed through misbehavior was being redirected productively. It also helped that he decided to go on meds to help with his ADHD.

The combination of meds, behavioral training, and academic success led to wonderful progress in all his mainstream classes. This young man knows that he will have to exceed everyone's expectations if he is to do well in a mainstream world. His reputation as a difficult student isn't going to vanish overnight, but he is willing to work hard to redeem himself in the eyes of his teachers. Mastering technology made him a leader in my class and gave him an opportunity to earn the respect of students in the general education classes as well.

He is currently making a successful transition and is even thinking of someday becoming a special education teacher—a future that was unimaginable just two years ago.

I make a promise to all my students when they arrive to my program that each day they walk through the classroom door it is a new start, a do over. Nothing is held against them.

They are safe and loved in my classroom. And I tell them this over and over again.

I finally figured out what was missing within me with regard to my master's program. I got in touch with my advisor and then reapplied for entry back into the program. My practicum project consisted of a portfolio project as a means for alternative assessment with my students. Subsequently, I finished my M.Ed. in 2000 from the University of Washington.

The Demands of My Job

Everyday I feel that I shortchange my students. As I enter my fourth year as a teacher, the demands of the paperwork, the endless meetings, and everyone else who needs me to do something now—my students take a back seat to all this. There are not enough hours in the day to deal with all the special education paperwork, plan challenging lessons, deal with mental health issues, teach the tools students need to deal with the triggers to their behaviors, the family issues students are plagued with, the abuse, the testing, new students sometimes one a week, and I wonder how I can keep up. I am successful with my students, but it is taking its toll on me, my students, and sometimes my doctoral studies. At times I feel that my doctoral studies cheat my students. I once used the weekends to plan my lessons, but now I use weekends for my doctoral studies. In the past I used most of my extra time at home as the time I needed to make parent contacts, plan lessons, and do paperwork.

Now, I do not have that time. I continue to be plagued with feelings of inadequacy. How can I give my students the best of the best and stay sane? On June 17, 2002, the school district superintendent announced that our principal would be leaving Northwood to become the new area director for the district. This was shocking to the staff. I felt my heart sink. Change is not easy for anyone. It was hard to say good-bye to our principal. I remember our conversation. I told him that the most heartwarming comment that he made about me was in a special education meeting. There was a young lady and her parents. She had been diagnosed with ADHD and she was having problems with her studies. Our principal looked at her and told her, "You know that everyone in this room is willing to help you however we can. But the greatest help you can get is from that teacher sitting down there. Ms. McNeil is just like you. She has ADHD and learning disabilities and she knows what you are going through. I know that she can teach you some strategies to help you with your studies. I also know that she would be a good person to talk to or check in with if you are having problems." This was the first time I had heard him say this. I had always been up front about my disabilities from the time I started at Northwood. I often disclosed my disabilities to parents and other students as a way of saying, "I know what it is like and I am here to help." In the beginning some staff cringed when I talked about my disabilities. Some became comfortable with it, some were not. I didn't care one way or the other because my disabilities are an important part of me.

Current Reflections of the Heart

Well, I am finishing my first year as a doctoral student. I still do not know my multiplication tables and I still have some difficulty with the writing process. However, this has not deterred me from continuing my education journey. I was surprised to receive a letter from the dean of the College of Education. She wrote that I had been named as a Morford Scholar for the 2002/2003 school year. I was shocked. It was the first time I had been recognized for my academic promise.

I will never forget the nay-saying educators of the past. However, I will continue to demonstrate to my students that academic and behavioral excellence can be achieved. I continue to believe that my ADHD and learning disabilities are gifts, and I help my students discover this also.

References

Morrison, S. K., (1997). An Apokni by any other name is still a Kakoo. In J. Harjo & G. Bird (Eds.), *Reinventing the Enemy's Language* (pp. 88–102). New York: W. W. Norton.

CHAPTER SEVEN
Teaching Social Justice in Partnership

Cleo Molina and Hutch Haney

We didn't know each other until six weeks prior to teaching, together, a course on multicultural ministry in partnerships. We were asked to design and teach a yearlong, master's level, site-based supervision course focusing on multicultural ministry. This request came from the School of Theology and Ministry at Seattle University. Hutch and I both have academic backgrounds in theology, teaching experience in multiculturalism, histories of advocacy for social justice, and understandings about oppression and reconciliation. We are also from different cultural and socioeconomic backgrounds.

The School of Theology and Ministry hypothesized that if students from different ethnic cultural backgrounds and life experiences worked in partnerships of two at multiethnic parish internship sites, they would first have to come to understand and deal with their own diversity. Cleo and I were chosen to be models and teachers from whom the students would learn about diversity, theological reflection, and ministry in a multicultural context. The course would have a strong focus on oppression, social justice, and personal reflection. We planned didactic sessions that included historical perspectives of the issues and that stressed developmental psychology, sociological, theological, and political constructs.

We focused classes on team/partnership development, self-awareness, cultural awareness, and majority group privilege; we problem-solved and dealt with conflict among ourselves as a class; and we taught specific skills such as observation, intercultural communication, and analyses of social situa-tions. We expected each pair of students to meet weekly, as well as with their supervisors/mentors at their internship site. Students were expected to enter their internship community respectfully, without a job description; observe for the first quarter; and then find appropriate ways to participate in the commu-nity while constantly reflecting on their experiences through papers and class discussion. And we, as faculty, helped them identify and, to some extent, work through family of origin issues that impacted their sense of social justice and that surfaced as they grew to see themselves more and more as ministers. Our classes became communities, and we, as partnership faculty, became friends and colleagues.

Hutch and I knew that any relationship has a power differential and that cross-cultural partnerships may be microcosms of larger communities. Conflict comes out of power struggles; oppression can happen when there is a major power imbalance, when there is no reconciliation or equity. Hence, a key component of our teaching and modeling for students was to understand power and its role in oppression and conflict in ourselves. We had to respond to our own questions regarding how we have been oppressed and how we have oppressed. We spent each week discussing the dynamics between us. Personal issues of oppression surfaced for the students as they related more and more to one another and to their internship communities.

Cleo and I spent additional hours sharing with the students, as they did with us. While we were models, we had eleven other partnership models that, in nine months, identified their differences, their similarities, their conflicts and power struggles. They described how they were oppressed and how they oppressed, and in time, how they reconciled and created equity. We told our stories and the students told theirs. Through these stories we understood the pain and joy of each person's experience, and the cultural, ethnic, gender, family, religious, regional, and socioeconomic values and other variables that influenced those experiences. The sharing of stories, often of pain, increased our empathy and appreciation of other people and other ethnic cultural experiences. We shared food, family pictures, drawings, poems, prayer, rituals, and music. Most importantly, we shared our lives, past and present. We often reflected in our weekly partnership meetings on how amazing it was that we were kind of thrown together and, yet, felt like we had known each other most, if not all, of our lives. It certainly helped that Hutch and I were born the same year, so we at least had the same social-cultural history. We also had children the same age, liked similar kinds of foods, and shared a passion for the Southwest and for great cars. Probably most important of all, we shared similar values and worldviews and were willing to risk being honest with our students. Yet, here we were—a Latina raised in a blue-collar home and a white, middle-class male who should have had more differences than similarities, working together in partnership. It became clear to us, even before the end of the first quarter of teaching, that what we were about was partnership teaching, not team-teaching, and that it was critical that we reflected and came to understand what that meant. Partnership teaching meant that we shared the responsibilty for every aspect of the course; we were, for all intents and purposes, joined at the hip. In our experience of team teaching, we would each have been responsible for a part or parts of the course and we might have divided the responsibility for delivery. Partnership is what we were expecting students to do, and we had to do the same.

Because this was a course on ministry, we knew that the two major content areas of this course would be partnership ministry and cross-cultural ministry. Based on the goals, structure, and format of the course, we agreed that both theological reflection and cultural reflection would be essential elements for students to better understand and integrate the concepts and re-alities of partnership and cross-cultural ministry. Because it was a course on multiculturalism, there was the focus on cultures; and because of the partner-ship focus, there was an emphasis on team development and dynamics. The course was also about conflict (the partnership's experience), oppression (multicultural and personal dynamics), and social justice (equity and fairness and spiritual and personal values) and reconciliation (a result of the desire for reconnection and the building of community).

To better understand how we became a partnership and how this experi-ence differed from any of the team-teaching we had done previously, each of us will share our histories and the personal experiences that shaped our de-velopment and enabled us to see more of our similarities than differences. We will further describe our class and experiences with our students. We will end with a partnership reflection on how our own experiences have influ-enced our teaching.

Cleo's Story

I would never have agreed to team-teach a class of this nature for a whole academic year with a white guy I didn't know, prior to completing my dis-sertation. The two-year intense process of heuristic research and writing on interpersonal reconciliation that I knew while writing my dissertation helped me understand the level of oppression I had internalized and its impact on my relationships with others. The anger, resentment, hatred, and fear that I felt toward my father for so many years still tainted the way I related to other white males despite the years of counseling and therapy that helped me heal from a painful childhood and adolescence.

One of my findings from my dissertation research was that reconciliation "is a way of living, a mind-set, a viewpoint, a process" and "not a conflict resolution intervention or technique." By studying forgiveness and recon-ciliation, I was better able to understand how my feelings toward my father had become generalized toward other white men. This had a huge impact on my work as well as my personal relationships. As a diversity trainer and edu-cator, I now felt some empathy instead of resentment or anger for the white men in my classes or groups who resisted being there and who felt that they did not need to change. Instead of withdrawing from them, I could now find ways to connect with them.

A common definition of forgiveness is the willingness on the part of an unjustly hurt person to deliberately give up feelings of hatred, resentment, and the desire for vengeance for an offender, while fostering the undeserved qualities of beneficence and compassion toward that offender, but at the same time, not excusing or condoning the wrongdoing (Augsburger, 1992; Coleman, 1998; Elder, 1998; Freedman & Enright, 1996; Enright, Freedman, & Rique 1998; Flanigan, 1998; King, 1977; Longaker, 1997; North, 1998; Smedes, 1998; Worthington, 1998). By forgiving and reconciling with my father, I lifted a huge weight from my soul—yet, I've never forgotten nor excused what he did.

He was a sick man, of that I'm sure, just as I am sure that we live in a sick society in which power continues to be way out of balance and in the hands of too small a group of white men. My father had far too much power in our family, and he often exercised it brutally. It was a good thing that I had other examples of power in my childhood that gave me hope and a more balanced perspective.

I was born in southern California during World War II to parents of very different cultural backgrounds—not at all the Ozzie and Harriet type. My mother is Mexican American and my father was Anglo of English, Scottish, Dutch, German, and Cherokee heritage. Both were raised in very different parts of the country and in very different circumstances. From them, I learned much about the cultures that are part of my heritage. I also learned about oppression and about human inconsistency in my parents, attempts to live out their espoused values.

My mother was the firstborn daughter of a very large, traditional Mexican family who moved to the United States shortly before her birth in 1910. She had twelve brothers and sisters, most of whom were younger. Because of the large numbers of children and the fact that my grandfather could not possibly support them all by himself with the manual labor sorts of jobs that he held, my mother had to quit school after the fifth grade to help my grandmother—her older brothers had already left school to work and supplement the family income. My mother had loved school so this was a big sacrifice for her and she did it willingly and lovingly. The impact that it had on her, however, was her dogged determination that her children would have good educations.

My mother's family was a pretty traditional Mexican family. Children were expected to be respectful and subservient to their elders (older siblings included) and were expected to give primary allegiance to the family and to the church. My grandfather had the ultimate authority—next to God and the local priest—and for being such a short person by U.S. standards (about 5 feet 2 inches) he was respected, loved, and, to some extent, feared by his children and valued by people in our small community. His authority was rarely, if ever, challenged. There is a great story that my mother tells (and I vaguely remember) about how I had confronted him as a baby.

I must have been around two years old because my mother said that I wasn't speaking clearly yet. (My mother, brother, and I lived with my maternal grandparents in a small room off the kitchen until I was six and a half years old.) It was late at night and my grandfather had been out drinking beer with his "compadres." My grandmother had put his dinner away when he did not come home, and we all had gone to bed. I was awakened by his yelling at my grandmother because his food was not hot and on the table waiting for him. I got up, went into the kitchen, stood in front of him, and shook my fist at him, scolding him in my own baby language. No one ever talked back to my grandfather, least of all a female. Apparently I caught him totally off guard, and once he got over the shock, he put his head back and laughed for several minutes. He then picked me up and put me back to bed, much to my mother and grandmother's relief. The story became a family legend and was told many times as an example of my spunkiness in standing up to my grandfather. I suspect it also held major significance in terms of pointing out, at least indirectly, his mistreatment of my grandmother. I don't recall hearing that he ever repeated that incident again. And, as family legends often do, this story helped shape my image of myself as an advocate for others.

While my grandmother was subservient to my grandfather, she carried out her role of primary nurturer and caretaker with a saintly, silent dignity. I was named after her—Clotilde—and felt a very special bond between us. I used to help her make tortillas (or so she would let me think) in the mornings, and she would tell me about her life as a young bride in Mexico, having moved from a city out to her husband's family's rancho and having to deal with a very stern mother-in-law who viewed her as little more than a maid. My mother worked during the day and I spent the days, until I started school, at my grandmother's side. I would get up early in the morning with her to get the day's food prepared. I can still remember her warm, white-flour tortilla smell and the faded colors of her two or three aprons, dusted with flour and spotted with chile. I saw that she had her own kind of power because of the level of respect paid her by her family, people in the community, and the priests who came to visit. She had a deep faith and a spirituality that grounded her during her most difficult times—deaths of four of her children, her husband's death, and her own illness. Her faith also made her open and generous to all God's people, and my mother would tell stories of the numbers of jobless, homeless men she fed during the Depression, regardless of color or creed.

She also instilled in me a fierce pride in my Mexican heritage. She would tell me to never say that I was "Spanish" (like some people did to make themselves "better" than others) and to be proud to be Mexican because of our culture and faith. So when I saw kids being spanked by teachers for speaking Spanish on the school playground, I was outraged. Or when kids

were called "dirty Mexican" by other kids, my mother would tell me to stick
up for them because we should never be ashamed. And I did, even though it
once cost me a black eye and a trip to the principal's office. We went to live
with my father in Arizona halfway through my first grade. I was not happy
about leaving my grandparents, my school, and all of my cousins and friends,
but I was still young enough to see it as some kind of adventure. Also, my
baby sister arrived a few months later, making my life busier. I didn't develop much of a relationship with my father; he was big, overpowering, and
very different from the men that had been in my life so far. He was also a
Protestant who, while he never went to any kind of church that I can remember, didn't think much of "those fish-eaters." He worked a lot and was only
home at night to eat and go to bed. He didn't seem to have much time to
spend with us as we became accustomed to a new home and a new way of
life.

Moving to Arizona into a predominantly Anglo community really helped
emphasize how different we were from other families. I had been aware that
I was "different" at an early age by my aunts' and uncles' comments attribut-
ing my talkativeness and bossiness to my Anglo blood. I was also taller than
most of my cousins and had reddish instead of jet-black hair like theirs. I
fully related to being Mexican, speaking Spanish first, and learning English
the summer before I started kindergarten. Also, my name was Clotilde Rita
Litchfield, but because no one could pronounce my first name, I had a name
specifically for school—Cleo. Living with my father, I learned that we
should always be proud of being American—but some people were more
American than others. I'm sure that Japanese Americans were never American by his standard and neither were those immigrants who continued to
speak their native tongue. Racial epithets were a part of his common vocabulary.

Poston (1990) states that while younger children may be aware of race
and ethnicity, they develop a self-awareness that is somewhat independent
from their background. It isn't until later, when racism and prejudice enter in,
that biracial individuals may tend to have identity problems if they internal-
ize the bigotry.

My question of Poston is "How might this internalization of prejudice be
impacted by one of the parents' bigotry?" Because my father was so racist
and at times referred to us as inferior, I became even more committed to my
Mexican identity and spurned the Anglo. This was reinforced by the kind of
injustices levied toward Mexican American children that I witnessed as well
as experienced in school from kindergarten on. I certainly did not want to be
like the kind of mean, white people that were in my life. Yet, I felt conflicted
as I entered adolescence because of the great love I had for my father's
mother and sister (both tall, fair-skinned, with reddish blond hair and blue

eyes) and because of my yearnings to fit in and be accepted and popular like all the white girls. I resented not being born with the blond hair, light skin, and blue eyes that fate had given my sister. She never had to bear being called "dirty Mexican" like my brother and I did.

I grew up with so many mixed messages about race and skin color. On the one hand, even though my grandmother would tell me to be proud of my Mexican heritage, my aunts and uncles would always call my sister the pretty one and refer to her blond curls and blue eyes. I would be warned to stay out of the sun because I would get "dark as an Indian." Yet, at school, girls would tell me that I was so lucky because I had "a year-round tan." All my dolls were blond, except for one. The images on television, in the movies, and in magazines certainly did not look like me. Nor did they look like most of the people I knew, with some exceptions, and they were the popular girls.

I had skipped the fifth grade because I was bright, well read, and had developed (physically) well ahead of my peers. The teacher felt that I would have no trouble with the jump in grades because "I was mature for my age." I felt like a misfit at my new school because everyone else in my seventh grade class had been to the same school since kindergarten and all were white and older than I. High school was easier. School was my refuge from the oppression at home. There was so much to do and I got involved in as many clubs and activities as I could and still maintained an almost perfect "A" average. I especially liked speech and drama and always did well in speech contests. I was in the honor society, the Y-teens, Spanish Club, the leadership club, and was elected student body social chairman my senior year. As many friends as I had, however, I invited very few to my house.

My father was a terrible bigot and I was terrified of what he might say or do. It had been a source of tension between us. I had developed an active social conscience and felt passionately about issues of racism and discrimination. When I attempted to confront or question him about his language, he would lose his temper and I would usually get beaten or severely punished. But strangely, his behavior was often inconsistent with his language and he was as likely to hire African Americans (long before other businesses in our town) launch food and clothing drives for Indian people and offer the Mexican American members of our family opportunities, as he was to call them the nastiest of names.

My father could be very violent and apparently had an explosive temper since his youth. He had sharp mood swings and we never knew when he was going to come home with treats and want to be playful or when he would be violent. It could be the most minor thing—a downcast look on my part, a meal he didn't like, or a simple request. All of a sudden he would start shaking; his face would contort and then he would lose it, smashing things, throwing his dinner against the wall, screaming, grabbing me and punching me with his fists, if I had been the one to provoke him. He never beat my sister or brother and only hit my mother once when she tried to get between him and me. Since we knew he kept a loaded gun by his bed, we were always afraid he would use it and he would have once, if I hadn't run out of the house and gone to the neighbors. (Unfortunately, I think they thought I was a hysterical teenager who had just had a fight with my parents. Who would have believed such things of the "Pillar of the Community"?)

A major theme that emerges in the recounting of my adolescent period is that of duality. I was the product of two very different cultures—Mexican and Anglo. I lived two distinct lives, at home and at school, and each hidden from the other. I had two different personalities to correspond with my two lives—one was outgoing and friendly and the other was sullen and fearful. All of this had major implications for my identity development.

All of this was compounded by the shame I felt about the abuse I was experiencing. Researchers refer to the difference between being ashamed and having a sense of shame; the former being disruptive and eliciting a painful self-consciousness as a result of "exposure of some discrediting fact or quality" and the latter as regarding relationship, the need to connect, and a kind of shyness or timidity that is needed to integrate us as humans to one another and to God. They refer to the ambivalence inherent in shame because it separates the self from others and at the same time indicates a deeper connection or desire for connection. I certainly wanted to be connected. I felt great pain at not fitting in. I was neither white nor Mexican; I felt stigmatized (Howell, 1996) by the abuse I experienced and felt nobody would ever want me because I was "damaged"; I did not see myself as having a family like everyone else. I had a recurring dream for years of peering in at a happy scene in someone's home with children and parents loving one another. I could see myself behind a thick plate glass with a very sad look on my face. Years later, I heard "my" dream described by a young Indian girl in the Upward Bound Program I worked for in Montana, and I knew I had found a niche. It was easy for me to listen, empathize, and support because I understood with every cell in my body!

My relationships with some key females were what I think saved me. Researchers write that girls' open relationships with their mothers in which they learn to perceive, respond, and relate to each other's needs are essential to the formation of self-worth and the ability to be empathetic. I was always very close to my mother and had a difficult time transitioning out of embeddedness (Kegan, 1982) because of our mutual need for one another. I remember her once telling me that I was her best friend. She thought we could talk about anything, which, of course, we couldn't. It was clearly a double bind for me. My close connection to my mother made it possible for my father to control me because I did not want to hurt her in any way. At the same time, her love and need for my companionship and our ability to comfort each other and talk about a range of subjects kept me from feeling totally isolated.

I always felt secure in her love. Kegan's (1982) statement, "we imagine that strong, robust connections are actually easier to separate from than conflicted, tentative, or ambivalent ones" (p. 168), clarified why it took me so long to separate from my mother. I don't think it happened until I was in my forties. I think that some of this mutuality can be explained by Kegan's notion of how all organisms order and regulate their relationships to the environment in which they find themselves.

My mother and I really needed each other for survival. Unconditional love from my two grandmothers and my Aunt Hazel (my father's sister) were essential in helping me feel grounded. I always knew they would love me no matter what, and my respect for them helped me develop at least some measure of self-respect. I knew they were women of high integrity, courage, and honor and that they had lived very difficult lives themselves; I knew I could, too. My grandmother Clotilde also influenced the development of my spirituality because of her example of daily prayer and her faith in Our Lady of Guadalupe. It was Our Lady and my guardian angel that came to me in some of my most desperate hours.

Kegan might refer to what I experienced as some type of psychotic delusion that helped me deal with my threatening environment. I wonder if in the context of my religious faith these "delusions" didn't serve as a safety net. Certainly, Catholicism is full of stories of visions and one of my favorite books was *Lives of the Saints*. Focusing on the Blessed Virgin enabled me to separate myself from my body. My body was not my self; my soul was my real identity.

The close relationship with my mother helped me develop close friendships with other girls. I always had a best friend. While only one of these friends ever learned of my hidden life at home, all helped anchor me. In many ways, the hell that I lived at home enabled me to be empathetic to others' pain and suffering and helped me be a compassionate, loyal friend and a good counselor, teacher, and consultant because I understood the need for such love. And ultimately, love, compassion, the desire for social justice, and the need to heal were what helped me forgive and, later, reconcile with my father.

Hutch's Story

I was asked to teach this course on multicultural ministry because I am a white male! It helped that I had a degree in theology and had already taught at the university, but because I was the second partner, and the first partner was a Hispanic woman, I was the multicultural balance. If I had been a Hispanic male with the same qualifications, I would not have been offered the job. Curious. White males, in the northern half of this continent anyway, don't always know that they can buy a house in any neighborhood, though they may know that others may not have that privilege. Understanding privilege is like understanding one's own oppression: it takes time and experience and often involves some sort of transformation. A friend who has been in a wheelchair all of her life had a transforming experience when she saw her reflection in a huge window in downtown Seattle. She saw how she looked in public, as others saw her, and had a transformed image of herself. If was not necessarily negative, but certainly different.

I was driving home from my parents' house with friends. One of them said "I didn't know your sister was retarded." Whoa, neither did I; but yes I did; but I never heard anyone say it out loud before. I was transformed. I also started to understand her oppression, and, interestingly, how I as brother had also been oppressed in a family culture that did not acknowledge differences: denial as oppression. Was this why I was a teacher for children in a school for students who had been rejected by the public school system (before public law 91-142)? Was this why I later became an advocate for persons with disabilities, why I marched in the streets of Selma in 1963, why I protested the Vietnam War? Maybe. I do know that I protested injustice for a long time before I understood how I had been oppressed and how I was an oppressor. The injustices by people toward people seemed clear to me (recognizing injustices to me and by me took time). Because this was the sixties, I was influenced by the changing culture around me, a new culture that I embraced and felt that I contributed to. And because the Vietnam War was a variable in the decisions I made, war, life, death, and justice were constant themes as I defended my beliefs and fears. They remain; they are teachable.

The most oppressive situation I have been in was at the age of eighteen when I went to a prestigious Catholic university. I was not allowed to express contrary opinions in class without being called in to the dean's office. I had to be in my room by 10:00 p.m.; I had to have permission to read certain books from the library; I was bombarded by injunctions about what I had to do and how I had to believe. I was truly in a different culture. I did find solace in a Crosier priest who allowed me to express my feelings about God and religion and everything else. This backfired, however, when the dean told me that I asked too many questions in this same priest's religion class, and other students were "losing their faith." It was time to leave, betrayed by God and appalled by what Catholicism had done to people's minds. Kennedy had been killed and the windows were tightly shut. My mother said that my grandmother would be very disappointed because I was the only grandson to go to a Catholic college. My grandmother said to always be true to myself and to do what I had to do. My mother didn't dispute this; my father never said anything, but he did give me my other grandmother's '55 Buick (which I was embarrassed to drive but would give anything for today), and this may have been a gesture of acceptance and love.

It took me two years to understand how oppressive it was for me. At this same time, I was differentiating from a very oppressive father. He did not come from an oppressive family; I think he was in a great deal of pain over events in his life and his way of dealing with that pain was through verbal hostility. He was not "The Great Santini," but he did not have tolerance for contrary opinions or behavior, refused to discuss anything but his own needs, and needed to dominate every conversation or interaction.

My father was a sort of Willy Loman, having never really "self-actualized." He viewed my ideas and involvement in social change as distorted and self-centered. Though he was extremely opinionated, he never talked about spiritual things, or values or the meaning of his life or mine; and if he had, I suspect I would not have taken him seriously. This was my salvation; I never took him seriously. My mother, the counterbalance, was and is very intuitive, trusting some inner sense. I think this was her greatest gift to me, though she often was fearful of this gift and afraid I might go too far (which meant I would embarrass her). I was raised in a culture that said (it has been changing) men can't be artists, men can't be emotional, men must play through the pain, and all the other things that have been written by and for white males. Some of it is true! I wasn't beaten, I wasn't denied access to a restraurant, but like many others, I had to understand my own oppression before I could understand, truly with empathy, how others had suffered, and whether or not it could be compared to my own by whatever scale we measure pain.

My sister has found no peace in her life, I would guess because she couldn't, for whatever reason, accept my mother's gift (packaged in a lot of expectations that she couldn't meet) and because she, and she alone, took my father seriously. My cousins and my aunts taught me that life was diverse and wonderful, my uncles that it was singular and dangerous, but my grandparents taught me to love and trust and they were revered.

Much of the richness of the period was in the stories of my Haney grandparents' life in the South and the dignity that must be preserved in the North. Some stories were about Ireland. I do not remember stories of the Hutchinsons, which I later learned were "shameful" and not to be told. But they were scary and had to do with being Jewish and the war. Somewhere in this richness, I learned that how I felt was not necessarily important or valid (you don't really feel that way?), but I always knew that whatever I felt or decided to do was my business and my privilege (that word again).

I believe that I learned to trust and hence, today I am both trusting and hopeful. I also learned to be autonomous but, because so many things were not talked about, I developed a sense of doubt or shame that manifested itself in the need to always be right and to never talk about anything that would cause me to appear to not be autonomous. Though I was an assertive child and took initiative, there were many shoulds about my behavior that led to guilt about being assertive. For many adult years I thought that I had no guilt, only to discover that my guilt was acted out in not taking responsibility for who I was. I did not pursue my truths because I didn't think they were right. This in actuality allowed me to control the world of shoulds in which I lived. Sounds like oppression.

I confronted my own oppressor when I heard myself saying oppressive, controlling things to my own son that my father said to me. Several times I had to stop, take a deep breath, apologize, and remember that his ghost did not need to speak through me. The oppressed becomes the oppressor! I oppressed in other ways; I had expectations for my son that were mine and not his; I can be very judgmental based on zero information; I haven't always spoken up when, for example, my cousin called his male cleaning person his "cleaning lady" because he is gay; I have not written many letters of protest that need to be written; I have wasted gas and other natural resources; I have smoked cigarettes and eaten too much sugar. I thought for many years that I had to be right and had to let people know that I was. These are common sins, but they contribute to the collective oppression of and to our world and the people in it

In my late thirties, a flyer landed on my desk. It described a program in health and the healing arts. It got my attention. A year later I read that an art school was opening close to my house. With great trepidation I enrolled in art school and finished a degree eight years later. To do this I had to give up several major life rules: you should already know how to do this; you should be an expert; never show that you don't know anything or that you are vulnerable. I don't think that these were necessarily parental injunctions, but rather survival tools. I learned that I must put on a happy, confident face to survive in a family and in a culture that expected that of me, or so I thought. Two years later, I saw a flyer announcing a workshop, *The Artist as a Spiritual Voyager*; I knew I was going to this workshop. I was being led by another force that I seemed to trust. I spent a week at the Institute for Culture and Creation, with Matthew Fox, Brian Swimme, and Company.

I became reacquainted with my spiritual self and understood that I could do this within the context of my life. I learned several truths: an artist is one that trusts his or her own images (hence being a cocreator of the universe); we are all from the same source (thus, no matter what we believe, it's all the same); that the planet earth is a source of healing (I knew this but never articulated it); this stuff is teachable.

In my late forties I decided to take three months off to complete a major art project and went through, in addition to completing this major work, a real dark night of the soul (though I would not have called it that at the time). During these years I completed a theology degree, did much reading, and spent several weeks each summer in New Mexico—summers filled with amazing spiritual experiences and insights that would take another paper to describe, but which convinced me that I could be in intimate contact with the forces of the Universe.

In my late forties I had several incidences that brought me face-to-face with a diminishing sense of invincibility, safety, and control. I was attacked on the street late one night. The young man who attacked me could very well be seen as a manifestation of my seemingly powerful, maybe angry, male ego that dictates that I can go where I want, do what I want, and have what I want. A hard part of this experience has been accepting that I can't go wherever I want, anytime I want. Another piece of this experience was that I blamed myself for being out on the street late. This was my first understanding of how victims blame themselves. An encounter with an old friend has taught me that my expectations of others and myself that were valid 20 years ago have changed; my adolescent assumptions are just assumptions. A loving confrontation with my son led me to openly acknowledge to him what I have been grieving, but have not shared; his life is his, not mine.

Events in my life have been like alarm clocks. Stephen Levine (1979), in *A Gradual Awakening,* says,

> Before, we were just lost in our problem; now, we're aware that we've got to work with it. That is awakening. When we don't know we are lost in it, there is no way out. When we are aware we are caught in it, we are already freeing ourselves. As we trust ourselves and experience this gradual awakening—not measuring it or weighing it or trying to taste it, but just seeing how it is without any score—it patiently steadies our feet on the path (p. 73).

The middle adulthood tasks are completed, leaving me to look at new roles and directions. The studying of theology is an example of the redirected energy. Letting go of adolescent ideation again allows me to account for who I am now, not then. The death and disease around me allows me to open up to my own death and disease, to my uniqueness and limitations.

I have begun a process of letting go of expectations of myself and others, of prejudices and beliefs far more rigid than I would ever tolerate in others, of the need to convert, fix, or solve, and of the need to control. But this is not dryness, for it seems that the more I let go, the more room there is for something fuller. The Hindus would call it "becoming closer to God." Peck (1987) would call it community: "touching on something perhaps even deeper than joy" (p. 106). These glimpses of freedom happen in moments of insight and in moments of silence. Charles Johnston (1991), in *Necessary Wisdom,* says, "Truth as the surety of knowledge gradually gives way to the more humble but ultimately more powerful reality of truth a wisdom" (p. 228). More and more I am experiencing and understanding, whether I need to or not, the wisdom of this truth. The healing and reconciliation are taking place, allowing for the transformation, choices, and acceptance.

And now, parents are aging and dying. Children are growing up. Friends have cancer. My body is changing, my memory tricks me, and the world seems to be changing very fast. There is a lot of pain ahead. I carry several jagged rocks in my chest that will always hurt. I do not have a God that is powerful enough to change my environment for the better or wrathful enough to change my environment for the worse. I do have a sense of the availability of a source of deep insight and warmth. The silence that once was loneliness is now a source of comfort. And I have learned from listening. This may not be teachable. We must listen to others' stories in order to learn.

Cleo and Hutch: The Course

In order to qualify for the course, students needed to have completed a group skills and an individual skills course; to have taken or be scheduled to take a prejudice reduction workshop; and to be willing to do an internship in a multicultural parish or congregation as part of a two-person cross-cultural team. We made the decisions of who would be paired with whom, based upon consultation with other faculty and staff, the ethnic cultural diversity of each team, information in the students' applications, and our prior experience with students.

Several congregations agreed to participate by committing to supervise, mentor, and coach ministry intern partnerships. These particular congregations had demonstrated leadership in the area of cross-cultural ministry and were willing to share what they had learned. This meant that supervisors would need to be chosen to oversee the interns' experiences, providing opportunities to learn from the congregation, meeting weekly with them to provide guidance and feedback, evaluating their efforts on a quarterly basis, and maintaining communication with the university by attending internship supervisors' orientation sessions and a closing celebration at the end of the academic year.

The sites provided the students (and the two of us!) with the opportunity to learn from very different types of contexts, leadership, and communities. Meeting with all the supervisors on a quarterly basis provided information on how students performed the tasks on their internships, how they interacted with the supervisors, the dynamics of the site, and of the varied strengths and capacities of the students. It was clear that the students and supervisors formed positive relationships and the students received guidance, mentoring, and wisdom. Students also learned how not to do things and what didn't work well, and they were able to hold candid discussions with their supervisors and share their insights in the classroom. The supervisors appreciated the focus on diversity and conflict resolution. The modeling of part-nership supervision and instruction was consistently viewed as valuable by the students and supervisors in the development of their own partnerships and as an archetype for "ideal" congregation administration.

We met weekly prior to each class to discuss course content, group process, group dynamics, and additional resources needed for the class. These meetings were also a good opportunity to discuss our own dynamics. We relied heavily on our past experiences in teaching, counseling, advising, training, and consulting. We also read new material and consulted with other professionals familiar with the course content and with the dynamic of team and partnership ministry in a multicultural setting. In addition to teaching and developing the course, planning, and leading the yearly orientations and daylong retreats, we met with each student to give feedback on course work and growth as a minister; we made quarterly on-site visitations, meeting with site supervisors to discuss the students' progress and specific challenges of the site; and we identified and scheduled guest speakers and planned and scheduled field trips.

We developed a nontext bibliography to acquaint students with theological and cultural stories in novel form. Students completed a variety of exercises in and out of class. A family life script facilitated a theological/cultural reflection paper on families of origin and ministry. The use of fiction as a way of reflecting on their own understanding of ethnicity, culture, and diversity was a successful way to increase the depth of cross-cultural awareness and communication. Exercises and debriefing on conflict management, and cultural identification were included. We used a Transactional Analysis model, for example, with role-playing to clarify the options that students in conflict had. Handouts were often given to students after a particular issue was discussed in class. Social justice and oppression were consistent themes in the readings, discussions, and assignments.

Student partners met weekly, shared professional and personal concerns, and worked on projects together. Students completed projects on their individual sites. Projects ranged from surveying parishioners about multicultural issues, to familiarizing young, low-income Latino students to the Seattle University campus on the possibility of college attendance. Students frequently expressed the need to "leave a legacy," and the projects often fulfilled this need. The influence of students on-site was often very subtle; for example, one team had some influence on the wording of a parish school survey, thus increasing the awareness of multicultural issues by both the survey designers and the survey takers.

Each class period included an opportunity for students to present issues from their site experience or from their own partnership experience. These were often personal issues and issues of partnership conflict. Our presentations were frequently amended, modified, or postponed in order to spend time on the issues raised by students. These issues were not always predictable, but the faculty, from years of teaching and from a passion for the subject matter, had an enormous reservoir of experiences to share, readings and films to recommend, and exercises to do. Any faculty teaching this course would, or should have, this reservoir of knowledge and experience as well as the creativity and flexibility to meet the specific needs of the individual student, the student partnerships, or course as a whole. On the other hand, we had certain concepts and issues, in addition to partnership and ministerial topics, which we felt students needed to know. We made more formal presentations that included discussions, references and resources regarding developmental psychology, conflict management, interpersonal communication, values clarification, and learning styles.

Thus, there was a tension between content and process, between paying attention to individual and group process and ensuring adequate time for theological reflection. Students frequently noted it. This course was not intended to be solely a process course, yet individual and community development are key parts of ministerial formation. We, therefore, had to decide on a weekly basis whether to stay with personal and interpersonal issues or move on to planned presentations. Sometimes, we chose incorrectly and students either resented the "counseling" mode or felt that we needed more time on their issues. Once in a while we were brilliant, spending the time on a personal or group issue that paralleled the content of the course.

We also noted the process of partnership bonding and hypothesized about its effect on the development of the group as a whole. We expected more group conflict than actually occurred. Group theorists and practitioners know that "pairing" is often detrimental to group process and progress. Students in this course were paired by design. Maybe pairing inhibited the group from entering into more conflict as a whole. In one discussion, a student defined partnership as "dancing with a person whose toes you don't have to worry about stepping upon. A partnership is truly a dance, toes are stepped upon, but that's okay." We observed that as partners, we sometimes disagreed about teaching methodologies as well as course content and assessment. We determined that partners do not have to agree but must be able to manage the conflict in a way that maintains the goals and integrity of the course. Partners must take care of each other; this course was very intense and talking about it helped manage that stress. The students discovered that sharing meals was valuable and that partnering takes time; at the very least, it requires a weekly meeting and frequent phone calls and e-mails to discuss the course, their internship, and partnership issues. It wasn't unusual to hear that the partnerships were developing into deep friendships.

Another source of tension was the role we played as faculty. We did not want to become oppressors to our students. We asked the students to share the responsibility for planning, evaluating, and presenting. We invited students to make decisions with us. We sought to model a course where all participants, students, and faculty had an equal responsibility for planning and delivery. This was greeted with some trepidation; some students expected us to oppress them: "Just tell us what to do," and "You are the teachers, you decide."

The power differential in academia has been learned by all of us. This was a serious source of conflict among all of us that served as an example of how we oppress each other. We became facilitators for understanding this oppression in our midst. We taught how to manage conflict, and we all learned how to share responsibility for the course.

The course was very time and energy intensive for us. Partnership teaching and supervision does not mean that the load is shared. Rather, the load is doubled because so much consultation between partners must take place. Yet, the experience of developing and teaching this course was a profound one for us. We developed new insights into the nature of understanding, valuing, and working with diversity in a classroom setting, as well as in the context of diverse ministries.

Cleo and Hutch: Reflection

Having read, and reread, our own stories, we have identified six themes that we feel contributed to our ability and passion to teach social justice individually and in partnership:

1. The Sixties: We "came of age" in the sixties. We celebrated social change and our power to contribute to the larger culture by acknowledging diversity, helping to change laws and attitudes, and attempting to influence the outcome of a war.
2. Counseling and Psychology: We both studied counseling and developmental psychology, and we worked with counselors and therapists to help resolve personal and family problems. We explored a variety of spiritual and religious traditions and have committed to ongoing spiritual development. We both studied, tried to undo, rebuilt, and created new social structures.

3. Oppression and Support: We came from families that had a marked contrast between oppression and support. We had oppressive fathers and supportive uncles; we had bigoted aunts and compassionate grandmothers. We also had mothers who loved us deeply and supported us unconditionally. We experienced personal and familial injustice and strong injunctions that we were a good son and a good daughter and would be treated fairly. We learned, therefore, to question authority without guilt (well, some of the time); and we recognized hypocrisy without doubt (well, most of the time).

4. Rewards: We were rewarded by immediate families, extended families, teachers, and peers for being leaders, teachers, and confidants; for being open to different cultures, languages, and food; for being both curious and confident (whether we felt confident or not); for being resilient when mocked or criticized (whether personally, or because of family or culture); and because we were intelligent and had wonderful senses of humor.

5. Life Events: Our life circumstances included associating with people from different cultures. We lived in diverse communities in Colorado and California, we worked in poverty programs and Upward Bound, we had friends and lovers who spoke different languages and had different skin colors. We married people from other cultures (Jewish and first-generation Italian). Before we became partners, we learned what it meant to be in partnership with people not like us.

6. Development: As adolescents in the 1960s, our advocacy and anger were influenced by family and social contexts. In early midlife, our personal, psychological, and spiritual growth was exemplified, and maybe "acted out," in our teaching and counseling. In later midlife, we have understood the universality of cultural appreciation and the continuing process of guarding that appreciation through justice and equity.

We hesitate to choose any of the many developmental models for comparison because we do not feel that we are necessarily linear in our journeys or we have reached a "higher" plane. But Fowler's (1984) faith development model does have concepts and language that parallel our parallel stories. At the "synthetic-conventional" stage, adolescents find authority outside of themselves, in families and schools especially, and either accept it or defy it (we did that); at the "individual-reflective" stage (20s and 30s), there is a relocation of authority from the external to the internal by reexamining old assumptions and taking on new responsibilities (we did this, too); and at the "conjunctive" stage, there is the acceptance of many truths, other ideas, and beliefs which precludes an interest in service to others (this fits). And at the "universalizing" stage, principles of absolute love and justice supersede individual needs for the needs of the community (we like to think we are here, at least part of the time).

By teaching this class, we were able to contribute to the understanding of social justice issues and to help students find ways to create equity and fairness. In the process, we learned about ourselves, individually. But unexpectedly, we learned the partnership became an entity itself. Students talked to us as if we were one person; we talked about "we" rather than "you" or "me." Students understood their own diversity and how to work with each other in partnerships as predicted.

We discovered that partnership teaching led us to a profound understanding of our commonality, our universality. We come from different cultural heritages, yet we share many of the same values. Our experience tells us that social injustice is often the result of a conflict of values, or perceived values, and an imbalance of power. Not unexpectedly, as we shared our values through our stories, and as students shared their values through their stories, the commonalities emerged, the conflicts melted, the empathy increased, and the dialogue about how we as teachers and ministers could create communities where there is less oppression and greater equity then began.

References

Augsburger, D. W. (1992). *Conflict mediation across cultures*. Louisville, Kentucky: Westminster/John Knox.

Coleman, P. (1998). The process of forgiveness in marriage and the family. In R. Enright & J. North (Eds.), *Exploring forgiveness* (pp. 75–94). Madison: The University of Wisconsin Press.

Elder, J. (1998). Expanding our options: The challenge of forgiveness. In R. Enright & J. North (Eds.), *Exploring forgiveness* (pp. 150–161). Madison: The University of Wisconsin Press.

Enright, R., Freedman, S., & Rique, J. (1998). The psychology of interpersonal forgiveness. In R. Enright & J. North (Eds.), *Exploring forgiveness* (pp. 42–62). Madison: University of Wisconsin Press.

Flanigan, B. (1998). Forgivers and the unforgivable. In R. Enright & J. North (Eds.), *Exploring forgiveness* (pp. 95–105). Madison: The University of Wisconsin Press.

Fowler, J. (1984). Faith development theory and the human vocation. In *Becoming adult, becoming Christian: Adult development and the Christian faith*. San Francisco: Harper & Row.

Freedman. S., & Enright, R. (1996). Forgiveness as an intervention goal with incest survivors. *Journal of Counseling and Clinical Psychology*, 64(5), 983–992.

Howell, P. J. (1996). As sure as the dawn: A spirit guide through times of darkness. Kansas City, Missouri: Sheed & Ward.

Johnston, C. M. (1991). *Necessary wisdom*. Seattle: ICD Press.

Kegan, R. (1982). *The evolving self: Problem and process in human development*. Cambridge: Harvard University Press.

King, M. L. (1977). *Strength to love*. Great Britain: William Collins.

Levine, S. (1979). *A gradual awakening.* New York: Anchor Books.

Longaker, C. (1997). *Facing death and finding hope: A guide to the emotional and spiritual care of the dying.* New York: Doubleday.

North, J. (1998). The "ideal" of forgiveness: A philosopher's exploration. In R. Enright & J. North (Eds.) *Exploring forgiveness* (pp. 15–34). Madison: The University of Wisconsin Press.

Peck, S. (1987). *A different drum.* New York: Simon and Schuster.

Poston, W. S. C. (1990). Biracial identity development model: A needed addition. *Journal of Counseling & Development, 69,* 152–155.

Smedes, L. (1998). Stations on the journey from forgiveness to hope. In E. Worthington, Jr. (Ed.), *Dimensions of forgiveness: Psychological research and theological perspectives* (pp. 341–354). Philadelphia: Templeton Foundation.

Worthington, E., Jr. (1998). Empirical research in forgiveness: Looking backward, looking forward. In E. Worthington, Jr. (Ed.), *Dimensions of forgiveness: Psychological research and theological perspectives* (pp. 321–339). Philadelphia: Templeton Foundation.

CONCLUSION
Claims Made—Claims Revisited

Roberto A. Peña, Kristin Guest, and Lawrence Y. Matsuda

The title *Community and Difference: Stories about Teaching, Pluralism, and Social Justice* came on Thanksgiving morning. This seems odd, as being different can leave one tired with life. As those who know difference, we know rejection and what it means to be oppressed. The experience of being set out of life has made us all advocates for social justice, and it has informed our lifestyles and teaching. There are times when we examine our feelings about social justice with students and colleagues and these self-reflections bring us joy and despair. This book describes our inner lives, but it also reveals feelings that come out from our hearts and souls.

We believe that we teach who we are and the educator's self is as legitimate a topic in discussions about teaching as the self is as legitimate a subject in discussions about life. We also define teaching as a joyful and compelling act, and we offer our stories as evidence of our experience with oppression and as our admission of the optimism we share.

Getting Started?

It was late December 2002 when Bob sent us the first draft of the individual chapters. The writers told about their journeys to find a place in society and how the process of writing for the book changed them. We were transformed from individuals working on a project to a family that shared ideas, worked together, and challenged and supported each other. We naturally expected the pressure of deadlines, but what we did not count on were those human events that make up the human experience but are never factored into the work. During the process a mother and a father passed away, and a daughter became ill. The workload shifted and someone from the team stepped forward to ensure the process moved ahead.

Even though we were a team, we also maintained our individual perspectives, values, and dreams. Naturally, when we discussed what the last chapter would look like, we had to resolve several issues. At first we thought an outside person should write the last chapter as a summary, but then that didn't come to pass. Then, we decided that each of us would try to bring closure to the work by summarizing major concepts and discussing the steps in the process. We asked what the last chapter would look like.

Should one of us take the different stories and fold them into a unified piece, or should each story stand alone? We decided to write summaries of our experiences and then decide. It was a very *Rashamon* like experience.

Rashamon is a Kurosawa movie about a murder on a road. The movie involves the story of what each witness perceived. Each witness told a different story about the same event in the movie. The stories that did unfold told more about the witnesses and their perceptions of selves, values, and what they ascribed meaning to than about the actual event. Like Rashamon, this concluding chapter does not pull together all of the loose ends into a nice, neat package. Instead, it raises new questions, discusses new revelations, and above all is a personal-perceptual account of what was meaningful for each of us. As such, it discusses revelations and changes generated by new ideas, perspectives, relationships, and their effects on our lives. Again, like the judge in the *Rashamon* court, it is the job of the reader to weigh the truth in the stories. The reader must judge, in relation to her or his values, who they are, what is meaningful, and what they perceive at this moment in time.

The process of reading the stories and discovering understanding in others and in self is similar to watching a movie at age fifteen and then watching it again at age 40. The movie is different the second time because we change and how we look at times, places, events, and others change as well. Respecting our individual viewpoints, it was decided that each of the editors' contributions would be presented in this final section as stand-alone summaries. Among other things, the editors hoped to touch and inform perceptions to promote action for social justice.

Ruffled Beginnings: Bob's Account

It was my students who first suggested this book. They'd completed their dissertation research and asked, "When, Professor, will you write your journey?" That was 1997 or 1998. I recall taking my seat, thinking I had little to say, stretching my collar and voicing what Mom and Dad had said about "myself last." The journey was inevitable I knew then. What remained was finding the courage, time, will, and affection to make the journey last.

The process of "internal search" that Moustakas (1990) describes where the traveler explores the "nature and meaning of experience" (p. 9); his assertion that heuristic researchers experience growing self-awareness, self-knowledge, and depth—I knew these well, held hands, and danced like children dance with these ideas and processes all my life. Heuristic became the name of what was and always had been cousin to me. I know this now and I fear that along with growing self-awareness, knowledge, and depth, heuristic processes and tinkering would probably spell the end of me. Thoughts put to words, words grown to actions—writing these probably meant giving human experience life and bringing the mysteries surrounding life death.

The actual writing of *Community and Difference: Stories about Teaching, Pluralism, and Social Justice* began during fall 2001 and then again during fall 2002. Kris Guest, Larry Matsuda, and I probably made careers about social justice, but in all likelihood, like so many before us, I sensed that we probably had not put our words and our own selves to the test of bringing teaching as social justice fuller meaning and life. Words communicate ideas and explain behaviors, and given that as teachers we expected so much from ourselves, our colleagues, and most important, our students, it also seemed by chance true that as advocates and soldiers of what we each held teaching and social justice to mean, we also were required to write and to put ourselves in the foreground.

Philosophies of education, leadership, and social justice—we all asked and continue to ask our students for statements, disclosures, and declarations like these, but as educators and students trained to study human experience, how many of us wrote and with that complied with our own wishes for learning and social justice? Works like Gary Howard's *We Can't Teach What We Don't Know* (1999), with his inspired story of his personal journey, had served as both a model and admonition for us, I believe, suggesting that depth of conviction and possibly depth of understanding teaching as social justice education was also related to our writing our experiences and beliefs.

We look back now and write about how writing our stories filled us with fear, uncomfortableness, and uncertainty of fit. We recall meeting to discuss and write about social justice with the understanding that we would address how it was reflected in our lives and teaching. We write about how some of our research backgrounds were born from empirical training and how heuristic research ran contrary to all the research techniques we had practiced and been taught. One wrote how a colleague at a nearby research one university called the approach drivel, accusing him of being a traitor for crossing over to the other side and pursuing less than scholarly research. This colleague's idea was that there was only one way to bring new knowledge into the world and it was not by what he called organizing gossip.

Following are Kris's, Larry's, and my thoughts about the experiences we had while meeting and writing and our stories. While the experiences are informing and for the most part potent enough, it seemed to each of us that teaching, social justice, heuristic, and other purposes might also be served by including our reflections and words about the lived experience. As such, the reflections about writing our stories that follow describe more than the experiences of writing the book as each of us understand them. Included are new understandings that describe time and place, the emergence of trust, friendship, understanding, and love, and how these sensibilities emerged from our working together toward social justice and from the organized and sometimes damnable process of ensuring social justice a place.

Kris's Account

Trying to describe the process involved in our writing for this book is a challenge because I'm not sure I still fully understand how it happened, how it is that we're now reflecting on a process that has occurred over approximately a year and a half. But I remember the beginning well, and it is somehow as if there was no turning back after an initially casual conversation that would not let go of me.

It was fall of 2001, and I had convened the first meeting of the academic year of our College of Education's "Justice Education Task Force." The initial meeting was well-attended, and I was pleased that we had some new members of the task force, possibilities for new ideas—including Roberto Peña, who had just joined our faculty from Arizona State University. The agenda involved thinking about the kinds of activities we would sponsor for our colleagues in the school over the coming academic year, and we began brainstorming possibilities. The meeting started with a round in which we shared with each other a brief version of our own "journeys toward justice." Then we moved into thinking about upcoming activities, and we brainstormed possibilities. I had just read Gary Howard's (1999) *We Can't Teach What We Don't Know* and been inspired by the story of his personal journey, and the depth of his convictions related to social justice education.

"What about inviting the faculty to read and discuss Gary's story as a stimulus to examining the delivery of our graduate curriculum through the lenses of equity and justice," I asked the group. Several people responded, and Bob looked lost in thought. After several minutes of listening, he looked at the group and said, "What about writing our own stories?" Surprised looks followed, and Bob said that he thought that we could put our own stories together in the form of a book, rather than looking to others' stories. Little response and the brainstorming continued. We stopped that day. I agreed to write up the suggestions for our review and some decisions about priorities at the next meeting.

The next meeting came at a time Bob was unable to attend. His idea of a book was listed, but generated no response. But I had trouble letting go of the idea—partly initially, I think, because I didn't want Bob to feel that we had just dismissed his idea without fair consideration. So when I ran into him next in the hall, I expressed that view. He looked me squarely in the eyes and asked the question I was afraid he might ask: "Are *you* interested?" I think I hemmed and hawed a fair amount; in listening to the short accounts of my faculty colleagues' journeys, I had realized that many of them had concerns about justice because of personal experiences with injustice. Such experiences were not mine, and I found myself asking the question that I asked myself many times during the course of my writing: how can I contribute when my background is one of privilege, not oppression? But Bob has a way of making it hard to say no, and I think I knew at some level from the time he first asked so directly, "are you interested," that this had the potential to be an important experience in personal reflection and growth, an examination at a deeper level of a commitment I professed but needed to examine further to see whether I could live that commitment more deeply.

"Damn," a part of me thought. I thought maybe the idea would just go away, and I wouldn't have to engage in this hard work. Unwilling to commit myself, I think I mumbled something about my willingness to talk further about the idea. "This guy just isn't going to drop this," I thought. And he didn't, and we didn't, and pretty soon it was too late to say "no" without having it feel like a cop-out. Much more comfortable, I kept thinking, to carry on with the task force as we had in the past—sponsoring several programs each year—than to look inward, to share with others, to have hard conversations about these matters which I professed mattered deeply to me. So Bob and I had another conversation, and then he told me that he had invited Larry Matsuda to join us in the book. Oops! It's no longer just exploratory conversation. Now he's actually talking about "the book," and talking as if this is something that is actually going to happen. This guy really doesn't let go.

And then amazing things began to happen. I went to the first of many subsequent meetings with Bob and Larry feeling quite anxious. I wondered if they did as well. What was the source of my anxiety? Many, many things. First, there continued to be the nagging doubts that I had a story to tell. "I thought we were talking about an edited volume," I protested. Editing I thought was something I could tackle; then I'd still be dealing with other people's stories. Then Bob started sending materials about heuristic inquiry our way. But he didn't just send them our way. After about two or three meetings he pushed the point I knew would come. As I said, this process somehow just wouldn't let go.

"I think that if we're going to ask others to write, we need to start writing ourselves," Bob suggested. "But what are we going to write about?" I protested. Being a linear thinker, I thought perhaps we should have a predetermined format for the chapters so that there would be some consistency across authors. Bob came back, of course, by reminding us that "heuristic" means to discover or to find, that the process of heuristic inquiry involves letting the writing help one discover the meaning of experiences.

It's not about predetermined format, but rather about a process that becomes a vehicle for personal search. And it begins with immersion. It was becoming evident that the role of noncontributing editor was not going to fly, and I was going to need to try my hand at telling about my own journey. Immersion, by definition, requires jumping in.

There was a remarkable unspoken assumption, I think, at this point. That assumption was that we each have a story to tell and, although our stories would be very different, Bob and Larry somehow communicated that they believed that I, too, might have a story to tell. But I felt a tension present as well; I believed that they were willing to give mine a shot (why, otherwise, were we proceeding and spending all this time meeting), and, at the same time, I felt that they were reserving judgment about whether my story could be as authentic as those who had experienced injustice.

Was this the beginning of some trust among the three of us, so different from each other, and coming together without knowing each other well at all?

I was sensing something larger than I could understand, that was to be trusted. I realized, anyway, that I was in too far to back out without at least giving the process a shot.

And so I began.

Writing and Sharing

I had the luxury of an ideal setting for the major part of my writing. My husband and I had applied and been accepted as "Whiteley Scholars," a marvelous opportunity provided by the University of Washington for academics from a variety of disciplines to spend time at the Whiteley Center outside of Friday Harbor, Washington. Set in a beautiful forest overlooking the saltwater bay off of Friday Harbor in the San Juan Islands, we had a study that provided a serene setting that was highly conducive to reflection and writing.

After letting my mind wander and ideas germinate throughout spring quarter, I approached my summer time at the Whiteley Center with a mix of apprehension and excitement. The time had come to start, so I promised myself that I would write every day. It was hard work but, somewhat to my surprise, I found myself enjoying the process. But then came the next scary step: sharing my work with Bob and Larry. It was one thing to write so personally for myself, and quite another to expose myself directly to these two colleagues. But the sharing and the conversations at our regular meetings became extremely important and meaningful to me.

We would read whatever new material we'd each written prior to our meetings, then gather and talk about one of our chapters at a time. We were certainly not always of one mind. The debates were sometimes vigorous; I felt challenged, often, by Bob and Larry, who would question what I'd written and, especially, push me to go beyond the description of events to my reactions to them. Wow. This was still tough. They weren't going to let me off the hook. Having been moved by Lillian Smith's *Killers of the Dream*, what had I done to confront racism? If I considered myself the product of white privilege, how did I use that understanding to confront my students about the nature of privilege and disadvantage in our society?

I remember some gentle pushing as Larry and Bob shared their experiences of injustice. They pushed about my statements that my life had been free of such experiences and so I needed to look to the experiences of others. Bob, in particular, kept telling me that he thought I had experienced injustice and could also, therefore, understand its nature from personal experience.

"How could he know whether I experienced a life event as injustice?" I thought rather defensively. But our dialogues were about trying to understand each other and help each other, through our heuristic inquiry, to discover some of the meaning in our life experiences. So I listened, and began to understand that perhaps some of my experiences and perceptions of them —e.g., being isolated religiously in childhood, being robbed and separated momentarily from my children in that horrifying moment in the Mexico City bus when I realized no one cared or was going to help me, having to leave a job and place I liked in New England because my husband's race was going to prevent him from receiving tenure—did involve forms of injustice.

While I'd had many fewer experiences with oppression than Larry and Bob, they helped me look at those experiences and recollect the feelings in new ways. There is still a difference, I believe, between my experiences and theirs. It has to do, I think, with the fact that mine were fewer in number, and largely in self-chosen situations that I could also choose to leave. Larry and Bob were stuck with oppression by virtue of their ethnicity and race. But in spite of these differences, their probing gave me a new perspective both on my experiences and on those of others.

More Learning and Difficulty

Another conversation I remember had to do with my statement that "I can't make my students learn or do anything." "I think you're using that as a cop-out," Bob challenged me. Larry listened, and supported me to the extent of validating that this was, in fact, my belief and therefore true to my experience. I think it was important for me to have Larry validate my experience, and it was also important for Bob to push me. I think in that conversation that Bob was trying to help me consider what I *can* do in order not to place all the responsibility on the students.

It was also clear from early on that when either Larry or Bob challenged my statements and my thinking, they were never trying to tell me what to think or lead me to their truths; they were only trying to help me think more deeply in arriving at my own. And I would like to think that it was precisely this reality, never articulated in words, that we all experienced. It was what created the trust that I think deepened over time, and allowed us to push each other harder, listen better, disagree more honestly, and learn far more over succeeding months as we wrote and met together.

One conversation we had was deeply troubling to me. How deep was my commitment if I could write that "To absorb completely all the suffering and injustice of the world would be to live in a state of chronic depression"? My original version read something to the effect that I, therefore, disengage at times in order to maintain my equilibrium. But my colleagues challenged me. If I disengage, do I really care about justice? Do I? I had to ask myself. I still believe my statement about chronic depression, but I think I understand that the challenge came from a place that I had not really considered. I can disengage when I choose because of my white privilege. Larry and Bob helped me understand, over time and through many conversations, that like others of color in our society, they do not have the luxury of disengaging. It's not a choice; they are, by being persons of color, impacted by their ethnicity every day of their lives. I don't think they were saying that they experienced racism every day of their lives, but rather that they can never escape the imprint of injustice that has come from their life experiences—never, never.

Their constructions of their experiences, of their interactions, their work, and their dreams are always through the lens of being a person of color. Yes, all of us construct our experiences, our interactions, our work, and our dreams through the lens of our life experiences. The difference that I think Larry and Bob were telling me and I finally understood is that my experiences do not involve a layer of pain and anger that can never be willed away. Larry and Bob have chosen how to deal with that pain and anger, and they believe that they do have the power to make those choices, but I have not had to make those choices because of my inherent privilege. Powerful teachers, powerful learning for me.

Larry's Account

In October 2002 Professor Roberto Peña, Professor Kris Guest, and I decided to write a book on social justice. Kris was as an active member of the College of Education Social Justice Committee and a veteran faculty member in counseling. She was to be on sabbatical later in the year and wanted to use the time to write. Roberto was a new professor from Arizona State and was teaching in the doctoral program. I was a visiting professor after retiring from the Seattle Public Schools as a K-8 principal in 2000.

Early Thoughts

As a visiting professor, the first time I met Kris was when I supported the Seattle University School of Education's National Council of Accreditation of Teacher Education (NCATE) review from 1993 to 1996. Since I was associated with the internal NCATE information gathering process involving the collection of documents, policies, and procedures from the faculty, I was at best tolerated and at worst openly challenged.

Kris and I, however, were always on good terms and we simply exchanged pleasantries whenever we met.

Throughout her career, Kris was very active in the College of Education and in 2002–2003, she was a member of the college's social justice committee. Her initial area of interest was the creation of a social justice course for education students. This course would support the Jesuit tradition of seeking truth and justice, and it would add a new and necessary strand to the teacher education component.

Roberto attended the social justice committee meeting and discussed his interests in heuristic research with Kris. The upshot was that they decided to write a book on social justice using heuristic research.

Roberto invited me to join and contribute a chapter since he read an article I wrote titled "Proving Loyalty," which appeared in the College of Education's magazine, *The Banner*. In it I discussed some of my experiences as a Japanese American born in an American concentration camp in Idaho during World War II. In the article I also discussed my 1995 trip to Hiroshima, Japan, to visit my relatives who survived the atomic bomb.

The article was timely because it was written after September 11, 2001, when the government was detaining Arab nationals without due process like the Japanese and because the government was discussing a nuclear threat from terrorists on U.S. soil with an outcome similar to Hiroshima.

Learning Heuristic Inquiry and Writing My First Draft

Our first meeting was in Kris's office. Roberto shared information and a book on heuristic research. We discussed social justice with the understanding that we would address how it was reflected in our educational lives. My research background was in empirical research, so heuristic research ran contrary to all the research techniques I had practiced and taught. My colleague at a nearby research one university called the approach drivel and accused me of being a traitor for crossing over to the other side and pursuing less than scholarly research. His idea was that there was only one way to bring new knowledge into the world and it was not by what he called organizing gossip. Nevertheless, I was committed to this endeavor since I had decided not to pursue a tenured position but instead, to work on small projects and grants as well as limit my teaching this year.

Robert explained that introspection, reflection, and authentically exploring a theme were essential elements of the heuristic approach. I still was not clear as to what the definition of social justice was. I knew it was part of the Jesuit tradition, but we still could not agree on a working definition. During our meetings, it became clear that we each had different points of view and saw the issue of social justice from different perspectives. During our discussion, each of us stated our thoughts and no resolution occurred. I guessed that part of the problem was that we were all professors used to being right. Differences were aired but we ended up agreeing only to start writing and to come together periodically to assess our work and progress. I started from a position of what I knew about social justice. As a result, I established myself as the primary audience for the work and began the work as if it were a dairy.

After I started I felt the presence and influence of my mother, who had passed away six years earlier. She suffered through the Great Depression, the incarceration and evacuation, and the resettlement and return to society. The experiences took a toll on the entire family. After the war, when I was growing up, my parents were constantly in and out of the hospital with other major illnesses. Before my seventeenth birthday, they were hospitalized five times, with the longest hospital stay lasting several months. Both lost jobs as a consequence of poor health. Years later at a dinner party with my friend Barry Grosskopf, a local psychiatrist, he and I compared our experiences since he was in a Jewish resettlement camp after the war. In his book, *Forgive Your Parents, Heal Yourself: How Understanding Your Painful Family Legacy Can Transform Your Life*, he stated that traumatic events often impact three generations. By examining the experiences of the grandparents, one can bring enlightenment regarding one's own situation. He also spoke about how emotions and fears can be transferred from the mother to the child.

His thoughts gave me comfort because I have suffered inexplicable waves of melancholy over the years that simply came on without provocation. After talking with Barry I concluded, rightly or wrongly, that what I felt was my mother's sadness chemically transferred to me before birth. Her sadness related to the indignity of the concentration camps, a stillborn child in camp before I was born, the loss of her relatives in Hiroshima, and the postwar racism in America. She and I were inextricably connected by these sorrows. I am and was my mother's child.

During the writing, I protected my feelings by creating a distance between me and the work in my first drafts. I consciously avoided trying to sound like a whiner who experienced injustice and simply wanted to complain. In addition, bringing up unpleasant memories was something that made me relive the pain and suffering of the original event. As a result, my first drafts were stiff and as Roberto said "not authentic." I bristled at his remarks and found fault in his work. We both stood our ground and it seemed like we disagreed about everything. If there was one thing that could be counted on, it was that we would disagree at all of our initial meetings.

Kris, as the counselor, managed to move our discussions to higher ground. Ironically, when Roberto and I disagreed, there was very little rancor or anger involved. We simply disagreed and decided to do what authentically suited the work. The other irony was that Roberto was correct and I needed to speak more authentically about my experiences and stories. Eventually Bob and I disagreed less and our relationship grew from a primarily professional relationship to one of friendship.

A New Audience in Mind

As my chapter took shape, I developed a clearer vision about what I was doing. I began to tell my story with a new audience in mind. I thought at first how my stories would speak to those who have been oppressed and who suffered from discrimination, with the hope of inspiring them to achieve their dreams. My stories later became more real and I was able to include the suffering I felt and the emotions without shame and experiencing my mother's sadness. My writing began to evolve into a very personal work as opposed to a purely academic piece.

Before each meeting we read and critiqued each other's work. In the process one assumption surfaced which took shape as a question: In order to write about injustice, should one have suffered to speak with credibility? Suffering was a large part of what Althe, Roberto, other contributors and I wrote about, and we used our memories to show how suffering transformed us. Since Kris was an attractive blond woman with a professional husband and two very attractive Nordic-type children who graduated from college, both Bob and I questioned her commitment to social justice. Kris was "privileged." She did not have to live with racial discrimination on a daily basis and above all, she could walk away and no one would question her choice to not participate. In our minds she could drop the social justice cause and easily take up the saving of the whales.

She had that luxury.

We, on the other hand, could not drop the cause because our people were being negatively impacted and we felt the pressure of being different on a daily basis. I myself believed that my cause was more important than the whales, the forests, or the spotted owl. As a matter of priority I thought, "Give my people equality and opportunity and they will be able to join in the campaign for whales and other endangered species."

Kris responded to our concerns and suspicions by focusing on what motivated her to work and teach for social justice. Her heart was touched by stories and experiences of segregation and inequality in America. It became obvious that these stories influenced her values so deeply that she taught her children, students, and friends about the need for social justice. She not only taught it, but she obviously lived it as well. Her motivation came from the external environment which she described as change generated from the Outside In. In contrast, Roberto, the other contributors, and I wrote about our experiences from the Inside Out. Reading Kris's work caused me to reexamine and reframe my audience again. I mentally expanded my audience to include people who experienced little suffering and could benefit from stories that touched their hearts. My primary audience, however, remained those who experienced injustice and needed inspiration.

Shortly after finishing my first draft of this summary section, I left for Paris. While on the plane I pondered our efforts as a writing team. I was still troubled about not fully capturing the essence of our work in my summary. The in-flight movie had just finished and I took my headphones off. My mind was wandering when a picture of a Native American appeared on screen. I promptly plugged the headset back in and watched the ESPN *SportsCentury* program on Jim Thorpe.

Thorpe had won numerous track and field medals including the pentathlon and decathlon Olympic medals at the 1912 Olympics in Sweden. Thorpe was later stripped of those medals when it was revealed that he played summer minor league baseball for money when he was a college student. Thorpe grew up on the reservation and was sent away to Indian schools because he had difficulty adjusting. As he grew older he used his athletic prowess to earn a place of respect in the Royal Courts of Europe, American mainstream, and the Native American nations. In 1950 he was selected as the most outstanding athlete of the early 20th century.

In the program, Thorpe's son commented on Jim's achievements in sports and life and said words to the effect that his father developed "the spirit to walk in two worlds."

The phrase was an epiphany for me because I sensed this was the theme of our collective stories on teaching as social justice. Our stories were about finding a place in society and ultimately finding the spirit to walk in two worlds. Roberto from the barrios, Althe from the world of abandonment, Kris from her world of privilegem and me from the Japanese concentration camps were stories I recalled and that brought the spirit of walking in two worlds home to me. We three and the other contributors described how we found the spirit to walk in two worlds and how that path involved finding social justice.

Reflecting on our book writing process, I can safely say that this heuristic research has changed my life. I continue to hear Roberto's words, "Be authentic." That phrase now permeates my life as I try to live each day with that thought in mind. The work also helped me put my past into perspective. What happened in the past has helped me become who I am today. I started as my mother's son. But as I work toward the goal of being authentic and someone who walks authentically in two worlds on the path of social justice, it is my hope that my son, like Jim Thorpe's son, will someday be able to claim with pride, "I am my father's son."

Understandings

Stories about Teaching and Social Justice describes how individuals experienced relationships. The nature of these relationships shaped understandings that contributors held about themselves and society overall. In their stories, status for contributors increased as others accepted them. Difference meant a decline in status so that likeness and difference appear to be the axes against which the conditions of belonging and not belonging rubbed.

In their stories, the measure of difference from a norm seemed vast and equal to the distance contributors needed to travel to gain acceptance and affirmation from society. Contributors believed that acceptance and affirmation came to those who were like and not markedly different from members of a reference group. Conversely, themes also suggest that the more they perceived themselves to be like members of a reference group, the more normal they felt and the more positively contributors judged themselves on both personal and interpersonal grounds. Similarly, the more each perceived they belonged, the more contributors believed in their own capacity to decide about their personal well-being and the well-being of others.

A logical possible challenge to assertions describing the importance of being accepted might come from those who frame personal and public acceptance as dependent upon perception about difference, situation, and place. This challenge comes from those who suggest that contributors experienced an infinite number of statuses when the numbers of infinite reference groups they knew are taken into account. Findings taken from the stories account for this by suggesting that while they did experience different statuses and an infinite number of different social groups, the perceptions that contributors held about different social groups did not weigh equally upon their minds. Instead, being different and sensitive to the isolation and inferior treatment that difference tended to bring led contributors to reflect more often on those experiences that brought anxiety, isolation, and pain. For contributors, being denied acceptance into desired reference groups tended to hold greater meaning than did those occasions when contributors were accepted.

Moreover, for some contributors, the desire to increase their chances for greater personal and social acceptance became synonymous with disguising and concealing their differences so as to more easily integrate with others in society. The importance of being accepted, in other words, took all and was the desired thing to do. Personal acceptance and obtaining the acceptance of others were important, and grew akin, for some contributors, to washing ethnicity, race, learning ability, sexuality, and birthright away. Unfortunately, not being accepted was not the sole reason for contributors to experience dismay. The effort made to belong also served to remind them that they were different, that they could not successfully negotiate certain borders, that they did not measure up, and that regardless of their attempts to gain acceptance, contributors would always be different and never the same and belonging with others.

Further, acceptance for different contributors appeared to depend upon the nature of their experiences overall. Different experiences held different levels of potency so that established norms in schools, churches, public airports, and other settings interacted with contributors' knowledge, wisdom, and beliefs to dominate their understandings and interpretations of self, others, difference, and their relative place in society. Discussions focusing on how difference limited access to learning and space elicited questions and magnified doubts within contributors about their personal legitimacy, adequacy, and opportunities for belonging. Doubts about personal identity and self-worth also emerged as contributors perceived difference as meaning inferior, as they perceived efforts to be more like others as an admission that they would never gain complete acceptance, and as contributors perceived they were more or less bound and unworthy as a result of their being inferior as different.

Finally, analyses and understandings of their stories suggest that discrimination and prejudice are more than thoughts and experiences resident in contributors' lives. As Allport (1979) suggests, discrimination and prejudice reside in the individual and in the collective story of society overall. Discrimination and prejudice, as discussed in contributors' writings, are conditions that were simultaneously present in their lived experiences and in the wisdom of others they knew, recalled, hated, and loved. This clarification is important because not only does it move the locus of discrimination and prejudice beyond contributors' experiences and lives, but it moves for understanding that a multifaceted plural approach to combating discrimination and prejudice is very much needed.

That said, one of many problems associated with discrimination and prejudice is that they generally position one against others so as to injure individual and all human experience. Approaches to addressing discrimination, prejudice, and difference, as Allport writes, call for "historical, sociocultural, and situational analyses, as well as [analyses] in terms of socialization, personality dynamics, phenomenology, [and] actual group differences" (p. 514). Allport's long-range policies for dealing with difference as well as his thoughts about plurality require additional scrutiny, however.

Allport's assertions that less educated groups favor assimilation policies, for instance, probably does some members of those "less educated" groups harm while simultaneously freeing those with greater levels of formal education and training from harboring bias and responsibility for injuring others. Discrimination and prejudice infect the consciousness and communities of the least and most differently educated publics. These viruses are therefore just as representative of ignorance among individuals as discrimination and prejudice are representative of the choices that less educated and more educated individuals deliberate on and make. That said, throwing blame around like manhole covers is neither always welcome nor always adequate or productive. Recognizing that discrimination and prejudice are not so easily located and fixed, however, may nonetheless also be important for developing approaches to ameliorate biases that strike against personal and human growth, freedom, and dignity.

Because the contributors are writing from an ideology that favors plurality, it probably comes as no surprise that while they are cognizant of numerous challenges that diversity brings, the process of writing their stories together has also altogether suggested that *community-in-difference* is possible and worthy of being achieved. Community-in-difference suggests that to combat discrimination and prejudice, and to enhance individual and social experience, it may be necessary to strive for plurality by continually examining the boundaries where difference as deficit and likeness as normalcy end and begin. Lacking such an analysis, it seems not only likely that discrimination and prejudice will continue to blossom but that because of practices and dispositions that favor discrimination and prejudice, individuals and groups will continue to lose opportunities to explore where freedom applies and where freedom oppresses individuals, groups, and society.

Plurality, when coupled with discussions about discrimination and prejudice—and it seems necessary and true that these discussions are comparable and need to coexist—requires that subjects like racism, sexism, and other forms of hurt are considered consonant with discussions about individual rights and how the rights of individuals impact on others. Discussions about discrimination and prejudice, when coupled with discussions about plurality, have the potential to serve individual and social values of the highest order without necessarily reducing the freedom that plurality gives. Likewise, discussions about discrimination and prejudice, when *absent* discussions about plurality and justice, offer promise as instruments of liberty whose very promise may be exceeded by the capacity of discrimination and prejudice to destroy what freedom with responsibility brings.

The methods used to analyze discrimination and prejudice, like the methods used to analyze individualism, plurality, and responsibility, probably ought to reflect the nobler purposes that difference, likeness, freedom, and plurality promise. Discrimination and prejudice limit human value and human experience, but the absence of analyses of discrimination and prejudice also hold the potential to create significant and permanent harm. To prevent oppression, the need for analyses of plurality, discrimination, and prejudice is clear. Through analyses of stories and human relationships, estuaries where discrimination and prejudice limit democracy, equality, and social justice will be discovered and go unpacked.

End

Stories about Teaching, Pluralism, and Social Justice is incomplete and has imperfections. Stories within stories went entirely untold. The value of teaching social justice for students often went largely unexplored. We have, thus far, surrendered ourselves and provided thoughts about what storytelling as heuristic inquiry did bring. It is necessary to correct the imbalance to a degree, perhaps; to go beyond the stories and reflection to some additional thoughts without abandoning our collective journey and resting when additional virtue might yet be obtained.

Any knowledge that can be transmitted, through heuristic inquiry, storytelling, or by any other means, can also be held, internalized, and understood anywhere and by anybody. Storytelling spreads knowledge of human endeavor, allowing educators and others concerned about teaching for social justice to know hope for an improved human condition. Heuristic inquiry, as a method of telling stories, allows writers and readers to share and altogether participate in making meaning of human experience, to know hope in caring and suffering and love as compared to counting and politics and dying alone and of greed.

Because heuristic inquiry as storytelling requires authenticity, continuity, unconditionality, and intentiveness of trusting and loving, it also offers unlimited potentiality, prosperity, and opportunity for cooperation and growth. *Stories about Teaching and Social Justice*, like heuristic inquiry, for all its imperfections, in its barest and most fundamental forms, attempts to render the essential condition of women and men. More than that, having written and told stories about growth and teaching for social justice offered each of us a way to know ourselves and to know each other better. Writing, telling stories of experience, and teaching for social justice also gave us a chance to know we belong, that a difference can be made, and it helped us to know that each of us is wanted and needed and loved.

If society did not want to read, then it seems likely that stories would not need to be written or told. Heuristic inquiry, as teaching for social justice, gave wings to experience, ideas, and dreams. We all dream, but for fortune and want of time, it may be that few of us do anything with our understandings and dreams. The hope, and in some ways the purpose, of allowing heuristic inquiry and teaching for social justice in was so that cooperation, hope, and balance might be experienced. Writing stories and being creative are probably not meant solely for practice during our spare time. Humans need to be clear about who they are, why they exist, and what is needed to define their lives.

Our salvation as a species probably lies in the authenticity of our stories and in the recognition that meaning and beauty beat deep in the human experience and heart. Moustakas (1990) writes that "behavior is governed and experience is determined by the unique perceptions, feelings, intuitions, beliefs, and judgments housed in the internal frame of reference of a person" (p. 32). Without storytelling, and possibly without works like *Stories about Teaching, Pluralism, and Social Justice*, we lose touch with human consciousness and lose knowledge about belonging and separateness, community and difference. Without the caring and generosity that heuristic inquiry as storytelling gives, we probably also lose chances to know resolution and the hope and opportunity that cooperation, love, working together, and teaching social justice bring.

References

Allport, G. W. (1979). *The nature of prejudice.* Cambridge, Massachusetts.: Perseus Books.

Howard, G. (1999). *We can't teach what we don't know: White teachers, multiracial schools.* New York: Teachers College Press.

Moustakas, C. (1990). *Heuristic research: Design, methodology, and applications.* Newbury Park, California: Sage. ISBN: 0-8039-3882-9

CONTRIBUTORS

ROBERTO A. PEÑA has published numerous articles and manuscripts about teaching and social justice. In addition to serving as a book editor and having spoken at numerous professional conferences on social justice issues, Professor Peña has also taught numerous seminars on social justice, teaching, education, and not-for-profit leadership across the eastern, midwestern, Southern, and northwestern United States.

KRISTIN GUEST has been a full-time faculty member at Seattle University since 1981 where she teaches in the Master in Teaching program and is the director of the School Psychology program. She was a school psychologist at all K-12 levels in Wisconsin and New Hampshire prior to moving to Washington. Kristin's areas of interest include classrooms as caring, moral communities, issues of social justice, motivation, brain research, personality types and teaching, and career development of school psychologists. She has presented and published articles and book chapters in these areas.

Kristin is a member of The Children's Alliance, a children's advocacy group, and has served on the boards of Teachers Recruiting Future Teachers and the Washington. Association of School Psychologists. She is a fellow of the Developmental Studies Center in Oakland, California, an organization committed to the development of schools as caring, moral communities. Sabbatical studies/work enabled her to live and work with teachers in Kathmandu, Nepal and in Bergen, Norway.

LAWRENCE Y. MATSUDA was born in the Minidoka Relocation Center (Block 26, Barrack 1) in Hunt, Idaho, during World War II. All of his stateside family was incarcerated in camps during the war without a crime or due process. Currently, Dr. Matsuda is a visiting professor in the College of Education at Seattle University. He is a former principal and assistant superintendent in the Seattle School District with extensive experience in the areas of multicultural/bilingual education, equity education, and educational administration. Dr. Matsuda was elected as the first Asian American president of the University of Washington's Alumni Association (UWAA) in 1996. In 1997, he was honored by the University of Washington's Multicultural Alumni Partnership (MAP) Club for his efforts as a volunteer: "for extraordinary service and commitment in promoting diversity in the University of Washington and the University of Washington Alumni Association." In 2003 he received the UWAA/MAP Dr. Samuel E. Kelly Award for contributions to diversity. In 2004 he received the UWAA Distinguished Service Award.

MARSHA D. HARRISON has numerous publications that discuss narrative storytelling as a means of enlightenment and transformation. Marsha currently works in Secondary Education at Arizona State University.

ALTHE ALLEN was graduated with her Doctorate in Education from Arizona State University in 2000. Her writing is excerpted from her dissertation. Althe is currently employed as an administrator in the Scottsdale School District in Scottsdale, Arizona.

JACQUE ENSIGN is an associate professor. Jacque has numerous publications that examine the relationship surrounding issues like race and student achievement.

KATHERINE NELL MCNEIL is a special education teacher in the State of Washington. She is currently enrolled in the Educational Leadership Doctoral Program at Seattle University. Her chapter is excerpted from her dissertation, which is currently in progress.

CLEO MOLINA was awarded her Doctorate in Education from the College of Education at Seattle University. Her scholarly interests focus on leadership, spirituality, multicultural education, and social justice.

HUTCH HANEY is currently a professor at Seattle University. He has served as chair and program coordinator of counseling in the Department of Counseling and School Psychology in the College of Education at Seattle University.

Studies in the Postmodern Theory of Education

General Editors
Joe L. Kincheloe & Shirley R. Steinberg

Counterpoints publishes the most compelling and imaginative books being written in education today. Grounded on the theoretical advances in criticalism, feminism, and postmodernism in the last two decades of the twentieth century, Counterpoints engages the meaning of these innovations in various forms of educational expression. Committed to the proposition that theoretical literature should be accessible to a variety of audiences, the series insists that its authors avoid esoteric and jargonistic languages that transform educational scholarship into an elite discourse for the initiated. Scholarly work matters only to the degree it affects consciousness and practice at multiple sites. Counterpoints' editorial policy is based on these principles and the ability of scholars to break new ground, to open new conversations, to go where educators have never gone before.

For additional information about this series or for the submission of manuscripts, please contact:

> Joe L. Kincheloe & Shirley R. Steinberg
> c/o Peter Lang Publishing, Inc.
> 275 Seventh Avenue, 28th floor
> New York, New York 10001

To order other books in this series, please contact our Customer Service Department:

> (800) 770-LANG (within the U.S.)
> (212) 647-7706 (outside the U.S.)
> (212) 647-7707 FAX

Or browse online by series:

> www.peterlangusa.com